This is a courageous book, exploring the frontiers and unspoken presumptions governing the ways in which otherness, ethnicity, race, migration, indigenous populations and social/linguistic estrangement have been thought, and have exceeded their cultural representations. This book addresses a broad international and multi-cultural audience with the key questions of cultural specificity, its social representations and its theoretical and political power in the context of key 1990s' debates in contemporary feminist and postmodern theory. Beyond guilt or indulgence, the essays gathered here all engage with the complexities and contradictions that otherness poses in a culture and in knowledges that pose themselves as singular, unified and universally representative. A brave and dangerous project directed towards the key social and intellectual issues of a political world now in crisis. I heartily recommend this book for all readers of culture, our own, and the others that make it possible.

Elizabeth Grosz

FEMINISM AND THE POLITICS OF DIFFERENCE

Edited by Sneja Gunew and Anna Yeatman

WESTVIEW PRESS
Boulder & San Francisco

Front cover photograph from Tracey Moffatt's film *Night Cries—A Rural Tragedy*: taken by Tracey Moffatt, hand painted by Jude Morrell.

First published in 1993 by
Allen & Unwin Pty Ltd
9 Atchison Street, St Leonards, NSW 2065 Australia

Published in 1993 in the United States by
Westview Press
5500 Central Avenue
Boulder, Colorado 80301

Library of Congress Cataloguing-in-publication data
available upon request

ISBN HB 0–8133–2063–1
ISBN PB 0–8133–2062–3

Set in 10/11 pt Sabon by DOCUPRO, Sydney
Printed by Chong Moh Offset Printing, Singapore

10 9 8 7 6 5 4 3 2 1

Contents

Illustrations

Acknowledgments

Versions of Jacki Huggins's 'Pretty deadly tidda business' have appeared in *Hecate* vol. 17, no. 1, 1991, I Indyk, ed.; *Memory* (*Southerly* 3, 1991) HarperCollins, Sydney, 1991; *Second Degree Tampering*, Sybylla Feminist Press, Melbourne, 1992. Laleen Jayamanne's 'Love me tender, love me true . . . ' was first published in *Framework* 38/39, 1992. A version of Smaro Kamboureli's 'Of black angels and melancholy lovers' appeared in *Freelance* (Saskatchewan Writers' Guild), xxi, 5 (Dec. 1991–Jan. 1992). Roxana Ng's 'Sexism, racism and Canadian nationalism' appeared in *Race, Class, Gender: Bonds and Barriers, Socialist Studies/Etudes Socialistes: A Canadian Annual* no. 5, 1989. Trinh Minh-ha's 'All-owning spectatorship' has also appeared in her collection of essays *When the Moon Waxes Red*, Routledge, NY, 1991.

For permission to print illustrations we would like to thank: Tracey Moffatt, for stills from her film *Night Cries*. The Australian Office of Multicultural Affairs (Chapter 8). Shogakukan Inc., Tokyo, for illustrations from 'The Heart of Thomas' and 'The Poem' (Chapter 11). Kadokawa Inc., Tokyo, for the illustration from 'Green Boy' (Chapter 11).

While every effort has been made to trace the copyright for illustrative material used in this book, further information would be welcomed by the publisher.

Contributors

Sneja Gunew taught for many years in literary studies at Deakin University and has recently accepted an appointment at the University of Victoria, British Columbia. She has edited or co-edited four anthologies of women's and multicultural writings. She is the editor of *Feminist Knowledge: Critique and Construct* and *A Reader in Feminist Knowledge* (Routledge, 1990). She has published numerous critical essays (nationally and internationally) on feminist literary theory and on multiculturalism in its various formations. She co-edited *Striking Chords: Multicultural Literary Interpretations* (1992) and was one of the compilers of *A Bibliography of Australian Multicultural Writers* (1992).

Efi Hatzimanolis is completing her PhD on multicultural women's writing and is a casual teacher in the Department of English at the University of Wollongong. She has published articles on Australian immigrant writing in *Hecate*, the *Journal of Narrative Technique*, *Span*, and *Striking Chords: Multicultural Literary Interpretations*.

Jackie Huggins is an Aboriginal writer and historian from Queensland. Before starting her studies and writing she worked for many years in Aboriginal community affairs. In 1984–85 she headed a national unit comprising 50 Aboriginal and Torres Strait Islander women whose task was to assess the needs of women, youth and children throughout Australia. She is now devoting time to preparing two collections of her unpublished essays and speeches on racism, history and colonialism and Aboriginal women's writings.

A biography of her mother, Rita, has just been completed. She has published in various journals, particularly *Hecate*, and looks forward to rewriting school history textbooks to give greater emphasis to the Aboriginal experience.

Annamarie Jagose teaches in the Department of English at the University of Melbourne. She is currently working on a book which critiques the textual production of the category 'lesbian' as synonymous with various spaces of alterity.

Laleen Jayamanne was born in Sri Lanka (1947). She completed her undergraduate degree at the University of Ceylon, and received a Master's degree in Drama from New York University and a PhD in film from the University of New South Wales for a thesis on 'Positions of women in the Sri Lankan cinema 1947–1979.' She teaches Film Studies at the Power Institute of Fine Arts, University of Sydney.

Margaret Jolly is convenor of the Gender Relations Project, Research School of Pacific Studies at the Australian National University. She studies anthropology and history at Sydney University and completed her doctorate there in 1979 on the changing gender relations among Sa speakers of south Pentecost Island. She has published many papers based on this research, in addition to the book *Women of the Place: Kastom, Colonialism and Gender in Vanuatu* (Harwood Press, forthcoming). Before her secondment to ANU, she was senior lecturer in Anthropology and Comparative Sociology at Macquarie University, where she usually teaches on the ethnography and colonial history of the Pacific, women and development, feminist anthropology and illness and healing. Over the past five years she has also been researching and writing on women in the colonial history of Vanuatu, political hierarchy and domesticity, the politics of tradition, and women, nation and state in the Pacific.

Smaro Kamboureli is associate professor of Canadian literature at the University of Victoria, British Columbia. Her publications include *On the Edge of Genre: The Contemporary Canadian Long Poem*; *A Mazing Space: Writing Canadian Women Writing*, co-edited with Shirley Neuman, and a long poem titled *in the second person*. She is currently working on a book about multiculturalism and ethnic writing in Canada.

Vicki Kirby works in several disciplinary areas, exploring questions about the representation of sexual and cultural differences through the problematic of embodiment. She has published in diverse journals, including *Australian Feminist Studies, Mankind,*

Inscriptions: Journal of Women in Culture of Colonial Discourse, Hypatia: Journal of Feminist Philosophy, Signs: Journal of Women in Culture and Society, Anthropological Quarterly, West and *Afterimage.* She received her PhD from the History of Consciousness Program, University of California, Santa Cruz. Her doctorate explores a corporal politics through deconstruction. In 1992 she was a visiting teaching fellow in Women's Studies at the University of Waikato in New Zealand. She is based in San Diego, California.

Wendy Larner was a lecturer in Geography at the University of Waikato, New Zealand. She is currently doing her doctorate at the University of British Columbia, Vancouver. Her research is on globalization, restructuring and changing sexual and spatial divisions of labour. She has published 'Women and Migration' in David Spoonley, David Pearson & Cluny MacPherson eds. *Nga Take: Ethnic Relations and Racism in Aotearoa/New Zealand,* Dunmore Press, 1991.

Midori Matsui was born in Yokohama (1959) and received her Master's degree in English from the University of Tokyo. She has also studied in the US and was a Fulbright fellow at Princeton 1986–88 as well as receiving an MA in Comparative Literature from Princeton in 1989. She is currently writing her PhD thesis on T.S. Eliot and Kobayashi Hideo and is associate professor in English at Tohoku University, Japan.

Roxana Ng migrated to Canada from Hong Kong in 1970. Since receiving an MA in Anthropology from the University of British Columbia in 1975, she has been concerned to understand the experiences of immigrant women from their perspective, and to develop 'immigrant women' as a legitimate area of inquiry in Canada. Out of her involvement in immigrant women's organizing across the country, she has written on issues of sexism and racism, and on the relationship between community organizations and the state. She teaches sociology at the Ontario Institute for Studies in Education. Her interests include reintegrating the body–mind dichotomy in intellectual endeavours.

Daiva Stasiulis is associate professor of Sociology at Carleton University, Ottawa. She has written extensively on racism, anti-racist politics, and the responses of the state, labour and feminist movements to ethnic diversity and racism. She has also worked with both labour and women's organizations on anti-racist campaigns. Her current research on domestic workers and nurses from the Philippines and West Indies examines the racial and gender boundaries of citizenship. Her recent publications include 'Theorizing Connections: Race, Ethnicity, Gender and Class', in Peter Li (ed.), *Race and Ethnic Relations in Canada,* Oxford University Press, 1990; 'The House the Parties Built: (Re) Constructing Ethnic Representation in Canadian Politics,' (with Y. Abu-Laban), in K. Megyery (ed.), *Visible Minorities and Ethnocultural Groups in Canadian Politics,* Dundurn Press 1991; 'Symbolic Representation and the Numbers Game: Tory Policies on "Race" and Visible Minorities', in F. Abele (ed.), *How Ottawa Spends 1990–91: The Politics of Fragmentation,* Carleton University Press, 1991; *Gender, Race, Ethnicity and Class in Settler Societies* (ed. with N. Yuval-Davis), Sage, forthcoming; and 'Ethnic Pluralism Under Siege: Popular and Partisan Opposition to Multiculturalism' (with Y. Abu-Laban), *Canadian Public Policy,* forthcoming, September 1993.

Trinh T. Minh-ha is a filmmaker, writer and composer. Her works include the films *Reassemblage* (1982), *Naked Spaces—Living is Round* (1985), *Surname Viet Given Name Nam* (1989) and *Shoot For the Contents* (1992); and the books *En minuscules* (Le Meridien Editeur, Paris, 1987), *Woman, Native, Other* (Indiana University Press, 1989), *When The Moon Waxes Red* (Routledge, 1991), and *Framer Framed* (Routledge, 1992).

Anna Yeatman was foundation professor of Women's Studies at the University of Waikato, 1991–93. She is professor of Sociology at Macquarie University, Sydney. Her research interests cover feminist theory, the implications of globalization for the polity, the restructuring of the professions and higher education. She has undertaken a number of public policy consultancies, including two research reports for the Australian Office of Multicultural Affairs. Recent publications include *Bureaucrats, Technocrats, Femocrats: Essays on the Contemporary Australian State,* Allen & Unwin 1990; editor and contributor to a special issue of *Social Analysis* (no. 30, 1991) on 'Postmodern Critical Theorizing'; and a book on *Postmodernism and the Revisioning of the Political,* forthcoming Routledge, New York 1993.

Introduction

Sneja Gunew and Anna Yeatman

In its third decade, a dominant area of debate in second-wave feminism concerns being able to deal with differences among women without losing the impetus that derives from being a coherent movement for social change. A manifestation of such differences is the fact that the editors of this collection of essays by feminists from around the world come from separate disciplines: the one from literary and cultural studies, the other from sociology and politics. What they have in common is the desire to work with poststructuralist critical theory in and around feminism. For both, the major concern is to shift debates beyond the current preoccupation with binary oppositions that invariably absorbs alterity into the hegemonic and familiar. Whenever such thinking prevails, we are merely in the business of juggling with traditional categories, privileging women rather than men, or some women at the expense of others, without changing the power structures behind such constructions. Such logic is homogenizing and universalist, built on the principle of exclusion and the tyranny of the familiar.

Poststructuralist theory (including deconstruction, psychoanalysis, postmodernism) offers a means of situating the speaking subject, of defining the intersections and contradictions of competing interest groups. It defines all knowledges as situated ones (Haraway 1991). Together with postcolonialism, loosely defined as a body of theories which offers a place to speak for those who have been excluded from Western metaphysics, poststructuralism gives us the tools to deconstruct these homogenizing categories so that it is possible to admit difference, not simply as the self-confirming other, but as the admission and recognition of incommensurabilities.

These essays also address in a range of ways the necessity for moving beyond identity politics, traditionally a premise for political activism. Three distinct suggestions are made in this context. The first is a recurrent theme: if we allow that identity politics may be an inevitable characteristic of a contemporary politics of difference, then it is critical that we foster what Denise Riley (1988) calls a spirit of deconstructive irony in relation to this politics. A second suggestion concerns the need to organise around local allegiances in order to dismantle once again the universal models which, however benign they may appear, work ultimately to confirm the old power structures, whether these be patriarchies or neo-imperialisms. A third suggestion, indeed a counter-suggestion to the second, refuses the binary of local and global, and proposes instead the usefulness of thinking in terms of local and global, and proposes instead the usefulness of thinking in terms of interested universalisms. The nature of all political claims is to work in terms of interested universalisms. The nature of all political claims is to work in terms of some kind of ethical universal. What poststructuralist theory permits us to see is that this universal exists only as it is particularised, and that this particularisation is always interested. In modern politics, universalism and interest are seen as mutually exclusive options. This means politics has to be about either ethics or interest. Yet all political vision has an ethical as well as an interested component. Politics concerns the contestatory and conversational dynamics of how these two components enter into the ways in which we work with shared conditions of plurality and alterity.

Rather than reinforcing disciplinary boundaries, this book is organised around a number of key questions: the nature of the intersection of race and ethnicity; the dilemma of appropriation and who is permitted to speak on behalf of whom; what makes a position or voice authentic, particularly in terms of minority claims; what are the structures of legitimation operating in relation to minorities; the problems posed by identity politics; how one may attempt to set up non-exclusive cultural and gendered positions; and, closely related to this, the problems with some strategies for subversion of existing paradigms. The frames for posing these interrogations are determined by the role various institutions can play in these debates, including national cultures and both the ideological and repressive dimensions of a national state apparatus. As well, there is a prevailing concern with struc-

tures of accountability and how one can construct policies in
relation to state and community.

   As editors, we should also point out that both of us have been
situated in ways other than simply calling ourselves part of
Australian feminism. This has involved our being caught up in the
battles over the past decades to secure for feminist work legitimacy
in a range of disciplinary structures, including the establishment
of women's studies. Both of us have been caught up as well in
the ferment around cultural difference, referred to as multiculturalism in the Australian context and as biculturalism in the New
Zealand arena, where assertions regarding multiculturalism have
been seen as deflecting attention away from the fight for Maori
rights. New Zealand feminism has been profoundly influenced by
this bicultural mapping of the national imaginary, and it is arguable that the dominance of a separatist orientation in New
Zealand feminism reflects the symbolic influence of the Maori
nationalist movement. While one of us has encountered versions
of cultural fundamentalism in New Zealand, the other has been
enmeshed in multicultural debates around Australian literary
nationalism. In the latter case, the attempts to deconstruct exclusive prevailing allegiances to English literature by promoting
recognition of all those writings that draw on other cultural
traditions and languages, have at times been undercut by appeals
to Aboriginal indigenous cultural claims. Here, too, there has been
another setting-up of implicit biculturalism. Between the rights of
the indigenous peoples and the Anglo-Celts, or Pakeha, there is
room for no other differences, and invariably these two categories
are also constructed as homogenous ones. There is no recognition
in terms of a simply defined activism for differences within such
groups. Ultimately, we would maintain, this is self-defeating. But
what are the alternatives?

Race and ethnicity

Many of the essays in this volume touch on this topic either
implicitly or explicitly. Some might argue that it is important to
keep these two areas separate, but most of the writers here would
adopt the approach that such discrete definitions are not so easy
to maintain. Gunew argues that at particular historical moments
race and ethnicity have been invoked with differing meanings, so
that while for a time ethnicity supplanted race, because of the
legacy of the appeals to theories of race during the Second World
War, now race has again become a way for minorities to assert
their irreducible differences. Nonetheless race has no essential or

indubitable markers of difference, and recent theorists have reas-
serted its constantly shifting and contested nature. The eventual
(as distinct from immediately strategic) value of asserting racial
difference as a ploy is dubious. Compromise might be more
constructively located by grounding difference within language
rather than blood, since the dangers of any appeal or legitimation
grounded in biological essentialism have often been canvassed.
Moreover, we need to ask what may be happening when race
displaces ethnicity and is taken to be the primary marker of
cultural difference. Often such constructions of race necessarily
occur in the face of racism and do not necessarily challenge the
traditional grounds of racist definitions of race.

Roxana Ng, tracing the intersections of sexism, racism and
class in Canada, also maintains that race and ethnicity are in a
constantly shifting dynamic. She argues that ethnicity and gender
constitute class relations rather than being separable categories.
She reminds us too of a point echoed by a number of the writers
here, namely that ethnicity is an element disavowed by those in
power, by the elite, as though this were inherently an admission
of vulnerable marginality. Wendy Larner's examination of labour
relations in New Zealand vis-à-vis immigration, women and globalization reiterates that different groups of migrants (e.g. Asian as
distinct from Pacific Islander migrants) are inserted into different
labour market segments, just as they have to negotiate their place
in the contemporary politics of migration and citizenship in quite
different ways. The regulatory function of discourses around race
and ethnicity have been confounded by globalization so that there
are no preordained allegiances in terms of race wedded to territory.
In other words, other alliances at local levels need to be forged
among women and inserted into 'the space of flows' which
describe prevailing market forces. These partnerships must incorporate other differences besides the traditional Maori-Pakeha ones.
Overwhelmingly in the past, acknowledgment of difference within
the New Zealand context has been played out around the binary
opposition of Maori and those descended from British migrants
(the usual inflection of Pakeha).

Margaret Jolly focuses on historical processes when she analyzes the differential access of white women to colonial history.
She critiques some revisionist feminist studies which construct
white women as simply the innocent victims of male representations, that is, often depicted as the bearers or guardians of colonial
values. Focusing on the lives and texts of two white women in
the Pacific and their relationship to the maternal, she illustrates
how Charlotte Geddie, a Presbyterian missionary wife, saw herself
as teaching indigenous women how to be good mothers (the

benign matriarch) whereas Beatrice Grimshaw, a traveller and writer, revealed another version of profound racism in her treatment of indigenous women as a threat to the regulatory structures of sexuality and motherhood within white 'civilization'.

Daiva Stasiulis analyzes the ambiguities surrounding race in particular when she asks the question: what constitutes anti-racism in writing? Within the shifting and shifty terrain of language, particularly fictional language, she ponders the attempts by Canadian feminist publishers to construct infallible guidelines which would protect the cultural rights of minority writers, particularly those of indigenous origin. Clearly, she argues, the issues cannot simply be solved by posting no-go areas for writers in terms of their rights to imaginative freedoms. Once again the danger is of blood too simply linked to signature, and we are returned to a limited essentialism which ultimately stifles creative possibilities and serves no one.

Appropriation: who is permitted to speak on behalf of whom?

One of the most fraught issues of recent feminism has concerned attempts to construct equable negotiations around minority rights. Depending on how one is situated, to what extent and by what means can one work to open up spaces for those who are labelled as marginal without falling into the traps of tokenism or appropriation? Clearly there are as many dangers in constructing certain figures as having to 'represent' their groups as there are, under the desire to engage with the issues of minorities, in oneself taking on/over the attempts to represent or designate their differences.

Stasiulis sounds the important warning that members of minorities are invariably constructed as being somehow representatives of their whole group and confined to this role, whereas other writers not so designated and not so limited remain free to write about 'universal' issues. Larner articulates the problem of appropriation as the importance of women learning to join with others without pretending to be these others. This is a common move, in which liberal feminists, in their desire to show solidarity with their oppressed sisters, take on in sentimental and problematic ways the accessories of difference. This gesture is of course a profoundly matronizing one and often results in what Trinh has called the nativist line of teaching the 'natives' how to be bona fide anti- or de-colonized others (Trinh 1989:59).

From the other side of the divide, so to say, in other words from a positioning as minority, Jayamanne reminds us that appropriation is in a sense not a one-way street. That is, the use of

assimilationist codes or icons in the hands of those positioned as
minority can open up an 'uncanny' space (in the Freudian sense)
within mainstream culture. She illustrates this in her Sri Lankan
reading of a film by Tracey Moffatt, an Aboriginal Australian.
Deploying the signs of popular culture, the stereotype of the
assimilated other can function as a profoundly subversive gesture
when it is situated within disjunctive uses of sound and image.
Annamarie Jagose tests the issue of appropriation from a slightly
different angle when she argues that certain figures may inherently
reinforce the familiar or same even though superficially they signal
difference. In her examination of border culture and the figure of
the Chicana *mestiza*, or cultural hybrid, she deconstructs its utopic
claims to show that they are predicated on the maintenance of
borders and 'proper' bloodlines. For example, the attempt to
locate Chicano Spanish as a deconstruction of the hegemonic in
fact reinstate a familiar oppositional duo in colonial language
hierarchies: English and Spanish.

Appropriation's insidious operations are analyzed in detail by
Trinh when she describes the misguided efforts of liberal white
feminists to 'remind' a Third World woman filmmaker of the
importance of class. Trinh shows the expectations projected onto
such figures and illustrates how 'the mandatory concern for class
in the exclusive context of films on and by Third World members
is in itself a class issue'.

Authenticity

Another, more insidious version of appropriation than speaking in
the name of the minority is to project the burden of authenticity
onto the minority. Even postmodernists who write easily concerning decentred subjectivity and metaphysics of presence in all forms
of writing sometimes return to the unified subject when it comes
to dealing with the minority or margins. In her critique of the
new ethnography, Kirby finds that even here, where anthropology
has engaged with poststructuralism, the emphasis on cultural
translation that remains at the heart of anthropology means that
a culture is rendered the 'same'. The emphasis remains on justi-
fying or shoring up the discipline rather than on opening it up to
difference. The same may be said, as she argues, about feminism
and postmodernism itself. Stasiulis, too, in her analysis of the
dilemma of indigenous writers, sees them as haunted by the burden
of authenticity: somehow, unlike other writers caught up in the
ambiguities of textuality, they are able to convey the plenitude
guaranteed by self-presence of their marginal existence in trans-

parent texts. Jayamanne notes that the apparent inauthenticity of
Moffatt's film, its use of popular culture including echoes of Albert
Namatjira's paintings (traditionally used to illustrate the supposed
Westernization of indigenous Australian culture), in fact makes it
a much more representative evocation of the condition of the
hybrid artist caught in the inevitable cross-cultural spectrum,
neither 'pristinely indigenous nor completely other'. Smaro
Kamboureli, critiquing official Canadian multiculturalism, reveals
how its inherent inauthenticity is displayed in its refusal to recognize any other differences than those set out in its regulatory
discourses and practices. Differences become segregated instead of
being allowed permeability and flow.

Trinh points out that differences are caught up in the oppositional binary categories of oppressor and oppressed. Authenticity
for the latter is thereby demarcated and controlled by the former,
a trick which renders oppressed totally dependent on the oppressor. Oppression and repression become commodified into 'codified
forms of resistance'. Thus the supposed authenticity of the Third
World is always refracted through the process of 'salvage' from
Westernization.

Legitimation

But if the dangers of appropriation can surface in their many
variations, how does one go about legitimizing minority positions?
What might these structures of legitimation comprise?

Anna Yeatman makes the central point that we must always
scrutinize who is authorizing whom to speak and that is an issue
as much within feminism as outside it in the familiar process
whereby men traditionally authorize women. When it occurs
within feminism, it is even more important that we understand
the ways in which this process functions. Stasiulis, in her delineation of the complex and often unresolved issues governing
attempts to legislate on non-racist or non-appropriative writing,
suggests that the only valid way forward is to ask who has access
to resources in relation to writing, publishing, reviewing, etc.
Ensuring that minorities have equitable access to such means is
the most useful apparatus of legitimation. Abstract theorizing on
these matters tends to catch one in the bind of legislating on the
most authentic and representative minority voice. The Canada
Council guidelines quoted by Stasiulis, in which minority writers
are asked to ensure the support of their community, mean, as she
points out, that certain individuals are arbitrarily appointed to be
the legitimate guardians of their culture. Something similar hap-

FEMINISM AND THE POLITICS OF DIFFERENCE

pens in Australia in relation to the Australia Council's program for multicultural arts. Here, these are often subsumed within community arts, which, aside from its connotations of amateur or developing status, also means that art forms in which artists work as individuals rather than members of a group are left out in the cold. In other words, when they foreground their cultural differences within their art form practices, artists are either landed within the community arts area or seen as being in a marginal relationship to the mainstream.

Hatzimanolis clarifies this further when she looks at the way in which multicultural literature, literature written by non-Anglo-Celtic Australians whether in English or not, is constructed within Australia as either safely lodged in the past or apprenticeship writing. It is perceived as a throwback to early or 'primitive' versions of Australian literature, structured around oral history or first-person accounts.

Kirby traces a somewhat different trajectory within this area of legitimating structures. Analyzing the call for a politics of clear meaning that is often attached to the direct activism of minority politics, including feminism in general, she demonstrates that this is usually predicated on an anti-theoretical positioning. In other words, everything must be rendered in terms of what is already known, and it is hegemonic discourses which tend to define the familiar, whether these be patriarchal matters or mainstream feminism. She shows how feminism itself is often built on the othering of some women, a point also made in Trinh's essay. Trinh analyzes at length the intolerance for non-hegemonic language that is particularly exercized towards Third World artists. Trinh describes this discourse as a linear lateral communication, a vehicle for quantified exchange. In a world of commodities, what other communication models would one expect? Against this, she explores the multitude of meanings of the colour red as they are refracted through cultural difference and gender.

No structure is inherently able to guarantee subversiveness. As Kirby asks, what is intrinsically radical or political about some forms of feminism? Often these forms are invoked as a convenient obstacle to critical inquiry, functioning as a feminist thought police. In the spirit of this question, Midori Matsui's analysis of Japanese 'boy-boy' comics, aimed initially at adolescent girls, shows how in the first phase, which she characterizes as the phallic, the characters (girls masquerading as boys) never leave the oedipal scenario, and are thus caught up in a phallic logic of desire. One way of putting this in a more idiomatic mode is to compare it with stages in second-wave feminism, when subversion at times was located in merely mimicking the accessories or external attributes of power possessed by men. Matsui describes the first phase as caught completely within the male gaze. One could also point out that in the film version of 'The Heart of Thomas' (one of her examples), the male director used girls to play boys and thus fully exposed the phallic economy of the text.

Jagose's analysis of the border *mestiza* figure demonstrates how its apparently revolutionary attempts to transcend the divisiveness of those excluded against those included ends up by reinscribing the inside/outside dichotomy. Like Kirby and Trinh, she reminds us that: 'Translation does not transgress but reinforces the border's jurisdiction, its production of the oppositional and hierarchic categories of inside outside'.

Trinh's description of the representation of postwar Vietnam reveals how it becomes a spectacle or commodity appropriated and owned by everyone, though superficially these moves appear to represent attempts to insert it into hegemonic history. The territory accorded it is always unified and represented within male commodity markets, which have room, according to Trinh, for only one feminism.

Finally, Jackie Huggins complicates the question of appropriation of the other by choosing to distance herself from her own immediate politics in attempting to represent the story of her mother. As she puts it: 'How much is "I" the writer?' To what extent does she need to situate herself as other in order to give centre stage to both her mother's immediate experience and its context—namely, a political climate and priorities that may be at odds with contemporary Aboriginal concerns?

Identity politics

Related to this topic of legitimating structures but invoked often enough to be designated a separate space is the issue of identity politics which haunts any discussion of minority rights.

As Kirby points out in her critique of the new ethnography, women still tend to believe that they have privileged access to gender truths, just as ethnographers trust that 'insiders' have particular access to ethnographic truths. But of course, any such designation returns the essential sovereign subject as guarantor of meaning, putting us back in the realm of truth claims and power structures which regulate the authority to speak. In her discussion of the New Zealand situation, Larner sounds a timely warning for minority groups which anchor their claims in identity politics and territory. Such moves are too easily recuperable by the Right. This has been seen in the Australian context, too, where indigenous spokespeople sometimes echo in alarming ways the anti-Asian racist rhetoric of the Right. In other words they single out particular and by no means random groups to bear the guilt for benefits through colonization. While all non-Aboriginal Australians are certainly beneficiaries of colonialism, it is precisely this kind of binary politics that leaves room for no other kinds of differences than those determined between colonizer and colonized, i.e. the codes of resistance identified by Trinh, mutually dependent on each other. Such formulations can also be used by racist forces within a society which certainly do not have the best interests of the indigenous or colonized peoples at heart.

Yeatman argues that politics is a contestatory relationship between those who name themselves as excluded by established policy and those who are positioned as the guardians of established policy. The identity of the former does not precede politics but is interpellated within the space of this contestation. The naming of the specific category of those who are excluded by established policy proceeds in terms of the claim that this policy wrongs a particular category by excluding them. This naming of the wrong presupposes both that the universalism of established policy is false and that this universalism can be made more inclusive. Thus the naming of the wrong constitutes both commonality and difference between those who are respectively the excluded and the guardians in respect of established policy. The politics of difference, then, does not work according to a strict binary, oppositional logic. However, a binary identity politics develops when it is forgotten that the identity of the excluded comes into being only within the political relationship of a contested universalism, when indeed this identity is retroactively projected as something that was always there and that is a given as far as politics is concerned. When identities are lived in this way, politics tends to be subordinated to the ritual enactment of ontologized difference. Such ritual enactment substitutes force of various kinds or the delicate and interlocutory contingencies of political contestation.

Identity politics is structured on the self–other principle and undoes the possibility of difference. The way beyond this is shown, for example, by Judith Butler, whose work is cited in Gunew's essay. Butler argues for local intervention into the repetitive processes which define and endorse identity positioning: 'The deconstruction of identity is not the deconstruction of politics; rather, it establishes as political the very terms through which identity is articulated' (Butler 1990: 148). In Huggins's story of her mother, the structure instantly counters the often-voiced suggestion that indigenous writers in particular are caught within the convention of the unified subject's first-person, authentic account. Huggins's narrative is clearly shaped by a number of public discourses constructing Aboriginal reality in the period she covers as well as being leavened by the stories conveyed by both her mother and other indigenous spokespeople of the time. Weaving through this montage is Huggins's own voice as narrator looking back on a younger self's reaction to her mother at various stages.

Non-exclusive cultural and gendered representations

Having canvassed all the dangers inherent in the politics of difference as commonly articulated, what are the possibilities for producing non-exclusive cultural and gendered representations?

Yeatman suggests some of the elements in such an attempt when she says: 'A politics of representation becomes a genuine politics only when it is played out as a context of debate, reciprocal accountabilities . . . it is locally anchored to whatever jurisdictional boundaries permit those who "speak for" and self-advocates to come together.' Stasiulis cites Trinh's statement on this topic as making possible the acknowledgment of the hybrid realities which are lived out every day by minority as well as majority peoples. Larner suggests that New Zealand needs to move beyond the exclusive focus on Maori–Pakeha differences, particularly when members of the latter category are confined to the descendants of British settlers.

Hatzimanolis traces the work of Anna Couani as illustrative of the possibilities of inscribing other temporalities and histories beyond universalist considerations. In her work the urban space becomes another kind of territorialization than those designated by white or black land claims. This is akin to Jayamanne's depiction of Mofatt's work, which is also played out in an urban space permeated by traditional indigenous culture. Neither is what it appears to be and both are juxtaposed to project an uncanny future in which the familiar home territory is rendered strange and perhaps a little monstrous, and by the same token not easily recuperable. Although none of the pages refers explicitly to Deleuze and Guattari's (1990) notion of deterritorialization, this comes to mind in some of the possibilities they discuss.

Kamboureli, drawing on Kristeva, suggests that the domesticated ethnic outsider of multiculturalism must be joined with the foreigner within so that difference becomes possible as a circuit of exchange. Matsui focuses on the second phase of the boy-boy comic (before it became part of mass culture and lost its specific adolescent female audience), in which androgyny and polymor-

FEMINISM AND THE POLITICS OF DIFFERENCE

phous sexuality are celebrated in a genuinely anarchic manner. This phase is represented by 'Green Boy', in which a young woman finds that her pet plant has many hidden metamorphic virtues. While traditional sex roles frame the narrative, within it endless variations are played out which confound the rigidity of such frames.

Finally, Trinh suggests that: 'In a society where they remain constantly at odds on occupied territories, women can only situate their social spaces precariously in the interstices of diverse systems of ownership.' They need to cross to and fro across borders rather than, fetishizing the border into a spectacle of difference which in fact, as Jagose points out, disavows difference.

What must be kept in mind throughout this volume is the disciplinary protocols that determine the ways in which texts are read. For example, some sociologists have a propensity to read fictional texts as though they represented transparent social truths and were not determined by generic and narrative conventions— the play of writing. As Kirby warns, reading is not simply retrieval or diagnostics; nor must we forget Trinh's injunction that every decoding is interpellated by ideology. Such considerations appear to be suspended in the interaction with minority texts even by sophisticated readers. The suggestion that minority writers are inappropriately read in terms of postmodernist strategies is one of the more patronizing gestures of 'well-meaning' theorists. They simply have, so it is argued, primitive stories which renders them fair game for salvage operations.

Conclusion

While on the one hand both Kirby and Stasiulis quote Said's salutary warning that: 'the fetishization and relentless celebration of "difference" and "otherness" can . . . be seen as an ominous trend' (1989:213), on the other hand there is no question that the ability to deal with difference is at the centre of feminism's survival as a movement for social change. That these differences inevitably constitute division is also a familiar conclusion which needs to be resisted and analyzed. The days of exclusionary solidarity as an unexamined strategy are long over.

Nonetheless, the dangers inherent in certain methods of accommodating difference need to be pointed out, and by now there is a sophisticated repertoire of these. Traditional methods of disavowal prevail. Whether these be simply talking about difference in order to displace dealing with it, as shown by Kirby, or the undeconstructed figures of difference traced by Jagose, we need to remain alert to their operations. The critiques presented in this book attempt to deal honestly with such evasions and wrong turns and thus provide the grounds or conditions for advances into the dangerous terrain of future possibilities.

References

Butler, J. (190) *Gender Trouble: Feminism and the Subversion of Identity*, Routledge, NY.
Deleuze, G. & Guattari, F. (1990) *A Thousand Plateaus: Capitalism and Schizophrenia*, trans. Brian Massumi, Athlone Press, London.
Haraway, D. (1991) 'Situated Knowledges: The Science Question in Feminism and the Privilege of Partial Perspective', *Simians, Cyborgs, and Women; The Reinvention of Nature*, Free Association Books, London, pp. 183–202.
Riley, D. (1988) *'Am I that Name?': Feminism and the Category of 'Woman' in History*, Macmillan, London.
Said, E. (1989) 'Representing the Colonised: Anthropology's Interlocutors,' *Critical Inquiry* vol. 15, no. 2, Winter, pp. 205–225.
Trinh T. Minh-ha (1989) *Woman, Native Other*, Indiana University Press, Bloomington.

1   Feminism and the politics of irreducible differences: Multiculturalism/ethnicity/ race

Sneja Gunew

so eager is he to name everything that he runs into the unnamable.[1]

Nationalism: cultural difference

Working for social justice is not necessarily at odds with a commitment to critical theory 'even' in its postmodern variants. It is necessary to state this in the face of consistent critiques which suggest that social justice issues inevitably translate into firmly entrenched binary oppositions, which are hierarchically positioned and involve mutual homogenization and reductionism. Whether these oppositions be men and women, or mainstream feminists versus minority women, or indigenous peoples versus settler societies, or biculturalism versus multiculturalism, nothing is served by holding to such crude characterizations. The dismantling of hegemonic categories is facilitated by the proliferation of difference rather than the setting up of binary oppositions that can merely be reversed, leaving structures of power intact. This is not to deny the fact that political manoeuvrings sometimes set these categories against each other, or that matters are somehow constructed in such a way that it appears a choice must be made between two parties, but this does not mean that we have to accept the terms of such manipulations. If we have a specific role as intellectuals it is precisely that of scrutinising and, if need be, redefining the conceptual terms of these debates.

This essay examines the tensions between ethnicity, race and women in relation to literature and multiculturalism. Since I have been primarily situated in Australia, it addresses the terminology and debates which haunt any discussion of cultural difference

1

within that context. I would, however, like to extend the discussion to encompass biculturalism within the New Zealand and Canadian contexts. For example, in the former, biculturalism often means simply the opposition between Maori and Pakeha, with the latter grouping usually encompassing only the descendants of British colonial settlers and not the many other groups that comprise modern New Zealand. In other words, I would like to explore some of the dynamics between biculturalism and multiculturalism. Interpretations are usefully complicated and qualified when one's own local debates are situated within a larger global schema. I will therefore not only refer to the diasporic phenomenon in general but also allude to Canadian women writers as well as New Zealand and Australian ones.

A central question in this paper is why debates around ethnicity are consistently conflated with those of race. Does the indisputable existence of racism and the need to oppose it require a concomitant adherence to traditional concepts of race? But before I move on to this topic I will attempt a quick summary of some of the ways in which multiculturalism resonates within Australia. It became enshrined as official policy in 1989 with the launching of the National Agenda for a Multicultural Australia which conspicuously did not deal with cultural matters, as they are usually figured, at all. In the wake of this quite recent event which calls on all government institutions and agencies to implement recognition of Australia's ethnic diversity, I find it ironic that I am increasingly asked to participate in panels and events, or performances, where I am to speak (authentically, of course) about ways of moving *beyond* multiculturalism—which increasingly generates a great deal of anxiety in Australia. At its simplest level, this development represents an instance of the classic conflation of multiculturalism as a system of government policies designed to manage cultural diversity, and multiculturalism insofar as it arises from the desires of various communities and individuals who feel excluded by the discourses and practices surrounding Australian nationalism. The two meanings of multiculturalism are very different but are often confused, so that cynicism with respect to government policies of any kind spills over into condemnation of legitimate challenges to the status quo which emanate from those groups and individuals conspicuously excluded by prevailing orthodoxies.

My own response to topics like 'Beyond Multicultural Writing' consists of emphasising that there have certainly been enough puerile and ill-informed debates around this theme and that I would prefer to ask the people who raise such a topic to do their homework and direct those interested in pursuing the matter further to the appearance of such publications as Bob Hodge and Vijay Mishra's *Dark Side of the Dream: Australian Literature and the Postcolonial Mind*; Kateryna Longley's and my own *Striking Chords: Multicultural Literary Interpretations*, and the recently published *Bibliography of Australian Multicultural Writers*, which includes around 900 published writers—not apprentices, but those who have managed to prevail, to continue writing, against the odds. Criteria for inclusion in the *Bibliography* were that the writer be either born in or have a parent or grandparent deriving from a language and culture other than those of England or Ireland. As it turned out, about one-third of such writers publish in languages other than English, another third in both English and other languages, and one-third in English only. This compilation represents a rather belated attempt to begin to analyze the contributions of those Australians whose cultural traditions and languages are from places other than England or Ireland, as well as to encourage critics to look at cultural location and differences across the spectrum of Australian cultural productions. Contrary to the opinions of some, these events are hardly a matter of marginalizing the writers concerned. Instead, they reveal that we have been operating within narrow definitions of the national culture, and they alert those interested in cultural matters to a new area which urgently requires detailed research. While I do not deny that there are problems with terminology in this field, one needs to think about what is being abandoned when discussion shifts 'beyond' these terms.

The term 'multicultural writer' is flanked by others such as 'migrant writer' and 'ethnic writer'. These often indicate simply that they are 'other', that is, not part of the mainstream. I agree that all have flaws and none pinpoints the real issue of contention, which is the role of cultural difference in Australian culture and specifically within literature. It may be useful at this point to indicate that my deployment of the term 'cultural difference' derives from Homi Bhabha's resonant formulation:

> Cultural difference marks the establishment of new forms of meaning, and strategies of identification, through processes of negotiation where no discursive authority can be established without revealing the difference of itself. The signs of cultural difference cannot then be unitary or individual forms of identity because their continual implication in other symbolic systems always leaves them 'incomplete' or open to cultural translation . . . Cultural difference is to be found where the 'loss' of meaning enters, as a cutting edge, into the representation of the fullness of the demands of culture . . . Cultural difference emerges from the borderline moment of translation . . . The transfer of meaning can

never be total between differential systems of meaning, or within
them . . . it is the articulation through incommensurability that
structures all narratives of identitification, and all acts of cultural
translation. (Bhabha 1990:313–317)

A few decades ago, battles comparable to the ones I've been
sketching took place around women's writing. Scandalously, very
few women writers were seen to be part of Australian or any
other writing. All this has changed, of course, and we certainly
no longer have anthologies that exclude women, though they may
not yet be automatically represented in equal numbers to men.

Not so long ago, too, Australian literature itself was not
recognized as a respectable territory. It is only relatively recently
that Australia has come of age, so to speak, and that it can rest
assured that its literature is a recognized field among the world's
literatures in English. And there's part of the rub. The fight to
establish Australian literature was intimately bound up with the
battle to secure Australia's cultural independence from its British
colonial heritage. On the one hand we had the love–hate relationship with the monuments of British literature and on the other
the need to separate from the paternal figure and assert Australian
independence. Some of this was bound up with the major dissenting strain in Australian culture linked to the Irish factor, which
ensures that Irish working class and Catholic experience dominates
the republican element in Australian political history in general
and cultural politics in particular. Ned Kelly becomes the quintessential Australian hero and writers from Furphy to Keneally
construct a literary genealogy conspicuous in which is a writer
called Henry Lawson or Henry Larsen whose father, it transpires,
was Norwegian. Recently, Michael Wilding (1992) and others have
explored Larsen/Lawson's non-Anglo connections. This is an
example of what I mean by suggesting that cultural difference
(including linguistic difference) is as indispensable a critical category as are gender and class. By cultural difference, I do not simply
mean mapping the influence of various European elements on
well-known writers or the fact that some Australian writers have
shown an interest in Europe or Asia. I mean, among other things,
that the monuments of British literature these days include works
by such writers as Salman Rushdie, Ben Okri and Kazuo Ishiguro.
I also mean that there is now a general awareness that literatures
in English are quite a different matter from English literature.

Back to Australia. After the great postwar migrations, the
various scatterings, had produced the next generation, people like
myself started to wonder what place there was in our picture of
Australian culture and its literature for our own or our parents'

experiences and their symbolic transformations. Our own diaspo-
ras connected us to places everywhere *but* England and Ireland,
yet this did not come through in the various narratives that
constructed the nation. By now, as everyone knows, 'we', those
who have come since the Second World War, represent about a
third of the population. Where were our histories, our writings?
This question has motivated my own work. Increasingly I had to
acknowledge the fact that this simple act of cultural retrieval
presented an enormous threat to certain interests. Nonetheless, a
number of us have produced bibliographies and established collections of these other writings. They will be here for future
researchers even if current work becomes the casualty of prejudice.[2]

So at this point let us explore some of the difficulties inherent
in prevailing terminology. If we use the term multicultural, we are
homogenizing more than 100 different cultural and linguistic
groups and this to some extent defeats the larger purpose of setting
up much-needed precise research into differences and specificities.
It constitutes a lumping-together of something which needs carefully to be teased apart. If we use the other favoured term of 'non
English-speaking background' (NESB), we are presented with a
definition in terms of a negative, as though these writers lacked
something instead of having something extra to offer, another
language, an intimate and insider's access to other cultures. In the
words of poet Ania Walwicz, 'foreigner has some extra at back
of head is another country' (Walwicz 1989:85). There is also some
truth to the charge that multiculturalism has been used to obscure
the differences relating to the rights of the indigenous peoples,
notably in relation to land claims.[3] On the other hand we do need
a mechanism, including terminology, for drawing attention to a
visible absence, the absence of these writers, languages and cultural traditions from acknowledgment as part of Australia's
differentiated culture.

Alas, these factors are not automatically taken into account in
the many festivals and celebrations exploring Australia's national
culture. This is partly because that culture has only recently gained
a measure of definition, and its architects, having won that
difficult battle, do not take kindly to further incursions into their
terrain or challenges to their assumptions. Interestingly, the
challenge which has (none too soon) been issued by Aboriginal
culture has somehow found greater purchase than those other,
'ethnic' ones. This is possibly due to the fact that Aboriginal
Australians number at most only four per cent of the population
and therefore simply don't constitute the same threat as the
'ethnic' 33 per cent. Symbolically their questions will, of course—

and rightly—upset the whole edifice of the carefully designed national culture. As will the interrogations which emanate from the other groups that constitute Australia, those 'English plus' people who are neither monolingual nor monocultural.

The time has now come to seek out and celebrate those differences instead of having to argue for their very survival. Focusing for the moment on the case of Canada, I am not saying that these writers of 'other solitudes', as they were called in a recent anthology (Hutcheon & Richmond 1990), have an entirely smooth run there. Indeed, one of the editors, commenting on that anthology's reception, noted that it had evidently 'hit a raw nerve in the Canadian psyche' (Hutcheon 1992:9). Nonetheless, many more such books are being published and put on curricula; this is perhaps partly because Canada was never simply English-speaking in the way that Australia was. Its policy of biculturalism, in relation to French and English, has operated for a long time and its recognition of multiculturalism in relation to other groups is also well-established. There is certainly a far greater curiosity there, a more earnest seeking-out of what these writers have to offer, and an acceptance that they may write in English or French or they may not.

Here is the Greek-Canadian Smaro Kamboureli:

> This is the first time I use the word immigrant with reference to myself. This word hits me in the face and in the heart. It ejects me from what I cannot leave (my past/my Greek language), and throws me into a place that constantly excludes me on the principles of difference. My ideas, my habits, my amorous moods, my temperament are, quite often, not seen as expressions of me, but as specimens of the Greek stereotype I am supposed to represent. How can I explain that, although I am a Macedonian like Aristotle, I am not a mimetic being, a signified brand. I am expected to be homogeneous at the expense of my personal heterogeneity. I've said 'No' to those who invited me to recite Homer by heart. I've given no response to those who described to me, very vividly, the dirty washrooms they visited in the small island towns of Greece. (Kamboureli 1985:8)

Such clear-sighted analytical distinctions are commonplace among those who inhabit more than one language and thus do not see any language as 'natural' or universal. They help remind us that the creative productions which are reinscribing the world are part of ethnic fermentations which are taking place every-where, particularly in the wake of the break up of the Soviet empire. And multiculturalism is a term that links Australia to these global upheavals. It does not function in the same way everywhere; in the US, for example, it relates very much to relations across racial divides and the claims of Hispanic and African Americans. But all these movements are marked by attempts to define local differences, to undermine the impulse to homogenize, and to deflect the suppressive effects of certain kinds of nationalisms. Such nationalistic endeavours unfortunately and inevitably constitute closures rather than an opening up to new cultural tolerances.

However, if we suppose for the moment that people really do want to know about these other influences and writers in Australia, the next step is to find out who they are and to ensure that they enter the cultural marketplace. Or, to quote Smaro Kamboureli in a different register: 'Only when multiculturalism becomes a circuit of exchange, only then will storytelling become circulation.' (Chapter 9, this volume). It was necessary to dispel the assumption that these writers had nothing but incompetence in the English language to offer. At the same time, it must be conceded that such studies, and the critical reassessments which accompany them, will radically change the face of Australian literature as we know it. To illustrate the kind of readjustments I am talking about, here is an extract from the introduction to the Hodge & Mishra text mentioned above:

> Our particular concern is with the roles that Australian literature has played in this unceasing and doomed quest for symbolic forms of legitimacy: Australian literature both as a set of texts and as an object constructed by various agencies attempting to prescribe what texts should be written, what they should be taken to mean, and what authors and texts should be deemed to count as major landmarks in the national tradition. We argue against both the competing views of Australian literature: that its claims to greatness (or fatal defect) lay in its heroic (or unfortunate) break with the culture of the centre. On the contrary we see the culture and its literature as still determined massively by its complicity with an imperialist enterprise, coexisting in a necessary but compromised symbiosis with moments and forces of subversion and resistance from within the society.
>
> In saying this we are not supposing that there is a single agreed object, 'Australian literature'. The term refers to a body of genres and texts that has always been stratified along social and political lines, with different orientations to the dominant groups in the society: and these lines have been drawn at significantly different places all over Australia's short history. In the past the Australian obsession with legitimacy has been translated into the project of establishing a distinctively Australian tradition, complete with a Great Australian Writer and a Great Australian Novel, whose manifest greatness would at last prove the colonists' right to belong, both to the metropolitan centre and in the territory that they had invaded and colonised, Australia itself. But this search

was doomed from the outset by a contradiction in the project
itself, a double message at its core. The concept of 'greatness' was
saturated with imperial connotations, with the value system
emanating from and controlled by the centre, while 'Australian'
was defined as an opposition to these values. (Hodge & Mishra
1991: x–xi)

This is the crux. If Australians are really attempting to create
something new, then they must stop making England and English
culture the sole reference point for defining their own differences.
If they acknowledged the influence of the other languages and
traditions that have long been a part of their (and 'our') lives,
they would facilitate the process of achieving cultural independence.

Imagined identities: Ethnicity and race

Let us turn now to the question with which I began, the intersection of ethnicity and race. The earliest uses of 'ethnicity' had the
connotations of 'heathen' or 'pagan', but in about the nineteenth
century the word acquired the implications of both 'race' and
'nation'. This shows, I suppose, that ethnicity and race were linked
from an early period, as well as indicating certain assumptions
about the nation and nationalism, namely that the secular is often
linked to the theological, that the secular narratives of nationalism
often require a sacred justification (Anderson 1983/91). The adja-
cent term 'ethos' had, in the seventeenth century, the sense of
'characteristic spirit, prevalent tone of sentiment of a people or
community'. This connotation underlies the current meaning of
'ethnicity', which is usually evoked as a way of distinguishing
between race in the biological sense and custom or history, or, to
put it another way, between body and spirit. But before we move
on to race we should note that a second meaning of 'ethos' links
it to aesthetic criticism and rhetoric and to the portrayal of
'character through mimicry'. Here, then, we have a highly charged
chain of meanings for which all of us can instantly forge contemporary significance. As with the old-fashioned distinctions between
sex and socially constituted gender, there is an emphasis in the
one on biological fact and in the other on socialised construct.
Nowadays, in the wake of the work of feminists such as Elizabeth
Grosz (1994) and Moira Gatens (1989), we know that sexuality
is as much a construct as gender and, indeed, that the body is as
much an inscribed terrain as any other signifying system. The old
body and spirit distinction no longer holds.

In comparable ways in the past, race was invoked as a science for differentiating in essential (and thus essentialist) ways among the various peoples comprising humankind and, indeed, as the work of Donna Haraway shows, distinguishing rather anxiously between humans and non-humans such as primates. Race was one of *the* irreducible differences and conveyed a certain reassurance, as all such irrefutable distinctions do. Male and female are another, but both categories, as we know, have been confounded. Ethnicity, in contradistinction to race, was seen as a 'function of sociology and culture rather than biology' (Outlaw 1990:60). For a while ethnicity was a favoured term because it was seen as a temporary state that eventually and inevitably resulted in integration or assimilation. As well, it was seen in terms of individualism rather than relationship to a group, and the individual is never as threatening or potentially disruptive to the status quo as is the group. Ethnicity had the quality of the self-chosen appellation, and this aspect remains a central way of distinguishing it from 'race': for example, ethnic communities and ethnic identity are self-identified.[4]

The category race fell into disrepute, especially after the Second World War, so that it seemed almost an insult to use it. Increasingly it became clear that whereas there is no question about the reality of racism, the notion of racial purity in biological or genetic terms, which underpins the concept of race, was a myth. At best one could talk only of 'clines', that is, 'gradients of change in terms of measurable genetic character such as skin colour' (Outlaw 1990:64). At this juncture, we recall that the link between genes and culture is always a problematic one and shapes such questions as: does one write differently as a woman or as an 'ethnic'? Nowadays 'race' tends to be spoken of as a social formation rather than in terms of bloodlines. Indeed, to quote a current theorist on the subject, it is 'an unstable and decentred complex of social meanings constantly being transformed by political struggle . . . political contestations over racial meanings' (Outlaw 1990:77). An illustration of this process occurs in Patricia Williams's account of a Jewish student's reaction to being informed that Beethoven was black:

> The determination that Beethoven was not black is an unspoken determination that he was German and therefore could not be black. To acknowledge the possibility of his mulatto ancestry is to undo the supposed purity of the Germanic Empire. It challenges the sanctification of cultural symbols rooted in notions of racial purity . . . if Beethoven . . . is not really white, if the word 'German' also means 'mulatto', then some of the most powerfully uplifting, inspiring, and unifying of what we call 'western'

moments comes crashing down to the aesthetics of vaudevillian
blackface. (Williams 1991:11)

But why are unproblematized references to race coming back,
and not always negatively? For instance, those involved in the
Black struggle (and bear in mind that this is a shifting term: I
have heard Southern Europeans and Arabs, for example, refer to
themselves as black) use the concept of race as a way of signalling
their determination to resist assimilation and to pursue cultural
difference and autonomy. The indigenous peoples of many cultures
use the term because their culture has been disenfranchised and
rendered invisible. And it is for similar reasons that other
'minority' groups also reach for the term race. It holds the magic
of irreducible difference, a non-negotiable space which heralds a
separate history, no less phantasmatic at its edges, however, than
all histories. It is also tied in disturbing ways to the notion of
primordial rights to land (Geertz 1973)—disturbing because such
claims about bloodlines and land have fuelled the fascist doctrines
of recent history, including the upheavals in what used to be
Yugoslavia.

Another phantasmagoric dimension of history is that as well
as a diaspora, a scattering of the genes/seeds across the globe, we
have myths of origin. These include the concept of the mother
tongue as traditionally constitutive of identity. In other words,
there is a focus on language rather than on originating territory
or geography.

But identity in our poststructuralist and postmodernist world
is also not unproblematic. We have come to identify identity with
the oppressive sovereign subject who is male and usually white.
Thus Descartes' famous dictum 'I think therefore I am' was fleshed
out according to a masculinist and Eurocentric model. In the past
few decades there has been an unprecedented assault on the
concept of this fixed subject by all those women, minorities,
non-Westerners who realised they were excluded from its purview.
Instead we have become more comfortable with the notion of
subjectivities or subject positions and a concept of identity in
which, to quote Judith Butler, 'identity becomes a signifying
practice—within a structure of repetition' (Butler 1990:12). Those
of us who also see our life's work as bringing about social
change—that is, once we have disrupted the sovereign (male)
subject to replace it with more democratic processes of cultural
participation—have been told repeatedly that without identity you
cannot have agency nor, therefore, a program for social and
political change. This is why postmodernism has so often been
accused of being anti- or apolitical. But is this necessarily so? On

the subject of agency without identity in the fixed sense, Butler comments:

> The critical task for feminism is not to establish a point of view outside of constructed identities; that conceit is the construction of an epistemological model that would disavow its own cultural location and, hence, promote itself as a global subject, a position that deploys precisely the imperialist strategies that feminism ought to criticize. The critical task is, rather, to locate strategies of subversive repetition enabled by those constructions, to affirm the local possibilities of intervention through participating in precisely those practices of repetition that constitute identity and, therefore, present the immanent possibility of contesting them . . . The deconstruction of identity is not the deconstruction of politics; rather, it establishes as political the very terms through which identity is articulated. (Butler 1990:17–18)

Translated into our local terms, it constitutes the responsibility for feminists to intervene whenever such 'identities' are being constituted, whether in nationalist or gender or class terms. It is crucial to shift the closures that operate within these repetitions as well as the terms of the debate, as Butler points out. In feminist debates it means insisting on the differences among women; in Australian nationalist debates it means insisting on the cultural work that draws on traditions other than those of England or Ireland and languages other than English. One notes as well Shirley Neuman's pertinent comments in relation to an autobiographical poetics of difference where there is a subject both

> . . . socially constructed and constructing . . . Such a poetics would conceive the self not as the product of its different identity *from* others but as constructed by multiple differences *within* and *from* itself . . . It is a complex, multiple, layered subject with agency in the discourses and the worlds that constitute the referential space of his or her autobiography . . . (Neuman 1992: 223–225)

So here we are, ethnics who are pagan or heathen in the sense that we are not part of the dominant ethos of this culture—hence we mimic its character at times in order to produce our own performative gestures of a different aesthetics, a different rhetoric. A tool we often wield is irony, described by Linda Hutcheon (1991:49) as that double vision which implicitly challenges any claims to universalism or speech in the name of humanity. It is this double vision that also informs the kinds of subversive local practices defined above by Butler.

So what might migrant and non-Anglo women have to offer in terms of irony and other textual innovations? In the first place,

they produce, necessarily, another version of history. In a charac-
teristically pyrotechnical essay about being a woman of Dutch
extraction in Canada, Aritha van Herk (1991) offers some valuable insights on the writing of migrant autobiographies, personal
histories. She distinguishes two stories, the covert and the overt
one and three themes: the shifts in time; the secret story which
the overt story covers over, e.g. the story of those who weren't
simply political refugees but who because they had collaborated
in wartime with the wrong side; and, most poignant of all, the
absent story of the self we would have been had we stayed in the
old country. This comes through for me very clearly in stories by
Canadian-Chinese writers. (Lee & Wong-Chu 1991). Often the
siblings who remain in China represent an imagined self. Haven't
we all fantasized in this way, wondering what our histories would
have been in Bulgaria, in Germany, in Greece? The other important point van Herk makes is that we are bound by the set pieces,
the traditional frameworks of such autobiographical histories,
which have been imposed or projected onto us. Elsewhere I have
written about this in terms of the burden of authenticity: we who
come from non-dominant groups suffer the burden of having all
our texts read only in terms of the authentic migrant experience,
just as Aboriginal writers are seen as being relevant only to
questions concerning Aboriginality or women are only concerned
with femininity and having nothing to say about either masculinity
or humanity—the last two often being synonymous but seldom
perceived as such (Gunew 1989).

The other double vision such positions potentially have is
related to language itself. Again, Smaro Kamboureli's writing
reveals an acute awareness of how the self is conditioned by
operating in more than one language, 'To live bathed in a language
other than my mother tongue, I have to partially drown the being
that was nourished by the mother tongue.' (Kamboureli 1985:10).
Another example refers to that uncanny space between languages:

> The borderline that marks the conflict between the first and second
> language marks as well the stage of language where words are
> beings in themselves prior to becoming the proper names of things.
> (Kamboureli 1985:10)

And elsewhere: 'I changed language, I grew a second skin,
wrapped around my self another self. I've become a metonymy of
my past' (Kamboureli 1985:21). In her book the new selves also
function as new inflections of the feminine. In other words,
femaleness itself acquires different forms in the new language, new
ways of performing the spectacles of femininity—and at the most
intimate levels. So another element we offer with our migrant or

non-Anglo female ironies is to extend that spectrum of signifiers which characterise femininity and femaleness within the dominant culture.

'Devouring language'[5]

Let me now tell you a story.

In a film produced by the Department of Immigration in the 1950s, *No Strangers Here*, there is a brilliant *mise en abyme*[6] which has haunted me since I saw it. The film is set in 'Littletown', a small Australian rural town, in the immediate postwar period. Narrative point of view is provided by the editor of the town's newspaper, a genial and overweight liberal. The story begins when he receives several anonymous letters, signed 'a true Australian', basically saying that foreigners are not wanted in Littletown. As the editor perambulates through the town kissing babies and talking to women, he notices the arrival of a foreign family, good-looking and nuclear. A voice-over traces their backgrounds briefly as refugees from totalitarian and war-torn Europe. Their exact provenance is carefully not specified. Suffice to say that they clearly gesture their astonishment at the abundance of material objects around them: food and particularly a bicycle, which the father craves. Remarkably quickly they find their niches. The father works in the brickworks, the son goes to school, and the fetching daughter ends up as an aide in the local hospital, where she sets the hearts of the male patients and doctors aflutter. The mother remains in the home, where the editor decides to pay her a visit. He enters her home with the immortal words: 'Please tell me the story of your life.' On the brink of answering, the mother rushes to the oven, where something more urgent is evidently calling for attention. She offers the editor a slice of home-made cake and he in turn requests the recipe. This proves to be the answer to his question. The recipe is published under the heading 'Easy To Mix' and the town's women respond appropriately. I will leave the rest for you to savour at your leisure.

This risible small tale is actually an extremely accurate metaphoric and metonymic delineation of the ideology at the heart of postwar migration and the various attempts to manage it. The film signals assimilation in certain ways, notably linking it to the digestive model from which the term derives. Crucially, the mother offers food instead of words. Food, as we know, has long been the acceptable face of multiculturalism.

As a way of exploring this signifying chain, I draw your attention to Kristeva's linking of the concept of abjection to language, food and the mother; I will return to this in a moment. But first, let me turn to two New Zealand women writers who do not fit easily into the prevailing structures of biculturalism as simply Maori versus Pakeha: Yvonne du Fresne and Antigone Kefala. The latter's published work to date has mainly been about New Zealand, although she has now lived for many years in Australia. I have chosen to look at their work in relation to two publications which deal with evocations of childhood.

I have written often about the ways in which 'migrants' are infantilized in a range of ways by the receiving culture (Gunew 1985; see also Hatzimanolis in this volume). The most productive reading is to see them as having to negotiate a new symbolic in the psychoanalytic sense so that their old languages (within the law of the father) are repressed, or become constructed as the abject in the Kristevan sense. To create a clean and proper language, they need to suppress and expel their previous language, so that not simply the mother but the mother tongue is denied.

Du Fresne's stories about Astrid Westergaard and Kefala's about her protagonist Alexia are characterized by their linking of language, food and propriety. For example, take du Fresne's story 'The Looters':

> At night the looters came home, bearing their prizes, hungry for their dinners. And what were their prizes? The English language. They looted the English language and brought home their finds. Examples. Typical expressions. They showed off to each other. I sat at the table, beaming, all ready for my dinner and the talk. I could never keep up with the talk, but how I watched, how I listened! Astrid the spy, watching the other spies, much more skilful than me, for they not only watched and listened—they could read. They read everything they could lay their hands on. And I could not read. That was my shame, you know. I listened to the reading groups at school and learned the words off by heart, for I too was a looter. But when I looked at the words of my *Beacon Reader*, the words turned into thin black shapes . . . I gazed at them in despair. Nothing spoke to me from those words. (du Fresne 1989:20)

'Astrid the spy' is an elegant way of characterizing the outsider caught between two languages and cultures. Instead of being depleted by this, she uses her double and secret knowledge of what lies beyond the surface appearances eventually to rewrite both traditions. In the process she casts a devastatingly satiric eye on the dominant Anglo culture—notably in the section where her father reads to her from stories about English schoolgirls. I mention in passing that this strikes a private chord because I recall devouring such stories as I grew up on the outskirts of Melbourne trying to understand the culture on whose rim I perched while concurrently enmeshed in a very different one. Astrid savours these stories 'like a secret drinker'.

It has been a standard gesture by Maori women writers like Patricia Grace and Ngahuia Te Awekotuku to utilise macaronic elements. This incorporation of the Maori language within their English narrative is a way of signifying the indigestible element that will not be assimilated or, more resonantly perhaps, the incommensurable and untranslatable which exists between languages (symbolic systems) and within each language—that is, the non-identity of language with referential reality. These lacunae and ellipses undermine the possibility of a universalist discourse.

Antigone Kefala's (1984) underrated book *Alexia* links language, experience and music. The disharmonies of the first two threaten the survival of the last. Alexia struggles with the new language and the bizarre realities conjured by its words and discusses these with her musician brother:

'Sounds had become superfluous things,' he said. It was no longer possible to play. He looked at the cellos they had carried for so long. 'These cages', he called them, now empty of resonance. This new country was not full of 'lotus eaters', as everyone said, but of 'resonance eaters'.

My final passage from this story occurs towards the end when the teacher invites Alexia and her friend Basia to tea:

Then she served them roast beef, mashed potatoes, which were very white and sparkled in the light, and boiled peas with sauce, and as she passed them one by one . . . she asked them: 'Are You Happy?'

And Alexia immediately went into a panic. For she felt Happy to be an Enormous Word, word full of flamboyant colours, which only people who had reached an ecstatic state had a right to use. She saw it as the 'apotheosis' so to speak, of a series of events, which as far as she could see, lay totally outside her life. But she could not explain this, for everyone on the Island kept asking, as if this Fantastic Word was the basic measure of their days—

'Are you Happy? Does this make you Happy? Isn't this Happiness?' and so on. And Alexia imagined them all dancing in the streets, flying above the houses, their hair blowing in the wind, surrounded by flowers and angels.

The more she thought about it, the more confused she became. Did Miss Prudence mean:

Was she happy eating her mashed potatoes?
Being in her house with the grandfather clock chiming?
Happy living on the Island?
or

Happy living in the World?

> There she was, with the salt-cellar in her hand which she had been
> asked to pass on to Mary, not knowing what to say, getting more
> and more confused between Happiness and Salt. (Kefala 1984)

In both these texts, subject formation is constituted in terms
of language and food. In Australia one of the few unthreatening
ways to speak of multiculturalism is in relation to food, in other
words, to say that all these migrants have improved the diversity
of the national cuisine. The usual way in which this diversity is
acceptably celebrated is through a multicultural food festival.

Julia Kristeva's discussion of the abject defines it as that
ambiguous area surrounding borderlines which threatens the stability of subject formation through problems of separation from
the mother. It is a place where meanings are lost, 'the in-between,
the ambiguous, the composite' (Kristeva 1982:4). Her introductory
example relates to food, namely, the inexplicable revulsion experienced at the prospect of ingesting the skin which forms on milk.
As the study goes on to explore, the abject is related to the mother
in the most primal sense, as that from which the subject needs to
separate in order to form a separate ego. The mother links food,
meaning and language, the entry into the symbolic and the law
which gives meaning to social negotiations. The mother is subsequently relegated to the semiotic hinterland where monsters dwell.
Interestingly, in Kristeva's analysis, the phobic who endures the
abject often displays remarkable linguistic versatility, hence the
reference to Little Hans and his obsessive need to name everything
as a way of warding off the fear of the unnamable:

> . . . the phobic object is a proto-writing and, conversely, any
> practice of speech, inasmuch as it involves writing, is a language of
> fear . . . the writer is a phobic who succeeds in metaphorizing in
> order to keep from being frightened of death; instead he comes to
> life in signs. (Kristeva 1982:38)

To some extent this relates also to Freud's uncanny, although
Kristeva differentiates it from this concept by pointing out that
there is nothing familiar in the abject, 'not even the shadow of a
memory' (Kristeva 1982:5). Elsewhere I have explored the notion
of the uncanny, linking it in a metonymic series to sickness for
and of the home; the familiar place or figure (the mother once
more) which suddenly reveals its archaic and monstrous elements
(Gunew 1988).

In her study of the monstrous female, Barbara Creed (1992)
relates the notion of the abject to the mother who must be expelled
lest she devour her offspring—the all-engulfing image. Again,

clearly, the mother, food, the loss of meaning are linked. My suggestion here is (and this is the subject of a work in progress) that foreign languages within a predominantly anglophone context function as the abject, as something which threatens meaning and subject-formation, including the notion of a coherent national identity. Words are feared because unlike food they cannot be assimilated, and words in another language emphasize the split within subjectivity. Words are able, like the non-introjected mother, to devour from within.

In a more expressive or commonsense vein, without necessarily reaching for this psychoanalytic apparatus, one could say that du Fresne's and Kefala's alertness to the precise contours of language, the frames which both exclude as much as they include and which construct precise versions of reality, is a characteristic of those who move with ease in more than one language, whether these languages be Maori, Greek, English or Danish.

Conclusion

In Australia now, the issue of cultural difference has become an inevitable qualifier of any questions to do with gender or class. Multicultural literature still signals those exclusions from received notions of the national literature and culture. We still need to make this absence visible, just as women's absence needed (still needs) to be made explicit. Universalist terms such as 'human' or 'writer' or 'Australian writer' don't, as a matter of course, incorporate the kinds of differences we have been exploring. Now in Australia we have the groundwork to research these differences: the first anthology of critical essays on multicultural literature (Gunew & Longley 1992); the first collection of multicultural literature at Deakin University, and specific language collections in a range of institutions across the country; and, at last, a bibliography of multicultural writers (Gunew *et al.* 1992). The hope is that these will change the ways we construct literature in Australia, for we will all need to become more informed about the literary and cultural traditions out of which these writers have emerged. It is not a matter of *Blut und Boden,* blood and geographical territory, but of ethos, that is, the 'characteristic spirit, prevalent tone of sentiment of a people or community'. Just as they are beginning to learn the iconography of Aboriginal culture, Australians will need to do their homework about all these histories and traditions in order to fully appreciate what is produced and written in all the languages of their country. It is a question not of elevating one aspect rather than another as more authentically Australian (or Canadian), but of being informed about all the various elements which converge, at times even in productive discord, to form a culture.

Notes

1 Julia Kristeva's reference to Freud's Little Hans (Kristeva 1982:34).
2 I am referring here to a debate which occurred last year and whose ramifications are addressed by a range of writers in Gunew (1992).
3 Interestingly enough, recent moves suggest that current debates around the concept of 'postcolonialism' have reversed this trend. Now issues concerning non-Anglo Australian are displaced by an exclusive emphasis on the opposition either to the old colonial power, Britain or between older settler cultures and the indigenous peoples. In other words, matters are reduced to the black-white opposition with no room left for positioning other differences.
4 The traditional qualities relating to ethnicity are rehearsed, for example, in Pearson 1991.
5 The phrase is borrowed from Kristeva 1982:40.
6 The concept comes from Dällenbach 1977 and the curious spelling of 'abyme' is noted in the introduction.

References

Anderson, Benedict (1983/91) *Imagined Communities: Reflections on the Origin and Spread of Nationalism*, Verso, London.

Butler, Judith (1990) *Gender Trouble: Feminism and the Subversion of Identity*, Routledge, New York.

Creed, Barbara (forthcoming) *Feminist Theory and the Horror Film*, Routledge, London.

Dällenbach, L. (1977) *Le récit spéculaire. Essai sur la mise en abyme*, Éditions du Seuil, Paris.

du Fresne, Yvonne (1989) *The Bear From the North: Tales of a New Zealand Childhood*, Women's Press, London.

Gatens, Moira (1989) 'A Critique of the Sex/Gender Distinction', in *A Reader in Feminist Knowledge*, ed. Gunew, Routledge, London.

Geertz, C. (1973) 'The Integrative Revolution: Primordial Sentiments and Civil Politics in the New States', in *The Interpretation of Cultures*, ed. C. Geertz, Free Press, New York, Ch.10.

Grace Patricia (1975/83) *Waiariki and Other Stories*, Penguin, Auckland.

Grosz, Elizabeth (1994) *Volatile Bodies: Toward a Corporeal Feminism*, Indiana University Press, Bloomington.

Gunew, Sneja (1985) 'Migrant Women Writers: Who's on Whose Margin?' in *Gender, Politics and Fiction*, ed. C. Ferrier, University of Queensland Press, St Lucia, pp.163–178.

——(1988) 'Home and Away: Nostalgia in Australian (Migrant) Writing', in *Island in the Stream*, ed. P. Foss, Pluto Press, Sydney, pp. 35–46.

——(1989) 'Authenticity and the Writing Cure', in *Grafts: Feminist Cultural Criticism*, ed. S. Sheridan, Verso, London, pp. 111–124.

——& Longley, Kateryna eds. (1992) *Striking Chords: Multicultural Literary Interpretations*, Allen & Unwin, Sydney.
——Houbein, L., Karakostas-Seda, A. & Mahyuddin, J. eds. (1992) *A Bibliography of Australian Multicultural Writers*, Centre for Studies in Literary Education, Deakin University, Geelong.
——ed. (1992) *Typereader 7* (1992) Journal of the Centre for Studies in Literary Education, Deakin University, Geelong
Haraway, Donna (1989) *Primate Visions: Gender, Race, and Nature in the World of Modern Science*, Routledge, New York.
Hodge, Bob & Mishra, Vijay (1991) *Dark Side of the Dream: Australian Literature and the Postcolonial Mind*, Allen & Unwin, Sydney.
Hutcheon, L. (1991) *Splitting Images: Contemporary Canadian Ironies*, Oxford University Press, Toronto.
——(1992) 'The Multicultural Debate: The Reception of *Other Solitudes*', *Italian Canadiana*, 8.2, pp. 7–14.
——& Richmond, M. eds. (1990) *Other Solitudes: Canadian Multicultural Fictions*, Oxford University Press, Toronto.
Kamboureli, Smaro (1985) *in the second person*, Longspoon Press, Alberta.
Kefala, Antigone (1984) *Alexia: A Tale of Two Cultures*, John Ferguson, Sydney.
Kristeva, Julia (1982) *Powers of Horror: An Essay on Abjection*, trans. L.S. Roudiez, Columbia University Press, New York.
Lee, B. & Wong-Chu, J. eds. (1991) *Many-mouthed Birds: Contemporary Writing by Chinese Canadians*, Douglas & McIntyre, Vancouver/Toronto.
Neuman, Shirley (1992) 'Autobiography: From Different Poetics to a Poetics of Differences', in *Essays on Life Writing*, ed. M. Kadar, University of Toronto Press, Toronto, pp. 213–230.
Outlaw, Lucius (1990) 'Toward a Critical Theory of "Race" ', in *Anatomy of Racism*, ed. D. Goldberg, University of Minnesota Press, Minneapolis, pp. 58–82.
Pearson, David (1991) 'Biculturalism and Multiculturalism in Comparative Perspective', in *Nga Take: Ethnic Relations and Racism in Aotearoa/New Zealand*, ed. P. Spoonley, D. Pearson & C. Macpherson, The Dunmore Press, New Zealand, 194–214
Te Awekotuku, Ngahuia (1989) *Tahuri*, New Women's Press, Auckland.
van Herk, Aritha (1991) 'Writing the Immigrant Self: Disguise and Damnation', in *In Visible Ink: Crypto-fictions*, NeWest Press, Edmonton.
Walwicz, Ania (1989) *Boat*, Angus & Robertson, Sydney.
Wilding, Michael (1992) 'Henry Lawson—Ethnic Writer,' *Outrider*, ix.1, pp. 104–109.
Williams, Patricia (1991) *The Alchemy of Race and Rights*, Harvard University Press, NY.

2 'Feminisms, reading, postmodernisms': Rethinking complicity

Vicki Kirby

If the uneasy conjunction between feminism, anthropology and postmodernism is a fertile and provocative one, perhaps it is because the resulting interchange generates more questions than we can comfortably answer. Much of my own work has been an exploration of what are commonly interpreted as the disabling contradictions that inhabit this awkward intersection (Kirby 1987; 1989a; 1989b; 1989c), for this particular 'meeting' engenders the anxiety and confrontational posturing of a high-noon stand-off. Amid the ensuing theatre of suspicion, threat and counter-threat, precisely what is at stake in this debate has become increasingly elusive.

The critique of ethnography, feminism's own internecine struggles, as well as contestation over the problematic category of postmodernism, are now arenas of such bitter, partisan dispute that the censoring hostility of rhetorical ambush tends to prevent dialogue. In an attempt to parry with the prohibitive strategies of closure that defend against debate, I want to explore a question about implication, contamination and the vagaries of identity. Put simply, I want to investigate the assumption that either a feminist and/or a postmodern ethnography is preferable to masculinist/traditional ethnographies. Or, recasting the question another way, I want to query a persistent belief that what identifies a practice *as* feminist and/or postmodern can be readily determined.

In a recent issue of *Signs*, a paper whose title promised to engage some of these fraught questions offered instead a troubling but not uncommon example of the way in which feminism can be made a convenient alibi to prevent critical inquiry. In 'The Postmodernist Turn in Anthropology: Cautions From a Feminist Perspective' (1989), the three co-authors, Frances E. Mascia-Lees, Patricia Sharpe and Colleen Ballerino Cohen, assume that a healthy political correctness can be secured by way of feminism's authorizing signature. Anxious to adjudicate ambiguities, they ask us to return to a 'clear politics' in which the tensions that complicate the discursive intersection between feminism, anthropology and postmodernism can be readily resolved.

Postmodernism is consequently characterized as apolitical obfuscation, as the fashionable hipster's updated *ennui* that 'beholds the world blankly, with a knowingness that dissolves feeling and commitment into irony' (1989:1). Postmodernism is apparently 'abstract and theoretical', caught up in dubious textual antics and decentring strategies that act to defer serious forms of political engagement. Postmodernism may even be another desparate ruse of patriarchy, one last attempt to disavow the inevitability of its own decline. Against this sinister force the authors project a salutary feminism that stands ready to set things right.

Mascia-Lees, Sharpe and Cohen acknowledge that 'there are many postmodernisms, just as there are many feminisms, and within both movements definitions are contested' (1989:1). But having given this caveat, they make no further mention of these other voices, nor of what might be at stake in their ongoing differences. Instead, feminism and postmodernism are staged as single, homogeneous categories, easily identifiable because in agonistic confrontation with each other. An unfortunate casualty of these monolithic representations is the sort of feminist practice that may find itself indebted to many of the critical theories that this article complacently describes with the shorthand label 'postmodern'. And it is a curious irony that the need to repress the existence of this apparently contaminated feminism, a difference *within* feminism, requires the authors' ready reliance upon a notion of purity and danger that women in anthropology have worked long and hard to call into question.

Feminism and postmodernism are, of course, not the unified terms that Mascia-Lees and her colleagues would rally us to choose between. It is arguable whether they are terms that can be successfully defended or condemned in quite this way. A more curious and equivocal approach to the question of the postmodern can have its rewards. Taking a critical distance from the hegemony of both Anglo-American feminism and Anglo-American interpretations of postmodern criticism, many feminists in Australia have been engaged in grafting, re-reading and recycling these exotic imports into products with different and local use values. With careful attention to their critical possibilities, they are made a pliable resource that can be put to work through new and hybrid forms. It can come as a surprise to an American audience, for example, that 'French theory' and its postmodern cognates were largely sponsored into Australia through the efforts of feminist and gay liberation activists in the 1970s.[1]

If feminism can and does occupy postmodern ground, what are we to make of Craig Owens's observation that:

> If one of the most salient aspects of our postmodern culture is the presence of an insistent feminist voice . . . theories of postmodernism have tended either to neglect or to repress that voice. The absence of discussions of sexual difference in writings about postmodernism, as well as the fact that few women have engaged in the modernism/postmodernism debate, suggest that postmodernism may be another masculine invention engineered to exclude women. (cited in Mascia-Lees *et al*.:1989:17)

Mascia-Lees and her co-authors rely on this particular citation as an accurate description of the situation and one that therefore validates their own argument. And indeed, both Andreas Huyssen and Jonathan Arac also express this same view.

In *The Pirate's Fiancée: Feminism, Reading, Postmodernism* , Meaghan Morris (1988:11) makes specific reference to what she calls 'this very curious doxa' that male critics, referring primarily to each other, like to reiterate. Morris is wary of their gesture towards feminism, arguing that this admission of an unwarranted and 'baffling' exclusion deserves further attention. For she recognizes that this assessment, even within the frame of these critics' own observations, works to blur the difference between what she describes as:

> . . . an act of re-presenting a presupposed historical not-figuring of women in postmodernism debates, and an act of re-*producing* the not-figuring, not counting, of women's work, by 'simple' omission (writing it out of history, by writing its absence into history). (1988:1)

In answer to this, Morris offers a long list of women whose work consistently engages issues and concerns that these same critics would consider postmodern. She thereby recasts the question from one that ponders the curious absence of women from this discourse, to one that asks what might motivate its dubious assertion. Importantly, Morris does not confine her list of writers to mostly white and Western women. She also acknowledges the contributions of those who are 'differently placed in histories of racism and colonialism' and who are also producing new theorizations of politics and culture (1988:13). Morris mentions, as examples, Rasheed Araeen, Homi K. Bhabha, Eduardo Galeano, Henry Louis Gates Jr., Geeta Kapur, Trinh T. Minh-ha, Nelly Richard and others.

Mascia-Lees *et al.* remain silent about this body of work within postmodernism, and this strategic oversight guarantees the simple force of their argument. For their primary concern is to secure anthropology's future, hence the need to construct feminism as a supportive ally against anthropology's postmodern critics, a useful 'tool' or supplement to the discipline's continuation. Having determined that postmodernism is implicitly reactionary, Mascia-Lees and her colleagues are then able to make favourable comparisons between feminism and anthropology. They assert that feminism 'knows its politics' and that anthropology too is 'grounded in politics' because, they claim, both discourses work towards the recognition of cultural and sexual difference.

However, their argument's organizational departure point is a censoring of the inner disunity of feminism. The authors are unable to admit the constitutive importance of this repression to their own perspective. It is through this very process of norming and repression (denial of a difference within feminism) that their own position is made generalizable: the notion of difference as something transparent and recuperable is thereby preserved. An ironic consequence of this is that talk of 'understanding difference' can become a way of disavowing irreconcilable tensions and ruptures beneath a *glissement* of seemingly admirable appeals to genuine and meaningful dialogue.

This last point deserves elaboration, and the issue of *Inscriptions* specifically devoted to 'Feminism and the Critique of Colonial Discourse' is helpful here. Donna Haraway (1988:95) emphasized the importance of 'women's multiple kinds of expressivity not easily caught by any of the disciplines, genres, or practices'. Acknowledging the violence within dialectical thinking, a violence that works to incorporate and synthesize difference, Haraway (1988:95) noted the way that contemporary feminism tries to intervene against this unifying tendency, attempting to 'hold simultaneously true what are otherwise considered contradictions'. She went on to temper this remark with the following observation:

> I also hear a trope in feminist discourse that appears to be against other feminisms. And this is becoming more and more a problem for me. As feminism develops, becoming broader and longer and shared among lots of other people, there is a kind of oppositional discourse set up within feminism as if one's positions about complexity were in opposition to prior feminists who fixed women's identity essentially. But I think this is historically not true,

and in fact, again part of an othering, part of a way that academic
discourses work by othering recent previous discourses. So I guess
what I'm asking is how to keep both the edge of one's criticism
without reproducing a history that others other feminists (1988:96).

Haraway's comments were in part provoked by a paper in the
same issue, in which Aihwa Ong had argued that feminism
retained an unquestioned investment in the critical value of an
emancipatory heritage, a masculinist heritage, where the rhetoric
of the West's salvage operation promised a secularized form of
redemption through global sisterhood. Uncomfortable with the
political interests that motivate the apparent benevolence of this
enlightenment narrative, Ong (1988:80) suggested that: 'If from
the feminist perspective there can be no shared experience with
persons who stand for the Other, the claim to a common kinship
with non-Western women is at best tenuous, at worst non-
existent'. What is being suggested here is that feminism capitalizes
on this political difference through the expression of its own will
to truth/power.

If we return to Haraway's comments, we can see both the
nervous apprehension that surrounds such a suggestion and the
way the threat is managed. Haraway (1988:97) mentions her
admiration for Marilyn Strathern's more recent work, because it
is 'an effort to describe geometries of feminist discourse in ways
that do not get caught in oppositional and taxonomic modes'.
Aihwa Ong's work is also included in this path-breaking enterprise. Yet, in a gesture that would seem to deny Ong's actual
argument, an argument that insisted that feminism is very often
complicit with neo-colonialism, Haraway generalizes that the
avoidance of oppositional thinking is exemplary of contemporary
feminist endeavour. In making this point, she separates feminism
from the wrongs of masculinism and imperialism, that is, from
the violence that motivates the need to explain differences from
one perspective:

> . . . I want to affirm that most of feminist discourse is not caught
> up or pinned by developmentalist and essentialist logic, or at any
> rate it has many ways to get out when it gets into it. I think I'm
> expressing a hope as much as a descriptive fact. (1988:98)

Ong's intervention, a critical perspective on Western feminism's
reluctance to scrutinize the interested nature of its political agenda
on a global stage, has here been subsumed to the higher order of
feminism's avowed good intentions. This remains something of a
qualified trust, since feminism's ability to avoid a universalizing
logic that pretends to speak for all women was described by
Haraway as 'a hopeful fact'. According to this view, my own work

would have to be read as a betrayal of such hopes, or at least as an unfortunate lapse. For in several articles I have argued that the narrative of feminism's own 'making proper', its claim to self-legit-imation, is *enabled* by 'othering'. I offer this perspective not because of any departure from feminist commitments, as the lament in Haraway's caution would seem to presume, but because of what I take to be most valuable in them. In saying this, I do not wish to denigrate the valuable contribution to feminist schol-arship that Haraway's work represents in many other contexts.

Haraway interprets the very process of 'othering' as the iden-tifying symptom of 'academic discourses' which, I take it, are to be interpreted as elite and masculinist. As the violence of their binary logic oppresses women, it is a logic that feminists must contest. Haraway's hope that feminism might extricate itself from the violence of dialectical thinking assumes that oppositional logic is an error to be avoided, a mistake that can be corrected. Hence her valorization of Marilyn Strathern's work because it 'do[es] not get caught in oppositional and taxonomic modes', and her expressed regret that some feminists still feel compelled, appar-ently unnecessarily, to 'other' each other. Haraway seems unaware that her own intervention is entirely dependent upon oppositional logic. Like the rest of us, her argument will proceed in terms of this as opposed to that; valuing this by way of devaluing that.

Haraway's remarks are, as Derrida (1981:251) might put it, '. . . without seeing or knowing it, *within* the very self-evidence of Hegel one often thinks oneself unburdened of'.[2] Similarly, Haraway's desire that feminism be judged a politically preferable discourse because it can escape (more often than not) the violence of representational dichotomies is itself an unwitting reiteration of a developmentalist and essentializing logic. This same desire for transcendence is at work in the argument by Mascia-Lees and her colleagues that considers the relationship between feminism and anthropology. There, the authors (Mascia-Lees *et al.*:1989:33) understand 'otherness' as something we should 'work to overcome', the site of an unfairness that can be redressed, rather than as an enduring structural asymmetry with constitutive force. This very notion of 'overcoming' repeats and reinvests the logic of a Hegelian *Aufhebung* (preservation and transcendence) that systematically denies the very differences that Mascia-Lees *et al.* would want to acknowledge.

As I suggested earlier, this trust in feminism's ability to deliver on its redemptive promise is seriously questioned by other, quite different forms of endeavour within feminist scholarship that have emphasized the inevitable complicity that all discourses share with masculinism's binary logic. This attempt to think the political 'otherwise' is a labour of reinscription that tries to do more than simply diagnose complicity as a pathology to be excised; a labour that Gayatri Spivak (1989b) aptly describes as one of 'negotiating enabling violations'.

Complex work of this kind is often criticized *because* it is complex. Scholars who commit themselves to this painstaking task are then found guilty of a lack of clarity, the stuff of their efforts turned into a deficit.[3] They are thereby made responsible for rendering the difficulties in this new material immediately accessible to those who have not engaged their challenges, as if the difference between doing the work and not doing it were of no particular value. This demand for clarity actually rules against the very possibility of a difference that might resist familiar frames of reference.

The force of this imperative is powerfully articulated in the belief that some feminists still hold in the self-evident value of a purportedly disinterested humanitarian benevolence. It is manifest in the desire to make 'the other' legible through love—and it is presumed in the conviction that political and ethical issues can be successfully adjudicated if we remain honest about our intentions. Phallocentrism and ethnocentrism are naturalized and disavowed in the benign appeal that feminists are the trustworthy translaters of cultural difference because, as women, 'otherness' is what also defines them. For example, Mascia-Lees and her colleagues credential their ability to empathize with the plight of subject peoples because: ' . . . from women's position as 'other' in a patriarchal culture and from feminists' dialogue and confrontation with diverse groups of women, we have learned to be suspicious of all attempts by members of a dominant group to speak for the oppressed, no matter how eloquently or experimentally.' (1989:33)

Despite this, their suspicions are conveniently suspended a few lines later when they come to authorize their own right to speak for others: ' . . . although ethnographers are speakers of the dominant discourse, *they know the experience of otherness*, albeit a self-inflicted and temporarily limited one, from their time in the field' (1989:33, emphasis added).

For these three ethnographers, it seems that feminism's principal contribution to anthropology will be the endorsement of its truth claims about fieldwork, that space in which 'otherness' is comprehended. Ironically perhaps, the presence of Bronislaw Malinowski, one of anthropology's founding fathers and a man who also believed he could 'grasp the native's point of view', is resurrected in these claims. Malinowski saw his work as of necessary benefit to the native. He wanted to 'make clear to traders, missionaries and exploiters what the Natives really need and where they suffer most under the pressure of European interference' (cited in Trinh:1989:74). Fifty years later, Mascia-Lees *et al.* (1989:33) still believe in an applied anthropology where ethnographers: ' . . . may be better able to overcome these power relations by framing research questions according to the desires of the oppressed group, by choosing to do work that "others" want and need'. The authors qualify their ability to satisfy the other's desire only inasmuch as they must: ' . . . be[ing] clear for whom they are writing, and [by] adopt[ing] a feminist political framework that is suspicious of relationships with "others" that do not include a close and honest scrutiny of the motivation for research' (1989:33).

This innocent vision of personal honesty and cross-cultural interchange, with its loyal recording of native desires, depends upon the notion of a self-present, Cartesian subject whose own motivations are transparent to scrutiny and therefore open to easy correction. The curious twist, as Chandra Talpade Mohanty (1987:35) describes it, comes in the attendant conviction that 'women have some kind of privileged access to the "real", the "truth", and can elicit "trust" from other women purely on the basis of their being not-male'. A similar logic motivates the call for repatriation anthropology, for shared and insider anthropology. Again, it presumes that certain subjects enjoy a closer relationship to the truth than others.

Many feminist ethnographers as well as most so-called 'new ethnographers' share an avowed desire to uncover a 'better practice' for anthropology, a practice that will redress the sexist and/or ethnocentric exclusions that the discourse of anthropology has perpetrated.[4] However, these often valuable interventions can at the same time install themselves as the limiting criteria for other forms of critique that are not predicated on any necessary allegiance to anthropology's future.

It is worth elaborating this problem in order to suggest that many of postmodernism's most challenging provocations have not been engaged by either feminist or 'new' (postmodern) ethnographers. For example, when a writer such as James Clifford (1988) explores the literary conventions that achieve an 'objectivity effect', he nevertheless relies on an unproblematized notion of subjectivity, with its attendant metonymy of attributes. Clifford assumes that a hermeneutic horizon of shared subjectivity does exist between different peoples and that the task is just one of more faithfully capturing its common experience.

The perceived failure of positivism's promise is then repaired by calls to reflexivity (another word for honesty), empathy, respect and reciprocity. Consequently, ethnographers are encouraged to reduce their truth claims, be more humble, eschew a detached stance of neutral observation, regard their subjects as collaborators and try to experiment with different writing genres that 'place more of the voices and perspectives of the researched into the narrative and that more authentically reflect the dissonance and particularity of the ethnographic research process'.

This particular litany is not proffered by James Clifford, although it could have been. Actually, it is a description of what many feminists have come to regard as axiomatic for their practice and it appears in Judith Stacey's (1988) 'Can there be a feminist ethnography?'. It attests to an investment that feminist ethnography has also made, together with much that goes under the banner of 'the new ethnography', in a pre-critical understanding of subjectivity, experience, authenticity and intention. The dividends from this investment are considerable, as they go towards sustaining the authority of the ethnographer, whether male, female or feminist, albeit in a different guise.

The ethnographer is now a caring ethnographer, sensitive, self-reflexive, sharing, sympathetic, consciousness-raised; in other words, a nice sort of person—someone you might trust. The problematic of the observer, however, with all those difficult political questions that address the very constitution of the anthropological *cogito*, tends to drop out of the picture in this personality make-over.

Perhaps feminist ethnography is more inclined to endorse this move because it has tended to define itself as research on, for or by women. This isn't a criticism. Anthropology's patriarchal and paternalistic history engendered the need for a feminist response, and the effects on the discipline have been hard won and, in general, valuable. Nevertheless, in feminist ethnography the common experience of female identity has, to a large extent, been presumed to underwrite a preferable and improved ethnographic practice. Stacey (1988:24) courageously questions the latter belief, with its implicit faith in feminist ethnography's ability to better safeguard and therefore represent the interests of informants:

> . . . the irony I now perceive is that [feminist] ethnographic method exposes subjects to far greater danger and exploitation than do more positivist, abstract, and 'masculinist' research methods. The greater the intimacy, the apparent mutuality of the researcher/researched relationship, the greater is the danger.

Stacey is concerned with the ethnographer's betrayal of personal confidences, the unresolved contradictions that emerge between subjects' competing interests and the summary pragmatism that accompanies the inevitable decision to 'write up'. Yet Stacey's hesitations do not extend to the more fundamental premise that motivates feminist ethnography. She does not go so far as to suggest that 'woman' is itself a questionable category of analysis that may not adequately authorize claims of shared subjectivity and shared knowledges. Feminist discourse has tirelessly interrogated interpretive models that understand 'woman' as a universal, biological given. The conservative agenda that such interpretations usually try to install is now well documented. But Mohanty (1984:337) notes the way the category re-emerges when 'the homogeneity of women as a group is produced not on the basis of biological essentials, but rather on the basis of secondary sociological and anthropological universals'.

Even when the differences between women are the proposed stuff of investigation, these differences must comply with feminism's, and/or anthropology's, essentializing frame. After all, cultural translation is a project that seeks to render difference commensurate, comprehensible, same. As Edward Said (1989:210) explains this ineluctable paradox, 'To convert them [the other] into topics of discussion or fields of research is necessarily to change them into something fundamentally and constitutively different.' Translation is always a transformation. This universalizing process is not a predicament that we can somehow get around, a mistake to be corrected or an arrogance that can be tempered by salutary humility.

Nevertheless, much of the rhetoric that pervades both feminist ethnography and its postmodern protagonists worries at how the ethnographer can *escape* the embroiling actuality of his or her imperial position. The desire to find a solution to the dilemma betrays an inadequate understanding of what is entailed in the problematic of representation. All too often, representation is narrowly interpreted as a question of who speaks for whom: who mediates the interests of others.[5] For example, Kamala Visweswaran's (1988) 'Defining feminist ethnography' interprets the problem of voice through the model of consciousness-raising: with courage and support, it seems that 'the other' will join us by speaking out. This Cartesian model of the subject also underpins demands that we be honest about ourselves, situate our truth claims and be made accountable. Such a desire for witnessing and confessional authenticity, in which some would name themselves real marginals and give testimony from the position of their subjugated selfhood, adjudicates the problematic of difference by appealing to the author function.

We see this again in the growing demands to have Third World and women's literature recognized—novels, diaries, autobiography—genres traditionally excluded from the anthropological canon. This is an important and necessary project. However, different modes of writing ultimately engender different ways of producing an object as knowable, and all of them involve an exercise of power. We would be naive to think that we could get out of the power/knowledge nexus simply by writing differently. Commenting on the desire to change the canon, Gayatri Spivak (1989a:28) charges us to think through the imperative at work in this:

> I'm telling you that your solution to enlarge the curriculum is in fact a continuation of the neo-colonial production of knowledge although in practice I am with you, because on the other side are real racists. The fact that this battle should be won does not mean at all that winning it does not keep a Euroamerican centrism intact. This is the real sense of crisis.

The political complexity that this would have us acknowledge is echoed by Said (1989:213), who notes that 'the fetishization and relentless celebration of "difference" and "otherness" can . . . be seen as an ominous trend'. Read against such cautions, can we remain comfortable in the belief that all those appeals to a moral goodwill are finally distinguishable from the process of empire?

I have suggested that feminist ethnography, like all ethnography, is caught and empowered by unacknowledged complicities with masculinism and, indeed, with imperialism.[6] I have also argued that feminist scholarship that attends to this bind is effectively censored when difference is conflated with pluralism. This explains why what norms itself as feminism within anthropology is increasingly impatient with other feminisms that engage poststructuralist and postmodern scholarship. The constant call by feminist and new ethnographers to experiment with innovatory writing genres is part of this 'resistance to theory', as these calls seldom address the difficult question of genre or, indeed, of writing itself.

Despite insistent suggestions that the problem of enunciation deserves more critical consideration, the literature in psychoanalysis, semiotics and discourse theory that actually attends to this most difficult question—to deixis, to the construction of the speaking subject and to the sexual inflection that articulates all modes of representation—is ignored. The reason for this might be that these discourses cannot uphold the dream of a sovereign subject caught in the embrace of an auto-affection that could thereby presume to know itself, account for itself, and be trusted to do the right thing.

What is at stake in feminist anthropology's refusal to engage other modes of feminism and other understandings of postmodern-

ism that include such critical analysis? Whose definitions authorize
and limit the field of political engagement in this way, and what
issues remain muted as a consequence? Has feminism become a
boundary rider against the discipline's would-be assailants?

An equally uneasy battery of questions hovers around
feminism's investment in the author function.[7] Some of these
questions might include the following: Is a feminist text determined by the sex of the writer and, further, by that writer's stated
commitment to feminism? Is it determined by the object of investigation? Is the style or genre of an ethnography a factor to be
considered, and if so, why?

Rather than subscribe too rigidly to any or all of the above
as determining requirements for feminism, we might consider the
work of writers whose work strays from these safe limits in
suggestive ways. To return to Meaghan Morris's provocative collection of essays, she argues that 'texts', and she doesn't just mean
books, are never passively received but are, in fact, actively
reinterpreted by both writers and readers. Consequently and
importantly, interpretation and criticism become performative and
political acts of transformation or, as Anne Freadman (cited in
Morris: 1988:3), another Australian feminist writer, has described
this enterprise:

> My major methodological presupposition will be that any text is a
> rewriting of the field or fields of its own emergence, that to write,
> to read, or to speak is first of all to turn other texts into
> discursive material, displacing the enunciative position from which
> those materials have been propounded. I mean that 'use' can
> always do something a little different from merely repeating 'usage'.

Morris's essays contest the need to define feminist criticism by
its traditional object of analysis. A preferred attention is given to
enunciative strategies and rhetorical conventions in order to transform accepted regimes of cultural consumption. For if reading is
work, then it must be able to *do* something: it must be able to
make a difference. For example, when Morris (1988:241–269)
explores the 'dead cleverness' of *Crocodile Dundee*, she does more
than diagnose the film's sinister ability to successfully negotiate
and capitalize on the gap between mass culture's politics of
production and specific patterns of reception in popular culture.
Morris wants to disrupt the complacency that sees cultural critics
looking to 'discover or retrieve' some essential meaning as it passes
across this divide between 'what the industry does' and 'what we
do with what it does'. For Morris, these meanings are much more
pliable than a so-called 'radical politics' would often care to
acknowledge, and *Dundee* offers some instructive lessons in this.

The task for cultural critics, then, might involve the imaginative labour of inventing different meanings and connections across this divide between production and reception. Indeed, the success of that labour could be measured by its ability to disrupt the very notion of a divide that fails to recognize that reception *is* production.

When Luce Irigaray (1985) finds *within* the texts of philosophers and theorists such as Plato, Descartes, Hegel and Freud, the very material she needs to read them *otherwise*, or when Barbara Johnson (1980) shows us that *how* we read can make a critical difference, we see exemplified what Spivak means by the challenging phrase 'negotiating enabling violations'; that is, the hard work of turning to our advantage what would otherwise oppress us. The challenge in this work comes from an appreciation that reading is an act of transformation, not a simple retrieval or diagnostics.

If the political density of the problematic of difference is confined to reparation, we repress the generative necessity that positions 'otherness/difference' as always/already finessed and suppressed in the construction of *any* identity. One can never simply surpass this bind. Yet in saying this, we are reminded of Spivak's caution that such interventions cannot be considered wrong or unnecessary because we have no choice but to struggle for them. This is the crisis. Although this irreducible bind does not prevent critical intervention, it does entail a careful attention to the apparent fact that the subject is *always* centred. If we are to intervene against this violence, our critical practice as feminists might well begin by addressing the scandal of this production.

Notes

An excerpt from this paper has appeared in revised form as a Comment in *Signs: Journal of Women in Culture and Society*, vol.16, no. 2, winter, 1991, pp. 9–15.

1 See, for example, the Feral and Working Paper publications from the 1970s that included the writings and translations of such young bloods as Paul Foss, Meaghan Morris, Elizabeth Grosz, Anne Freadman, George Alexander, Paul Patton and a host of others.
2 For a discussion of the inextricable ways in which our thought is immersed within Hegelian, dialectical logic, and why we will consequently need to develop different strategies for intervening in the violence of oppositional modes of understanding that can acknowledge this contamination, see Derrida (1981).
3 See, for example, Cowlishaw and Lea (1990). Despite their very different perspectives, Strathern and Kirby are nevertheless both accused of deliberately employing 'alienating language', 'obscurantism

and incomprehensible jargon', 'unnecessary abstraction and conceptual complication'. This judgment is handed down by Cowlishaw and Lea (1990:88) with the following explanation: 'It may be that the terminology is simply unfamiliar to readers not in the swim, but when the precise meaning of a passage eludes several experienced academics who are loyal readers of [*Australian Feminist Studies*], even after readings aloud, then something is amiss.'

    Unfortunately, the assumption that language can deliver up a precise meaning to anyone, let alone these judges who resort to 'readings aloud' when faced with terms and expressions that are unfamiliar, or that loyal subscription to a journal that only very occasionally publishes poststructuralist work is sufficient authorization for 'being in the swim', exemplifies the problem. By definition, 'the clarity test' must diagnose as pretentious and irrelevant the difficult complexities of continental philosophy that women who are prepared to do some homework have found useful for feminism.

4 The term 'new ethnography' is something of a catch-all, grouping together writers whose aims and efforts are arguably quite disparate. The collection of essays in *Writing Culture* (Clifford & Marcus:1986) brings together some of the better known writers whose work falls under this vague rubric. See especially the essays by Tyler, Clifford, Marcus, Fischer and Crapanzano.

5 For an elaboration of this point, see Kirby (1989c).

6 Gayatri Spivak's work offers a persuasive argument for the need to learn to read by way of unravelling our immersion within, and complicity with, networks of power. This involves a relentless shuttling that can never be finished, a tireless enterprise that must continually re-work (by re-reading and re-writing) the weave of texts into different habits. See for example, Spivak (1989b).

7 For a provocative discussion of the author function and feminism, see Grosz (1990).

References

Clifford, J. & Marcus, G. E. (1986) *Writing Culture: The Poetics and Politics of Ethnography*, University of California Press, Berkeley.

Clifford, J. (1988) 'On Ethnographic Authority' in *The Predicament of Culture: Twentieth-Century Ethnography, Literature, and Art*, Harvard University Press, Cambridge, pp. 21–54.

Cowlishaw, G. and Lea, T. (1990) 'On Vicky (sic) Kirby Versus Marilyn Strathern Vers(us)', *Australian Feminist Studies*, no. 11, Autumn, pp. 87–89.

Derrida, J. (1981) 'From Restricted to General Economy: A Hegelianism without Reserve' in *Writing and Difference* (trans. A. Bass), Routledge, London, pp. 251–277.

Grosz, E. (1990) 'Feminism after the Death of the Author?', unpublished paper.

Haraway, D. (1988) 'Panel Discussion 2', *Inscriptions: Journal for the Critique of Colonial Discourse*, nos. 3/4, pp. 94–104.

Irigaray, L. (1985) *Speculum of the Other Woman* (trans. G. C. Gill), Cornell University Press, Ithaca NY.

Johnson, B. (1980) 'The Critical Difference: BartheS/BalZac' in *The Critical Difference: Essays in the Contemporary Rhetoric of Reading*, Johns Hopkins University Press, Baltimore, pp. 3–12.

Kirby, V. (1987) 'On the Cutting Edge: Feminism and Clitoridectomy', *Australian Feminist Studies*, no. 5, Summer, pp. 35–55.

——(1989a) 'Capitalising Difference: Feminism and Anthropology', *Australian Feminist Studies*, no. 9, Autumn, pp. 1–24.

——(1989b) 'Re-writing: Postmodernism and Ethnography', *Mankind*, vol. 19, no. 1, April, pp. 36–45.

——(1989c) 'Corporeographies', *Inscriptions*, no. 5, pp. 103–119.

Mascia-Lees, F. E., Sharpe, P. & Cohen, C. Ballerino (1989) 'The Postmodernist Turn in Anthropology: Cautions from a Feminist Perspective', *Signs: Journal of Women in Culture and Society*, vol. 15, no. 1, Fall, pp. 7–33.

Mohanty, C. Talpade. (1984) 'Under Western Eyes: Feminist Scholarship and Colonial Discourses', *Boundary 2* , vol. 2/3, pp. 333–358.

——(1987) 'Feminist Encounters: Locating the Politics of Experience', *Copyright*, vol. 1, Fall, pp. 30–44.

Morris, M. (1988) *The Pirate's Fiancée: Feminism, Reading, Postmodernism*, Verso, London.

Ong, A. (1988) 'Colonialism and Modernity: Feminist Re-presentations of Women in Non-Western Societies', *Inscriptions: Journal for the Critique of Colonial Discourse*, nos. 3/4, pp. 79–93.

Said, E. (1989) 'Representing the Colonized: Anthropology's Interlocutors', *Critical Inquiry*, vol. 15, no. 2, Winter, pp. 205–225.

Spivak, G. Chakravorty. (1989a) 'The New Historicism: Political Commitment and the Postmodern Critic' in Veeser, Aram H. (ed.), *The New Historicism*, Routledge, New York, pp. 277–292.

——(1989b) 'Feminism and Deconstruction, Again: Negotiating with Unacknowledged Masculinism' in Brennan, T. (ed.), *Between Feminism and Psychoanalysis*, Routledge, London, pp. 206–223.

Stacey, J. (1988) 'Can There Be A Feminist Ethnography?', *Women's Studies International Forum*, vol. 11, no. 1, pp. 21–27.

Trinh T. Minh-ha (1989) *Woman, Native, Other: Writing Postcoloniality and Feminism*, Indiana University Press, Bloomington.

Visweswaran, K. (1988) 'Defining Feminist Ethnography', *Inscriptions: Journal for the Critique of Colonial Discourse*, nos. 3/4, pp. 27–44.

3 'Authentic voice': Anti-racist politics in Canadian feminist publishing and literary production

Daiva Stasiulis

> The imagination is, alas, not pure, but contains a social structure in the speaking voice. (Moure 1989:4)
>
> Authenticity can be a slippery and limiting term when applied to Native literature for it suggests cultural and political boundaries past which we should not let our writing wander. (King 1990:xv)

In 1988, the process of developing an anti-racist politic within Canada's best-known feminist publishing house, Women's Press, detonated an explosion within the Press itself, which sent shock waves reverberating throughout the Canadian feminist and literary communities. Even before the smoke had cleared, the old Women's Press had divided into two—to form the new Women's Press, with a mission to build an anti-racist feminism, and the Second Story Press, dedicated to pursuing a more 'mainstream' feminist mandate. Women's Press was not the first test of what constitutes racism in Canadian feminist publishing and writing.[1] However, the Press' disputes were the first to gain national notoriety and widespread (both mainstream and alternative) media coverage.

The highly publicized debates over the institutionalization of anti-racism at the Women's Press also prefigured the intense and often polarizing discussions within other organizations in writers, and publishing circles. For example, issues of racism and representation of Aboriginal women, Black women and women of colour formed the dominant theme at the Third International Feminist Bookfair, held in Montreal during June 1988 (*Broadside*, 1988/1989, 4). The Writers' Union of Canada (TWUC),[2] PEN Canada,[3] and the League of Canadian Poets are three prestigious national writers' organizations that have recently formed arenas for heated debates on racism and exclusion of racial minorities in writing and publishing.[4] In the case of the Writers' Union, the events surrounding Women's Press's anti-racist politics served as a catalyst for formulating a Union policy on racism.

35

The development of strategies for anti-racist change in the personnel, decision-making processes and publishing priorities within Women's Press raised a battery of unsettling questions about wedding anti-racist and feminist principles within cultural, and specifically literary, production. In this essay, I focus on one aspect of the anti-racist policies instituted by the Press that engendered a long and intense debate within Canadian feminist and literary communities pertaining to issues of 'appropriation of voice and culture'. This essay will flesh out some of this debate and provide a critique of the essentialist position on 'authentic voice'.

One's history and various social identities—both individual and collective—affect what one chooses to write about and one's capacity to write 'authentically' about them. But that relation is not one of fixed determinism. Research, analysis, skill in the writer's craft, commitment and imagination all affect the quality, integrity and verisimilitude of writing, both fiction and non-fiction.

In a context where writers are sensitized to issues of appropriation of oppressed groups' voices and cultures, they increasingly feel compelled to identify their race, ethnicity, gender and sexual orientation. While the motives underlying this practice are laudable (desire to show awareness of racism and appropriation), the new convention of credentialism by race, gender and other identities is fraught. It suggests that what is written ought to be judged according to how close or far from the cultures and identities of characters the writer is positioned. I have therefore decided to forgo this convention of racial, ethnic, etc., self-identification on the grounds that to do so would be inconsistent with the anti-essentialist thrust of my argument. My argument must be judged on its own merits, rather than on the basis of my skin colour, ancestry or any aspect of my multi-faceted social identity.

My analysis of anti-racist politics in literary production suggests that all efforts to prescribe or proscribe 'authentic voice' leave themselves open to undesirable outcomes. In particular, white writers may feel pressured to write only about white people, thus precluding exploration of the relationship between racial and ethnic groups, surely of critical importance in racially and ethnically diverse societies. Similarly, there may be a narrowing of what is sought or expected of Native and minority women writers. These outcomes are clearly inimical to any anti-racist project. Much more beneficial are policies that seek to widen access to resources and audiences of new and marginalized voices in a manner that valorizes plurality and diversity in writing and publishing.

The discussion on 'authentic voice', raised provocatively by the

Women's Press, initially spawned a hostile environment where protagonists and many within the larger feminist community took up polarized positions. Neither the debate in Women's Press, nor similar ones conducted in other literary or feminist organizations, have engendered consensus. The questions of authenticity and cultural appropriation are vexed ones which have led to diverse and emphatic individual and policy responses (e.g. from agencies such as the Canada Council) (Godfrey 1992). One outcome of the debates has been to heighten consciousness within writers' and publishing circles about race- and gender-based relations of power and authority within literary production. As importantly, the debates on voice and authenticity have given rise to collective multi-racial action focused on questions of Native[5] and minority writers' access to the resources and infrastructure of literary production. This essay concludes with a discussion of some of the creative strategies employed by Native and minority women writers to build autonomous cultural-political institutions and open up spaces in the Canadian literary mainstream.

The experience of dealing with racism in literary and other forms of artistic production has been described by both women of colour and white women as traumatizing and silencing. According to some white women who have been anti-racist activists, the women's movement has not learned how to deal with complexity; it has too easily polarized over issues of racism, and treated some participants as irredeemable. Women of colour who have been subjected to the unconscious racism, patronizing attitudes, tears of guilt and confessions of white feminists have decided to leave whited-dominated feminist organizations and redirect their energies elsewhere.

When questions of 'authentic voice' and cultural appropriation enjoin a politics that is easily polarizing, efforts to understand, so as to better confront, all forms of racism are often unlikely to be 'politically correct'. Nonetheless, it is only by developing analyses of those things which divide us, and render our experiences as different, that progressive women (and men) can build meaningful alliances.

There is a pressing need for feminists and others wishing to take racism seriously to clarify the nature of racism. Even while many white feminists express their commitment to anti-racism, confusion reigns over what racism is, and what combating racism means for their politics, writing and scholarship. Part of the problem resides in language. 'Racism' refers to the racially motivated violence of the white-sheeted Ku Klux Klan and the Aryan Nation. It also refers to the myriad of verbal and non-verbal gestures constituting the 'unconscious' and learned racism of individuals which serves to define and circumscribe some people not just as 'other' or different, but as unequal.

Both racism and anti-racism are historically constructed, and they are defined and re-defined in political practice. For example, to be non-racist in North America within the context of white leftist organizations in the 1970s meant to support Third World struggles. Such commitment has since been criticized for its positioning at a safe remove from the lived realities of First Nations and Black people, or other people of colour within Canada. It avoided racism on the home front, and did nothing to better the lives of oppressed peoples in Canada.

Within creative writing, to be non-racist and even anti-racist for many white writers in the 1970s meant to write sensitively and evocatively about Native people and people of colour, whereas in the late 1980s and 1990s, this is being defined by some Native and racial minority writers as 'usurping their voice', and appropriating their cultures, which constitutes a racist act. It was this latter definition of racism, reflected in a set of editorial decisions and anti-racist guidelines, which made the Women's Press the centre of the storm over questions of authenticity in creative writing.

Women's Press's definition of racist expression

Among the controversial attempts to define anti-racist literary practices instituted by Women's Press was its (internally contested) decision to reject the short stories of three authors for an anthology of fiction, *Imagining Women*, on the basis of perceived racist language, structure and style.[6] One story, about a white woman's first visit to Africa (Somalia), was criticized for presenting an exoticized, naive, tourist's vision of Africa. A second story, set in Guatemala, was censored for stereotyping Latin American politics from a white perspective, and for the athor's taking on the 'voice' of people of colour. A third story, found objectionable for being written in the first person from the point of view of an Aborigine suffering in a fictional Latin American country was called 'imperialistic (neo-colonial) by virtue of cultural appropriation' on two additional grounds—for appropriating the Latin American genre of magic realism, and for portraying the speech of the protagonist as fragmented and thus seemingly unintelligent (Fitzgerald 1988; Cole 1989:10).

It is beyond the scope of this paper to evaluate the particular judgments made about the racist properties of the rejected stories. What they had in common, however, was their authorship by

white women, and their subject matter—the cultures and lives of
colonized peoples in Third World countries. Explicit anti-racist
guidelines for submissions by authors were issued soon thereafter
by Women's Press.

These guidelines state that 'to make Women's Press a racially
integrated publishing house which is anti-racist in all aspects of
its work', the Press will avoid manuscripts

> . . . in which the progragonist's experience in the world, by virtue
> of race or ethnicity, is substantially removed from that of the
> writer . . . We will avoid publishing manuscripts in which a writer
> appropriates the forms and substance of culture which is oppressed
> by her own.

Also on the Press's 'to-be-avoided' list were 'manuscripts which
contain imagery that perpetuates the hierarchy black=bad,
white=good', and 'manuscripts which use terminology that reinforces stereotypes and words which are indelibly associated with
prejudiced usage'.

The responses to Women's Press's anti-racist guidelines from
Native writers, writers of colour, and white writers—feminist and
other, female and male—have not been uniform and have not
followed any simple ethnic, racial, gender, or ideological demar-
cations. However, the lengthy debates sparked by the guidelines,
both within feminist publications (e.g. *Broadside*) and within the
Writers' Union, unquestionably focused on the spectre of censorship—either by publishers or by authors themselves. Much of the
discussion in the 'Writers Confidential' section of the Writers'
Union newsletter repudiated any restriction on what and how a
writer should write, and ran up the flag for freedom' of the
imagination.

The arguments advanced in support of this position were
compatible with liberal-humanist discourses that privilege individual subjectivity and freedom. Some writers argued accordingly that
writers should not respond to political expedience and that the
ethical constraints governing good writing were different to those
governing good citizenship. Many writers argued from a position
of universal humanism that good, talented or 'real writers' can
transcend the limits of personal experience and of nation, sex,
race or class.

Several writers displayed their repugnance for any type of
censorship, viewing proscriptive guidelines as 'tyrannical', 'racist',
'inverted prejudice', akin to forms of censorship found in dicta-
torships, and stultifying to the creative process. Restrictions on
the use of characters or symbols from other cultures were seen to
lend themselves to a 'slippery slope' argument, narrowing the

subject matter to a point where writers were confined to writing autobiography (see also Atwood 1991: 22; Bissoondath quoted in Godfrey 1992:C15).

Although white feminist writers were to be found on both sides of the 'voice' issue, they were prone to be particularly sympathetic to the 'anti-censorship' argument for three reasons. First, while some of the most prominent writers in contemporary Canadian literature are (white) women,[7] some feminists contend that in general, women continue to face greater barriers to publishing than men. These barriers pertain not only to the overall weaker financial position of women (exacerbated if they are poor or working class) and constraints on women's time associated with the 'double day', but also to their under-representation within the range of institutional sites which structure the field of literary production (publishing, state cultural institutions and granting agencies, universities, literary criticism, literary prizes, anthologies, and writers' associations).

Ethnic relations of power are also perceived by writers of non-British, non-French origin to marginalize their creative writing from the literary mainstream and place their work into a 'multicultural ghetto'. Upon finding her name entered in the *Oxford Companion to Canadian Literature* under 'Ukrainian Writing', Myrna Kostash, a Canadian-born writer of Ukrainian descent, asked:

> Could it be that, given my origins outside the Anglo-Celtic and Franco founding nations, I shall *never* be considered to belong because it wasn't there at the beginning when the naming took place? That CanLit is a category and a practice hi-jacked and held captive by a very exclusive gang of men and women who all come from the right side of the tracks? (1990:19, emphasis in the original; see also di Michele 1987)

Thus, many white feminists maintained that women writers continue to be disadvantaged or marginalized, especially when they find themselves in subaltern positions with respect to other types of social relations (defined by ethnicity, sexuality, religion, age, etc.).[8] They met efforts to impose restrictions on their literary production with anxiety and opposition. The 'fear of being gagged' (Warland 1988:8) compelled many white feminists to adopt a vehement position in defence of principles of freedom of expression and imagination. Having won 'the permission to say the unsaid', after having been 'told endlessly, *thou shalt not*', Atwood (1991: 24) argues, women writers 'don't need to hear it again, and especially not from women'.

A second source of opposition to any policy that prompted

censorship for many feminist writers was the recent legislation aimed at combating pornography. It provoked:

> . . . [a] long, hard-fought struggle with the Tory government over Bill C-54, a piece of proposed legislation that would have endowed the government with broad censorship powers over artistic and educational production in the name of stamping out pornography. [Given their recent battles with censorship,] the nervousness of the artistic community over freedom-of-expression issues [was] more than understandable. (Scheier 1989:9)

A third objection to proscriptive guidelines stems from a wariness about new forms of essentialism inherent in any position that assumes that the race, gender and class of the writer is the guarantee of the authenticity of the text. While Chris Weedon (1987) identifies this essentialism as a property of Black feminist literary criticism, Henry Louis Gates Jr. notes that 'the belief that we can "read" a person's racial or ethnic identity from his or her writing runs surprisingly deep' (1991:1). Posing serious challenges to the 'ideology of authenticity' is the whole genre of celebrated yet 'fraudulent autobiographical' writing such as eighteenth- and nineteenth-century American 'slave narratives' authored either by white or free Black writers (Gates 1991).[9] Rejection of essentialist notions of authenticity is likely to find fertile ground in Canada where French-English linguistic and political duality, the continued demographic importance of immigration, and high levels of inter-marriage have combined to make the lived experiences of many Canadians bicultural and even mutlicultural.

Many questions are raised by proscriptions on cultural sub-ject-matter, style and character, including the 'voices' permitted or judged 'authentic' for the growing number of individuals who identify with more than one ethnic origin, from both dominant and oppressed cultures.[10] For instance, are the attempts by writers of colour to adopt the voice of white characters or characters from cultures different from their own (e.g. black authors writing about Native characters) to be assessed differently from the white adop-tion of the voices of non-white characters? Is one Native or Black woman's voice to be taken as automatically speaking for a whole group (rather than merely expressing an individual's point of view about her interpretation of a collective experience)? To what extent are proscriptive guidelines on voice likely to repress and paralyse, rather than enable and vitalize the production not only of white, but also of minority and Aboriginal writers?[11]

The defence of the Women's Press's anti-racist guidelines has come from feminist writers of colour and Native writers, such as Jamaican-born Dub poet Lillian Allen (cited in Scheier 1988),

Ojibway poet Lenore Keeshig-Tobias (1991), and Metis writer Lee Maracle (1991). The position that white writers should refrain from writing fiction which incorporates characters and cultural elements from Aboriginal and oppressed racial groups is based on two major arguments.

The first is that writing by whites drawing from the cultures of oppressed groups contains stereotypes and distortions which reproduce cultural racism against these groups. There are both strong and moderate versions of this argument: the strong one is that presentation by white writers of Native and minority cultures is *necessarily* racist. The moderate version is that writing by whites about Native and minority cultures *tends* to stereotype these cultures and thus tends to perpetuate racism. The first version is a form of essentialism and as such, is beleaguered by the problems identified above. As explored below, the second version is supported by the scholarly exegesis of fiction-writing in Canada by Craig (1988), Goldie (1989), and Godard (1986) among others, and raises serious issues.

The second argument providing justification for anti-racist writing guidelines is that the appropriation of treasured contents and modes of expression of colonized cultures by writers from the dominant culture has led to the suppression and silencing of the voices of Native writers and other writers of colour. While historical support exists for this argument, the proposed solution is inadequate to rectify the effects (silencing, marginalization of colonized writers) of appropriation. In placing the blame for the problem and the burden of the solution on writing by individuals, attention is deflected from the sources of systemic racism (or exclusion through dynamics other than racism) existing in publishing, distribution, educational curricula, and literary criticism.

Proscriptive guidelines also tend to shift the discourse of the debate from that of racism to that of censorship, thus undercutting the anti-racist impulse behind the guidelines. Because of the impasse reached in debates on 'authentic voice', writers sensitized to issues of appropriation have shifted the terrain of debate and politics to the means of widening *access* for the voices of Aboriginal and minority writers. This approach has proved to be more productive of building multi-ethnic movements for anti-racist action.

Appropriation and racist distortion in English-Canadian fiction

There is considerable support for the idea that the tradition of English-language fiction in Canada is marked by prevailing racist and ethnocentric beliefs and myths. In his critical overview of racial attitudes in English-Canadian fiction, 1905–1980, Terence Craig (1987) has called attention to a Canadian literary tradition rife with assumptions of predestined Anglo-Celtic superiority and patronizing attitudes towards Indians and people who deviated from English and Scottish ideals of political and cultural superiority. The moral virtue of characters from immigrant groups was evaluated according to their cultural proximity to the English and Scots, and their Canadian-ness was in part judged in terms of their willingness to fight for the British Empire. Craig argues that underlying many of the racist depictions of non-British groups were class prejudices. He also emphasizes that while different writers appeared to harbour their own idiosyncratic prejudices against different groups, there was a general tendency to treat ethnocultural differences as differences in 'race'. In much popular literature, the word 'white' referred less to skin colour than to virtues of honesty and integrity which Britons were assumed to monopolize, leaving Jews, Mediterranean and other European groups 'not truly white'.

With the notable exception of Hilda G. Howard's (1921) *The Writing on the Wall*, Craig argues, vitriolic pieces of racist fiction are virtually absent from the twentieth-centry English-Canadian literary canon. Nonetheless, the most derogatory, threatening and patronizing fictional stereotypes were reserved for Asian and Black characters, who were, not coincidentally, from groups considered by Canadian authorities to be least desirable as immigrants.

With the emergence of greater numbers of writers from ethnic minority backgrounds, a self-conscious attack on racist, ethnic and anti-semitic stereotyping became a feature of Canadian fiction. In most instances, writings by 'ethnic' writers have targeted the stereotypes of members of their own ethnic community. Only a few writers, such as A.M. Klein and Rudy Wiebe, have risen 'significantly above [their] own regional ethnic enclaves' to embrace a 'true internationalism'. Craig defends 'cultural variety and contrariety' within the fiction of writers who simultaneously insist 'that discrimination which results from any form of pschological "centricity" be it ethnic, religious, or racial, is negative and harmful'. Or in other words, anti-racist intentions and meanings are compatible with textual representation of 'the eclectic delight of a multicultural world' (Craig 1988:147).

The most developed exhortation that white authors and other artists should desist from appropriating the cultures of colonized peoples has comprised arguments advanced by both Native and non-Native writers about the literary uses of Native spirituality and culture. The history of Native contact with whites has been one of active and state-enforced suppression and outlawing of customs such as the Potlatch, the Sweatlodge and Sundance cere- monies, spiritual practices, and Native languages. In addition, First Nations people have suffered the loss of their cultural icons, taken from them to be displayed by museums as evidence of dying or dead cultures. Visual artist Joanne Cardinal-Shubert contends that once an art is viewed as dead or primitive, it becomes 'vulnerable to appropriation and vast pillaging by the dominant culture' (1989:25).

This viewpoint finds echoes in work by critics Terry Goldie (1989) and Barbara Godard (1986), who have each turned their gaze on the treatment of Native peoples within fiction produced by non-Native writers. In tracing the image of the 'indigene' in the creative literature of Canada, Australia and New Zealand, Goldie (1989:5) argues that the overwhelming facts of the invasion and oppression of Native peoples has awarded semiotic control to the invaders, and since then the image of "them" has been "ours".

In order to efface their own alien status and 'otherness' to become 'native Canadians', Goldie (1989:155) argues, whites in Canada have adopted a process of 'indigenization'. The process of indigenization is complex. It involves attributions to Aboriginal cultures of power, mysticism, liberated sexuality, and harmony with nature. These cultures are then entered into and appropriated by white protagonists via processes of shamanic initiation, dreams, or the simple evocation of Aboriginal signifiers. But it is the *prehistoric* Aborigine who is valorized, so that contemporary First Nations people are either (as in Margaret Atwood's novel, *Surfac- ing*) vague glimpses or (as in W.P. Kinsella's 'Indian Stories') deviants, drunks and prostitutes. Dead tribes (e.g. Beothuks of Newfoundland) and dead heroes (Louis Riel) permit authors to avoid the question of 'indigene as social problem', prompting Goldie (1989:160) to exclaim, 'the number of indigenes which represent the dying gasps of their culture seems almost limitless'! Goldie (1989:222) claims that white culture has created an image of the indigene 'through an extended intertextuality, national and international', such that neither textual nor visual representations can escape it.

Goldie (1989:218) argues that the representation of the indi- gene in the works of Maori and Australian Aboriginal writers is prone to problems similar to those faced by white authors. Aborig- inal writers must see themselves through the prism of the dominant culture's view of the 'indigene' for reasons such as the absence of Aboriginal literary traditions. The reproduction of the 'indigene' in texts by Aboriginal writers is also linked to the infusion of

these writers' self-images with racist stereotypes, and the constraints associated with writing in English and thus within a
European language which does not express Aboriginal thought
processes.

If Goldie's conclusions are accepted, several difficult choices
with regard to the question of authorial responsibility present
themselves. Goldie (1989:214) rejects the static image of the
indigene as an immutable product of society, opting instead for
the establishment of 'an awareness of our semiotic snare' so as to
reverse the status of 'the Other' historically given to Aboriginal
peoples. He also argues (1989:222) that avoidance of Native
characters and cultures by white authors creates only an 'emphatic
absence which appears as a denial of the indigene's position in
the writing of these countries'. Thus, 'because it is so encompassing, the de-brainwashing cannot be limited to the indigenes'
(1989:221).

Barbara Godard's (1986) comparative examination of the literary productions of Native women, and of white women authors
drawing upon Native myths, reaching similar conclusions to
Goldie's about the romanticization of the image of the Native and
of Native spirituality within white-authored texts. Drawing on the
language of the nineteenth-century Canadian novelist Frances
Brooke, Godard describes this literary reflex as 'going squaw'.[12]
For Godard, the appropriation within feminist literature of myths
about Native women is 'feminist revisionist myth-making', the
'remythologizing of a lost Amazonian world in order to restore
white women's lost powers' (1986:95).

Unlike Goldie, Godard discerns a fundamental difference in
the texts produced by Native women and non-Native women
guided by their different purposes in referencing aspects of Native
cultures, and by their different relations in oral traditions. Whereas
Native women write 'a miscellany, discontinuous tales rather than
coherent quest narrative, symbolic events rather than psychological descriptions', the writings of white women evince full
development of sacred tales connected with ritual, and anecdotes
drawn from life histories (1986:87). Godard (1986:87) locates the
distinctiveness of Native women's writing in the predominance of
the oral tradition in Native cultures, performances and 'events in
which meaning is actively negotiated' contrasting with the pre-
constituted meanings of written texts. Another difference between
white women's use of Native symbols and mythology and Native
women's writings resides in the conditions governing the appropriateness of telling stories within Native cultures, the importance
of the Native 'copyright system' which governs the transference
of stories within Native communities. For instance, Native women

writers choose to deliberately shroud some of the sacred rituals in silence, whereas the use of Native tales and shamanic initiation rites by white women is not similarly governed by taboos (for a further discussion of the protocol for the telling of Native stories, see Keeshig-Tobias 1991 and Cameron 1991).

While there are undoubtedly differences in the quality of writing by Native and non-Native women, Godard's assertions about these differences appear more than a little over-drawn, romanticized (as they pertain to Native women's writing), and essentialist in their assumptions. At the heart of Godard's view of the duality of Native/non-Native women's writing is the assumption that writing, at least by Native women, transparently conveys the authentic, unmediated experience of their Nativeness. However, what is obvious from the diversity of recent writing by Aboriginal writers is the influence of heterogeneous literary structures and styles of expression—*both traditional and non-traditional to Native cultures*. The contemporary Native literary landscape contains both writing with explicit literary connections to First Nation cultures (through the Trickster,[13] orality, the natural elements, etc.) and writing from which traditional Native characters, use of oral literature or strong sense of Native community are absent (King 1990:xv). While 'traditional' Native symbolism is in principle more politically available to Native than non-Native writers, its complex appearance in works such as the plays of Tomson Highway (1988, 1989) suggests a critique by Native artists of static celebratory Native imagery ('defeathering' stereotypes) and subversive textual strategies against indigenization.

A more persuasive argument than Godard's concerning the relationship of Native identity to the writing of Native stories, characters, etc. is offered by Atwood (1991) who takes into account the relationship between writers and the political contexts in which they write. Atwood suggests that, in general,

> . . . the best writing about . . . a group is most likely to come from within that group—not because they are more likely to vilify it, but because they are likely, these days and out of well-meaning liberalism, to simplify and sentimentalize it, or to get the textures and vocabularly and symbolism wrong . . . Also, writers from outside a group are less likely to be able to do the tough, unpleasant, complex bits without attracting charges of racism, sexism, and so forth. (1991: 23)

While the first objection to the adoption of Native voices by white writers revolves around issues of the authentic, racist, good or bad quality of the writing itself, the second speaks to the effects of such writing on the suppression of the voices of Native writers. Because of the history of colonial oppression of their communities, the argument here is that Native writers have less access to the resources necessary for the development of self-expression through writing and publishing such as education, financial resources, time, a 'room of one's own', etc. Moreover, given the depths of racism inscribed in publishing, the entrenchment of the hegemonic image of the indigene identified by Goldie, and the comparatively greater resources of white writers, the latter are ironically given greater leeway and legitimacy than Native writers to write such as Beth Cuthland, Jeanette Armstrong, and Maria Campbell have all spoken about the danger posed to Native women's writings of the 'image of the squaw' presented by white women, which threatens to become the literary norm against which all creative writings, including those produced by Native women, would be measured (Godard 1986:88). Similarly, Lenore Keeshig-Tobias (1989) expresses concern about the standards used by non-Native publishers in judging Native-produced manuscripts. She pointedly asks, 'Just what is "too Indian" or "not Indian enough" in a Native-produced manuscript—the inclusion or exclusion of a beaver pond, a worn-out moccasin, a horse, a drunken Indian?'

Metis professor of literature and poet Emma LaRocque provides anecdotal evidence to support Keeshig-Tobias's fears about the repressive and silencing effects of the hegemonic images of Native cultures and peoples in the practices of gatekeepers to publishing. In one instance, LaRocque received a rejection slip for poems that she had sent to a new Winnipeg magazine of poetry that read, 'Not Indian enough'! In another instance, she (1990:xix) speculated that the choice of one poem from a group of about twenty she had submitted to a major literary journal was probably based on the inclusion of one Cree word.

Although the majority of Native writers who have publicly addressed the topic are concerned about cultural appropriation, their definitions and proposed solutions to the issue of appropriation differ. Unlike Keeshig-Tobias, Maracle, and Delaware playwright Daniel David Moses, who have all asked non-Native writers to stop writing Native stories, LaRocque (1990:xv) argues that non-Native writers must take responsibility for fighting racism in literature.

By necessity, LaRocque's injunction would mean that non-Native writers would extend their writing beyond their 'own' experience, and would engage with Native cultures, symbols and characters, at least in some of their literary production. To remain confined to writing only about themselves, and silent about the experiences of 'others', would be to consign white writers to a whitewashed image of Canadian society, thus perpetuating a well-established tradition of ethnocentric and Eurocentric fiction-writing.

Self-monitoring by white women does not automatically or necessarily empower women writers of colour (Philip 1989). The development of a self-censoring climate within the literary community is aesthetically stultifying and may in fact encourage white writers to distort (by omission of minority or 'other' cultures) the depiction of the situations, characters or contexts which form the material of their texts. This would seem to be antithetical to any anti-racist intent. Self-censorship may also lead to a defensive posture, a politics whereby writers from the dominant culture abrogate responsibility for confronting racism. Clearly, other strategies for the empowering of excluded or silenced voices are required.

Rather than restrict the debate to ethical dilemmas facing 'the individual writer sitting before a word processor with only the imagination for the company' (Philip 1989:210), writers such as Marlene Nourbese Philip and Libby Scheier have enjoined the literary community to match the energy expended in fighting censorship with a similarly concerted effort to combat racism in writing and publishing. Scheier (1991a:16) has opined that 'it's wrong to oppose the position that white writers should not write in non-white voice, without simultaneously decrying the racist injustices that underlie the debate'. Indeed, through the formation of the 'Ad-hoc Committee on Racism in Writing and Publishing', the Writers' Union has shifted the debate on 'voice' away from the paralysing issue of 'authenticity' to focus on the political and economic issues of access to print by new or excluded voices.

Modes of exclusion in literary production

All new forms of cultural expression and all new voices have to fight for access to public attention. This process is not only inevitable but also productive in that the fight itself is part of the process which actually 'creates' the new voice. But in addition to the 'normal' barriers that exist for the acceptance and inclusion of new authors and experimental or innovative writing, there are a variety of specific barriers to publishing for Native and minority-group writers. It is admittedly difficult to disentangle racist from other types of operating principles in publishing, especially when all writers have at early stages of their career experienced rejection from publishers, funding agencies, etc. (Kulyk Keefer 1991:105). This does not, however, negate the existence of racism in literary production nor diminish the need to develop anti-racist practices.

The mechanisms for exclusion from literary production and publishing exist in a myriad of linked sites and practices, across a network of institutions—publishing houses, state granting agencies, the mass media, universities, etc. It is within these institutional sites that the hegemony of the Western, liberal-humanist discourse operates, informing the criteria used by the gatekeepers of publishing to evaluate manuscripts. Writing from the perspective of a Third World 'aesthetics of opposition', Arun Mukherjee (1988) elaborates the inadequacies of criticism based on the Western canon in dealing with both the stylistic innovations and political content of the texts by many Native writers and writers of colour. Western critics, writes Mukherjee, show a preference for 'existentialist-universalist lamentations on the "human condition" ', and for 'cosmopolitan' and obversely an aversion or the local and the historically specific—common features of creative writing by Third World and colonized peoples (1988:11–13). Trinh T. Minh-ha (1991:230–231) argues more simply that the lack of familiarity with Black, Chicana, Asian, or Native American women's experiences among 'Caucasian' critics breeds contempt and patronizing attitudes towards the artistic production of these other voices.

Another mechanism of exclusion of fiction by some writers of colour is the tendency of publishers to valorize 'standard' English', and devalue dialects common to the Caribbean. Black writers employing particular dialects have been told by publishers that their language is inaccessible to a broad readership. Norma De Haarte (1990), a Guyanese-born writer whose first novel was published by Sister Vision Press in 1991, was informed by several publishers that she would have to rewrite the Creolese dialogue into standard English, something she steadfastly refused to do.

In general, writing by minorities has less chance of getting into print because of a perception among publishers that new writing or 'new voices' cannot promise to deliver an audience (Atwood 1991:19; Fawcett 1989:3). The systems of grants in aid for publishing are also stacked against relatively new Canadian publishers such as Sister Vision, whose priority is to publish books by women of colour.

Racist rationales such as 'women of colour do not read' or 'there is no market for these types of books' operate to limit the distribution of books by women of colour (Silvera 1990). An assumption that books by women of colour would not be of interest to multi-racial audiences often lies behind such arguments, which are ostensibly based on the neutral logic of markets and economies of scale. The critical and commercial success of American women writers of colour such as Toni Morrison, Alice Walker and Maxine Hong Kingston provide dramatic evidence that such prejudicial thinking is being successfully challenged.

Voices on the margins: Subverting exclusion

Thus far, I have directed attention to the suppression and silencing of the voices of Native women of colour. But there are counter-trends in contemporary literary criticism and in feminist, Native, and social-movement politics that are facilitating the expression and inclusion into the cultural mainstream of new and marginalized voices.

At variance with the liberal-humanist tradition of the literary academy is the growing trend, in postmodern feminist, leftist, and (for want of a better term) Third World deconstructionist approaches to literary criticism, to discount the notion of 'the universal' altogether, and embrace the idea of 'difference', the universality of difference as it were (Appiah 1991; Hutcheon 1991; Mukherjee 1988; Scheier 1988, 1991a). This trend intersects with the social reality of the emergence of a new generation of Canadian writers whose works are informed by racial and gendered subjectivity, by experiences of having been born and lived in countries with histories of colonialism, and by confrontation with otherness within Canada.

The innovations in genre and form as well as the social relevance of the themes addressed by Native writers and women of colour are increasingly received by literary circles as among the most vibrant and innovative being produced in Canada (Scheier 1988, 1991a). These experimentations reflect the complexities and disjunctures of Aboriginal, Third World and émigré experiences: the use of pastiche and collage, 'parabolic structures, indigenous story telling conventions, folk tales, parodies of western and indigenous forms and rituals' (Mukherjee 1988:17), and the fidelity of speech patterns from the Caribbean and elsewhere. In addition, many of the 'new voices' especially those of Native women and women of colour, relate accomplished journeys of comprehending and resisting both racial and gender oppression.

Frequently locked out of mainstream publishing venues, these writers have adopted the strategy of constructing autonomous spaces. This has included the editing of 'special issues' of journals, the self-publishing of work, the development of support or advocacy groups, and the establishment of presses and magazines by and for Native writers or women of colour.

The current prodigious creative output by a younger generation of university-trained Native playwrights, poets, novelists and short story writers is remarkable. The phenomenal explosion of creative writing by Aboriginal artists has been accompanied by their efforts to assert artistic control over all aspects of production—in publication and editorial work, as well as writing; and in creative direction, acting, and technical support in the theatre. This has entailed the creation of small publishing houses such as Pemmican in Winnipeg. It has involved the formation of groups such as The Committee to Re-establish the Trickster, whose goal has been been to promote the literature of Native writers and to encourage literacy on all levels and in all languages used by Native peoples (Keeshig-Tobias 1991). Native writers have founded new magazines which provide access to writers from their communities— such as *Trickster*, a magazine of 'new Native writing', *New Breed*, published by prairie Metis, and *Sweetgrass*, a Native news and cultural periodical.

As in the past, the cultural production of Native communities is affected by decisions made elsewhere. For instance, in 1990, Native newspapers in many communities across Canada were axed as part of the round of budget cuts by the federal conservative government. Indeed, until these cuts, virtually every Native nation in Canada had its own communications society, usually publishing a newspaper, some even producing radio and television programming. There has also been more than ten years of film production at the Inuit Broadcasting Corporation.

Encouragement of Native writing has also occurred through the formation of schools (such as the En'owkin International School of Writing in Penticton, British Columbia), theatre groups,[14] and workshops to hone writing skills, and the staging of festivals to introduce new plays and playwrights. There have always been local audiences within Aboriginal (including circumpolar) communities for the literary and other cultural production of Native artists. What appears to be most novel about Native literary production is its increased acceptance within the Canadian literary mainstream.[15] Animating the impressive, varied and frequently collective activities within the literary production of people of Native heritage has been the vitality of Aboriginal politics, seeking self-determination for First Nations peoples in all aspects of their lives.

Women of colour from other communities have also made use of many sites of struggle in efforts to get their voices heard. 'Special issues' or anthologies of writings by women of colour gave many authors their first experience of having their work published, and offered many readers their first exposure to writing by women of colour or by women from their own community. A further benefit is that such anthologies offer a sense of whole communities, a means of contextualizing the writing by women of colour (Gupta 1990).

Particular communities of women of colour are producing new magazines which provide a venue for the expression and self-affirmation of women who share common identities and experiences based on culture, racist oppression and sexuality. *Diva*, a quarterly journal of South Asian women, and *Tiger Lily*, are two Toronto-based magazines produced by women of colour.

Although self-publishing is devalued within the literary mainstream, it has permitted the development of new audiences for 'noncommercial minorities'. For instance, both the Writers' Union and PEN Canada do not accept self-published books as a qualification for membership. But for Caribbean-born dub poets Lillian Allen, Devon Haughton and Clifton Joseph, self-publishing was a means of both demystifying the publishing process and reaching an audience not accessible through the mainstream publishing houses. *Rhythm and Hardtimes*, the first published book to include dub poetry in Canada, had sold 8000 copies as of January 1988, a total that would make it a best-seller in academic publishing terms (Allen, 1987/88)!

Some of the most important and sustaining work on subverting racism in publishing has been accomplished by publishing houses founded and run by women of colour. Williams-Wallace in Stratford publishes works by people of colour, 'discovering their history, rediscovering their identity, and struggling for their just place in Canadian society' (Mukherjee 1988:8). Battling many obstacles, including lack of access to block funding by the Canada Council (which requires a minimum of sixteen titles), rejection by bookstores and by reviewers, and the high cost of printing, Sister Vision, a press for black women and women of colour, has survived for seven years and produced eight titles. The importance of Sister Vision lies not only in its provision of access to women of colour but in its work in nurturing and imparting skills to those who are not accomplished writers but are thought to have something to say. This sort of work is regarded as too costly even by many alternative presses facing the exigencies of staying in business.

Sister Vision's choices of manuscripts to develop, such as *Blaze a Fire*, a book profiling Caribbean women, are based on a perspective of 'global feminism'. The members of Sister Vision also hope to publish work by lesbians of colour, for they see a real need to provide access to works or genres that are not represented in the lists of either mainstream or alternative publishing houses.

Makeda Silvera, a founding member of Sister Vision, maintains that the very existence of a press for women of colour both validates the literary voices of women of colour that have been stifled for so long and has also aided in influencing other alternative presses (Women's Press, Between the Lines, Press Gang, Coach House) to bring out writing by women of colour. In addition, alternative arts magazines such as *Fuse* now regularly include contributions by (female and male) Native and minority writers and cover events and debates pertaining to work in the visual and literary arts by women of colour.

Just as the efflorescence in Native artistic production is infomed by the Native movements for sovereignty and self-determination, so too the literary production of women writers of colour is supported by anti-racist, feminist, identity and 'difference' politics, constituted by gendered and racialized subjectivities, and forged in the experience of exile and struggle. Dub poet Lillian Allen (1987/88:14), whose poems address such issues as the indentured condition of Caribbean domestic workers, apartheid and racism, and male domination, acknowledges that 'it was the massive support of the women's movement that first made it possible for me to garner national prominence'. Through the adoption of affirmative measures to support the inclusion of women staff and writers of colour, Women's Press has made itself a more welcoming place for such women (Gupta 1990). Its commitment to anti-racist publishing is apparent in recent releases by Native and racial minority authors such as Dionne Brand, Beth Brant, Lee Maracle and Marlene Nourbese Philip; the priority given to anti-racism is also evident in its provision of advertising and distribution to Sister Vision (Black Women and Women of Colour) Press.

This link between literary production and politics affirming 'difference', and especially a commitment to anti-racism, has been empowering—both redressing the historical exclusion of these voices and subverting the negation and falsification of the cultures of Aboriginal peoples and minority groups within a long history of colonized texts. It also, felicitously, ensures that the representations of Native women and women of colour in the creative writing of white women are less likely to be read as the literary norms against which writing by Native women and women of colour is judged.

Conclusion

The questions of racism and cultural appropriation, recently fought over within feminist publishing and literary organizations, have ushered in both a new awareness among writers about the perils of writing in a voice other than their own, and new processes and mechanisms to facilitate the emergence and recognition of 'new voices'. But the embrace of 'difference' within both the feminist and literary mainstream, which, as I have indicated above, supports and validates Native and minority voices, is accompanied by its own contradictions. Several intellectuals from Aboriginal and minority groups are voicing some scepticism about what Edward Said (1989:213) regards as an ominous trend involving the 'fetishization and relentless celebration of "difference" and "otherness"'. Writers of colour, and particularly Native writers, are at risk of being treated as 'otherness machines, with the manufacture of alterity as [their] principal role' (Appiah 1991:357). The growing demands that the literature of women writers of colour be produced and recognized increase the risk of their being read from the vantage point of 'politically correct' feminist dogmas such as the now ubiquitous mantra, 'race, class and gender'.

Does an editorial decision to reject a white-authored story that employs the writing style of magic realism (on the grounds that this is a style 'indigenous' to Latin America) lead to the expectation that authors born in Latin America should employ this style? In drawing distinctions between European/First World and non-European/Third World styles, is one in danger of perpetuating exotic and 'otherness' of expectations of writers of colour?

The sheer output and increasing diversity of literary production from Native and racial minority/feminist communities provide grounds for optimism that the tendency towards fetishization of 'otherness' in the writings of people of colour can be, and is successfully being, resisted. Notwithstanding the asymmetry in power between Native and non-Native cultures, for instance, linguistic and cultural appropriation can go both ways (LaRocque 1990:xxvi). As Native writers have 'appropriated' and mastered the colonizers' language and culture without abandoning their indigenous ones, their art bears the imprint of two or more (Native, non-Native, reserve/rural-urban) cultures, none of which is monolithic or uncontaminated by other cultures.

In an edifying discussion of the relationship between African and American cultures, Kwame Appiah (1990:354) has written of the falseness of static dualisms, a position which is equally applicable for Native/non-Native, East/West, and white/non-white cultures:

> If there is a lesson in the broad shape of this circulation of
> cultures, it is surely that we are already contaminated by each

other, that there is no longer a fully autochthnonous *echt*-African culture awaiting salvage by our artists (just as there is, or course, no American culture without African roots).

Appiah challenges us to abandon the 'binarism of Self and Other [as] the last of the shibboleths . . . we must learn to live without' (1990:354). There are major problems inherent in proscriptions on 'authentic voice' that tend to undercut the anti-racist intent of such policies. The whole notion of 'authenticity' is slippery, limiting, and prone to essentialism. It also discredits the artistic process, which, as Trinh (1991:232) writes, requires that boundaries be ceaselessly called to question, undermined, modified, and reinscribed'. It ignores the role of the imagination, and of learning and research, which makes 'cultural impersonators' of all writers regardless of their race, class or gender (Gates 1991:29). Offering personal credentials, or proof of connection with those possessing 'the right' credentials, does not explain why characters are believable or why narratives are compelling.

For these reasons, I question the wisdom of the emergent policy on 'authentic voice' of the Canada Council, the major Canadian arts funding organization, which requires fiction writes to obtain the permission of minority group, through consultation or collaboration, in order to write about minority cultures (Godfrey: 1992). Not only does such a policy fail to guarantee the authenticity of such writing, it also problematically assumes that by virtue of their birth or social identities, some individuals are the legitimate 'keepers' of a culture. Policies which decree that the fictional depiction of groups or cultures other than one's own is encroachment on 'the Other's' territory will encourage writing by white writers solely about white characters and white culture, a consequence that is antithetical to any anti-racist objective. Such policies may inadvertently expect minority voices to abide by the bounded styles, forms, languages and subjects that dominant critics associate with minority cultures. They also ignore the growing number of artists with 'hyphenated identities and hybrid realities' (Trinh 1991:73). Policies of silencing one's own or other voices to accord with an over-simplified dichotomy of oppressed and oppressor cultures are not only aesthetically stultifying. They also divert energy and resources from developing inclusive politics in publishing. And ultimately that is what the politics of voice should be about—facilitating new or marginalized voices, valorizing plurality and complex diversity, and encouraging a rich flowering of creative writing that depicts the whole spectrum of humanity.

Notes

An earlier version of this paper was presented at a conference on 'Immigration, Racism and Multiculturalism: The 1990s and Beyond', Department of Sociology, Saskatoon, Saskatchewan, March 22–23, 1991. I am grateful for insights provided to me by several writers, editors, publishers and others involved in literary and artistic production, who generously gave me their time during research conducted in May–June 1990—Barbara Carey, Sue Findlay, Nila Gupta, Norma De Haarte, Liz Martin, Rona Moreau, Susan Prentice, Libby Scheier, Makeda Silvera, Laura Skye, Rhea Tregebov and Margie Wolfe. I would also like to thank Frances Abele, Yasmeen Abu-Laban, Alan Hunt, Radha Jhappan and Jeanne Laux for their careful comments and valued advice on earlier drafts.

1 In the early 1980s, the Toronto-based feminist journal *Fireweed* had gone through similar battles.

2 The Writers' Union of Canada is a national organization founded in 1973 that promotes the interests of writers vis-à-vis government and publishers.

3 PEN Canada is a national writers' organization affiliated to PEN International, which addresses itself to the plight of banned, censored, imprisoned and disappeared writers around the world.

4 In the case of The Writers' Union of Canada, the debates over racism and authorial voice were caried out within the 'Writers Confidential' section of the Union's newsletter. Debates over racism resurfaced at the May 1989 general meeting in the form of a panel discussion on racism in publishing, and a resolution introduced on the floor to establish a task force on racism in publishing. The stunning defeat of the resolution led to the formation of the Committee on Racism in Writing & Publishing. During the May 1990 general meeting, the unanimous passage of the anti-racist resolution formulated by the committee was greeted by a standing ovation by some 150 writers from across Canada (*FUSE* 1990).

Allegations of racism against PEN Canada were raised by Vision 21, a group of writers formed around issues of cultural representation, racism and the arts. Vision 21 alleged first, that Native, Asian and African writers were underrepresented at the 54th Annual Congress of PEN held in Toronto and Montreal during September 1989. Second, members of Vision 21 called into question the behaviour of June Callwood, president of PEN Canada, when confronted by leafleting members of the former organization (*Globe and Mail*, September 26, 28, 1989; October 2, 1989; *Books in Canada*, December 1989; January/February 1990; March 1990; April 1990; Philip 1990:18–28).

In 1984, at the annual general meeting of the League of Canadian Poets, three dub poets—Lillian Allen, Clifton Joseph and Devon Haughton—were rejected from membership in the league for failing to satisfy league standards. The reason given was that they were not poets but performers. To which the poets responded, 'What do you think we perform, newspaper articles?' (Allen 1987/1988:14).

5 In this paper, I use the terms Native peoples, Aboriginal peoples,

indigenous peoples and First Nation synonymously. The term Indian (which would exclude the Inuit) is also used where appropriate, as are the names of particular First Nations such as Cree, Ojibway, etc. While many of these terms are contested, my nomenclature reflects the diversity of terms used by First Nations artists and writers.

6 This decision was particularly controversial given that it involved breaking contracts with writers whose work had already been accepted and edited, thus raising questions regarding the rights of the writers, the possible defamation of their writings on the charge of racism, and the possible violation of publishing ethics by Women's Press. The Writers' Union of Canada became engaged in the defence of the three writers whose contracts were broken. Its Rights and Freedoms Committee advised members not to have any dealings with the Press until it had demonstrated 'professional standards, for contracts' (Cole 1989:10).

7 Significant gains were made during the 1960s and 1970s. Female authors such as Margaret Atwood, Margaret Laurence, Gabrielle Roy, Mavis Gallant, and later Alice Munro and Marian Engel won recognition as part of the mainstream of Canadian literature. Moreover, women attained positions of power and editorial control within important publishing houses such as McClelland & Stewart and Macmillan Press. Explaining her sense that male Canadian publishers were consistently encouraging and non-sexist in their professional behaviour, Margaret Atwood argues that, 'In general, the Canadian publishers were so desperate for any book they thought they could publish successfully that they wouldn't have cared if the author were a newt' (Atwood 1991:19). The increased visibility of white women in CanLit was aided by the flurry of activity in literary production during the 1970s among white, university-educated women determined to guarantee women's liberation a voice. Several feminist magazines, newspapers and journals were founded, and feminist publishers (such as Women's Press in 1972) were established. The market for books authored by women was greatly augmented by the emergence of interest in feminist material, and by the institutionalization of women's studies in universities.

8 See Tregebov (1991) on the disadvantages of being a Jewish woman writer.

9 In Gates's (1991) exploration of the issue of authenticity in fiction, he also examines the infamous case of the best-selling 'autobiography', *The Education of Little Tree*, by Forrest Carter. Forrest Carter was later found out to be a pseudonym for the late Asa Earl Carter, a Ku Klux Klan terrorist, fascist and anti-semite, and author of the 1963 'segregation forever' speech by Governor George Wallace of Alabama.

10 In the 1986 Canadian census, 28 per cent of respondents identified their ethnic background as including more than one ethnic origin.

11 According to Gates (1991), the tendency to categorize authors according to their social identities has elevated the works of minority authors that contain minority characters while burying other novels whose main characters are white. For example, 'James Baldwin's *Giovanni's*

Room, arguably his most accomplished novel, is seldom taught in black literature courses because its characters are white and gay' (1991:28).

12 'Squaw' is an offensive term applied to Native women. It is unclear why Godard chooses to use this epithet, except possibly in an ironic fashion to emphasize the literary appropriation by non-Native women.

13 The trickster is a figure found in many oral cultures, but is special to the Native cultures of North America. Among the names by which the trickster is recognized are Nanbush (Ojibway), Weesageechak (Cree), Glooscap, Nanabojoh, Napi, Raven, Hare and Coyote (Keeshig-Tobias 1991:173; Kelly 1978).

14 Native theatre groups include the Native Earth Performing Arts in Toronto, the De-ba-jih-mu-jig Theatre Group on Manitoulin Island, the Spirit Song Native Indian Theatre Group in Vancouver, and the Saskatoon Native Theatre Group in Saskatoon.

15 I would like to thank Frances Abele for bringing this point to my attention.

References

Allen, Lillian (1987/1988) 'De Dub Poets', *This Magazine*, 21(7), pp. 12–14.

Appiah, Kwame Anthony (1991) 'Is the Post- in Postmodernism the Post-in Postcolonial?' *Critical Inquiry* 17 (Winter).

Atwood, Margaret (1990) 'If You Can't Say Something Nice, Don't Say Anything At All', in L. Scheier, S. Sheard & E. Wachtel eds., *Language in Her Eye: Views On Writing and Gender By Canadian Women Writing in English*, Coach House Press, Toronto.

Books in Canada (1989/1990) 'Field Notes', December; 'Letters', January/February, March; April, Toronto.

Broadside (1988/1989) 'Take Our Word For It', 10(3), p. 4.

Cameron, Anne (1991) 'The Operative Principle is Trust', in L. Scheier, S. Sheard & E. Wachtel eds., *Language In Her Eye*, Coach House Press, Toronto.

Cardinal-Shubert, Joanne (1989) 'in the red', *FUSE Magazine*, Fall, pp. 22–26.

Cole, Susan (1989) 'Writing Our Racism', *NOW Magazine*, March 23–29, p. 10.

Craig, Terence (1987) *Racial Attitudes in English-Canadian Fiction*. Wilfred Laurier Press, Waterloo.

De Haarte, Norma (1990), Author interview, May 8, Toronto.

di Michele (1987) 'Writers from Invisible Cities', *Canadian Women's Studies*, 8(2), pp. 37–38.

Fawcett, Brian (1989) 'Notes from the Inner Circle', *Books in Canada*, August/September, p. 3.

Fitzgerald, Maureen, 'Letters', *Broadside*, 22(10), August/September.

Fuse (1990) 'Writing Authentic Voice', 1 (1&2), Fall, pp. 1–15.

Gates, Henry Louis Jr. (1991) ' "Authenticity", or the Lesson of Little

Tree', *The New York Times Book Review*, November 24, 1, pp. 26–30.

Globe and Mail (1989), 'Charges of Racism Spark Protest at Writers' Congress', September 26, A19; 'All Abroad! Writers' Express Heads for Montreal', September 28, C11; 'PEN Organizers Stress the Positive,' October 2, C7, Toronto.

Godard, Barbara (1986) 'Voicing Difference: The Literary Production of Native Women', in S. Neuman and S. Kamboureli eds., *A Mazing Space: Writing Canadian Women Writing*, Longspoon/Newest, Edmonton.

Godfrey, Stephen (1992) 'Canada Council Asks Whose Voice Is It Anyway?' *Globe and Mail*, March 21, C1, C15.

Goetz, Anne Marie (1991) 'Feminism and the Claim to Know: Contradictions in Feminist Approaches to Women in Development,' in R. Grant & K. Newland eds. *Gender and International Relations*, Indiana University Press, Bloomington.

Goldie, Terry (1989) *Fear and Temptation: The Image of the Indigene in Canadian, Australian and New Zealand Literatures*, McGill–Queen's University Press, Kingston.

Gupta, Nila (1990) Author interview, May 10, Scarborough, Ontario.

Highway, Tomson (1989) *Dry Lips Oughta Move to Kapuskasing*, Fifth House, Saskatoon.

Highway, Tomson (1988) *The Rez Sisters*, Fifth House, Saskatoon.

Hutcheon, Linda (1991) 'The Particular Meets the Universal', in L. Scheier, S. Sheard & E. Watchtel eds., *Language In Her Eye*, Coach House Press, Toronto.

Keeshig-Tobias, Lenore (1991) 'The Magic of Others', in L. Scheier, S. Sheard & E. Wachtel eds., *Language In Her Eye*, Coach House Press, Toronto.

——(1989) 'Letter to the Editor', *Globe and Mail*, June 6.

——(n.d.) Letter in 'Writers Confidential', *Writers Union of Canada Newsletter*.

Kelly, M.T. (1987) 'The Trickster', *This Magazine*, 21(1), March/April.

King, Thomas (1990) 'Introduction,' *All My Relations: An Anthology of Contemporary Canadian Native Fiction*, McClelland & Stewart, Toronto.

Kostash, Myrna (1990) 'Pens of Many Colours', *Canadian Forum*, 64 (790), p. 19.

Kulyk, Keefer (1991) 'A Response to Margaret Chritakos' "Axioms to grind",' *Room of One's Own* 14. pp. 97–118.

LaRocque, Emma (1990) 'Preface', in J. Perreault & S. Vance eds., *Writing the Circle: Native Women of Western Canada*, NeWest Publishers, Edmonton.

Maracle, Lee (1991) 'Native Myths: Trickster Alive and Crowing', in Scheier, S. Sheard & E. Wachtel eds., *Language In Her Eye*, Coach House Press, Toronto.

Moure, Erin (1989), 'Watching the watchwords', *Books in Canada* 18 (8), November.

Mukherjee, Arun (1988) *Towards An Aesthetics of Opposition*, Williams-Wallace, Stratford.

Philip, Marlene Nourbese (1989) 'The Disappearing Debate', *This Magazine* 23(2), July/August, pp. 19–24.

Said, Edward, (1989) 'Representing the Colonized: Anthropology's Interlocutors', *Critical Inquiry* 15(Winter).

Scheier, Libby (1988) 'True Confessions Transformed: On Writing Our Emotions', *This Magazine*, 22(6), December, pp. 31–34.

——(1989) 'Phrase Fraud', *Saturday Night*, November, 91.

——(1991a) 'Chopped Liver', in L. Scheier, S. Sheard & E. Wachtel eds., *Language In Her Eye*, Coach House Press, Toronto.

——(1991b) 'Whose Voice Is It Anyway? *Books In Canada*, January/February, pp. 19–24.

Silvera, Makeda (1990) Author interview, April 27, Toronto.

Tregebov, Rhea (1990) 'Some Notes on the Story of Esther', in L. Scheier, S. Sheard & E. Wachtel eds., *Language in Her Eye*, Coach House Press, Toronto.

Trinh T. Minh-ha, (1991) *When the Moon Waxes Red: Representation, Gender and Cultural Politics*, Routledge, New York.

Warland, Betsy (1988) 'The White Page', *Broadside*, 9(10), August/September, p. 8.

Weedon, Chris (1987) *Feminist Practice and Poststructuralist Theory*, Blackwell, Oxford.

4 Pretty deadly tidda business
Jackie Huggins

I remember all my mother's stories, probably better than she realizes. Not only have I heard them a hundred times over, but she is a fine story-teller, recalling every event of her life with the vividness of the present, noting each detail right down to the cut and colour of her dress.

I have listened to her stories of being allowed to go only to fourth grade at school; stories of the cohesiveness of Murries on the reserve; stories of how none of them ever saw the money which was paid into their trust accounts. These stories continued after she met and married my father, who had been a prisoner of war on the Burma–Thailand Railway during the Second World War, in the days long before he and his people were even citizens of this country. There were also stories of the excitement of the 1967 Referendum and how Aboriginal[1] people began politically organizing themselves; and stories of the love and loss of her family. Yes, I too have lived through every one of those stories as she related them to me.

Recording the memories of elderly Aboriginals is an urgent task. If it is not done, much information about australian history will be lost forever. The life stories of older people illuminate much about what it was like to live in earlier days, how people experienced the world they knew, and the coping strategies they developed which have led to present-day survival. They also create a picture of what it has been to be 'on the other side' of forced assimilationist policies.

Aboriginal writing is deeply concerned with precise knowledge of the history of Aboriginal existence, gleaned if necessary from white records and prised out of white archives. Although archives and documents are white inventions, Aboriginal writers have developed a stronger sense of history than their white counterparts, along with a more intense concern for the social reality of Aboriginal people both today and in the past.

In attempting to analyze the writing of my mother's life, it is necessary for me to elucidate the vital role history plays in the recording of Aboriginal stories and how it has changed over the years, specifically in queensland, where my mother and her family lived. In the 1920s the queensland government pushed tribes out of their traditional areas and placed them on mission stations and government reserves, ostensibly to protect them from whites but in reality to place them under the control of missionaries and government officials. Traditional customs and practices such as corroborees, ceremonies, religious beliefs and marriage laws, as well as the use of tribal languages, were condemned and actively discouraged by missionaries and managers.

Ever since those forced movements, first from traditional areas in the 1920s and then from isolated communities in the 1940s and 1950s, Aboriginal people have become increasingly dispersed in rural towns and cities, resulting in the continued fragmentation of Aboriginal history and oral tradition. When people were living together in larger, enclosed communities, history and tradition were passed on orally by the older ones, and while the community remained together traditions were maintained. This was one of the many resistance strategies that Aboriginals employed against the colonizing forces.

The queensland government's long-term plan was to eventually absorb Aboriginal people into the white community so that they and their cultures would become extinct. This plan did not succeed, and it is a testament to the power of the Aboriginal sense of identity, history and place that Aboriginal people have been able to withstand these deliberate forces of complete annihilation. Aboriginal people still have a rich tradition of oral history, storytelling, philosophy, autobiography and biography, stored particularly by the older people.

Aboriginal studies are now concerned with the transformation of that oral literature into a written literature without necessarily destroying the original form in the process. Through writing, material that was previously contained to a large extent in a particular local or regional setting becomes available for more general distribution and reinterpretation.

Research by Aboriginal people tends to be concerned with discovering particular matters relating to individuals or communities; requires that the observer be an insider; and recognizes that observations depend on the relationship between the observer and observed and also on the particular time and circumstances of the observation. These concerns have shaped my writing of Rita's story.

Rita Huggins was born Rita Holt on 10 August 1921 at Carnarvon Gorge via Springsure, central queensland. She was born of two 'half-caste' parents, Albert and Rose Holt, whose traditional Bidgara–Pitjara area encompassed what is now known as the national park of Carnarvon Gorge.

Rita was never given a tribal name that she could recall. She may have been given one, but it would most certainly have become redundant when her family was forcibly removed to Barambah Aboriginal Settlement (as Cherbourg was known in the late 1920s). This redundancy was due to the white expectation that Aboriginal people would no longer continue their 'heathen' ways and practices, and to concomitant attempts to Anglicize every aspect of their culture and lifestyle. The prime signifier of personal identification was concealed. Like her parents, Albert and Rose, Rita's brothers and sisters were prescribed european names— Barney, Margaret, Clare, Harry, Thelma, Rita, Jimmy, Lawrence, Violet, Ruby, Oliver, Albert, Isobel and Walter. It is known that the three eldest children had traditional names, but Barney's daughter, who instigated a wide search for her father's name some years ago, has been unable to ascertain what it was. The person most likely to hold the key is the second eldest sibling, Clare, who has since passed away as a patient in a psychiatric nursing home.

Tindale's research into Aboriginal tribes in Australia, now held in the South Australian Museum, has also revealed Rita as 'Rita'. Aboriginal people despair at such lack of information about their people's genealogies and language groups. However, Rita was able to trace her maternal grandmother in the Tindale documents—she was known as Lucy 'a "full-blood" from the Maranoa'.[2]

Anguish and confusion filled the Holt family as they awoke one morning to the clamour of horses and troopers riding through their camp. Rita remembers her mother shielding the children protectively from the troopers as her father cautiously investigated. Soon after, the whole tribe was transported in the back of a cattle truck to Barambah.

Rita vividly recalls her grandmother wailing as the 'mob' was rounded up. 'Don't take my gunduburris![3] Don't take my gunduburris!' she screamed repeatedly. Much later, Rita was told that her aged grandmother wandered off aimlessly into the bush that day, and was never sighted alive again. It is presumed she died alone somewhere out there with a broken heart. When her body was found it was buried in Woorabinda, where her 'full-blood' relations lived.

On the basis of skin colour, the 'half-castes' were sent to Barambah and the 'full-bloods' to Woorabinda, in accord with the colonizers' ideology that children with white blood would be easier to assimilate than their darker counterparts. The lighter-skinned children were also segregated from the darker children in classes to accelerate their acceptance as white people. Teachers and missionaries were astounded when this strategy did not succeed.

School was the primary site for Aboriginal children to be socialized and imbued with european education. Rita attended school from the age of eight to the age of thirteen, or fourth grade as it was then. Subjects taken were basic reading, writing and arithmetic, with particular emphasis on british history, captain cook and sewing. Happy memories of school still remain with Rita, not because of the challenging educational content, but because it was a place where kids could socialize.

Outside school, other duties took precedence. As one of the middle ones in the family, Rita undertook most of the jobs her brothers and sisters performed. The egalitarian nature of family relationships was such that no one had specific jobs or ever felt 'picked on'. At a very young age Rita helped gather firewood as well as attending to other chores which included washing up, cleaning the yard, helping prepare food and looking after younger brothers and sisters while her mother rested.

Rita was sent to the mission dormitory at the relatively late age of twelve as punishment for dating boys. The life in the dormitories was one of control, regimentation and discipline. Boys and girls were segregated and all were required to do a range of domestic chores such as making their beds, rinsing soiled linen, washing and scrubbing out the dormitory and picking up papers. After breakfast the children would go to school for several hours. Some play time filled in the rest of the day before prayers, dinner and bed.

The dormitories segregated children from their parents as a strategy of social control, which did its damage in its attempts to sever ties between the children and their traditional way of life. The considerable time absorbed by dormitory routine succeeded in limiting the depth and richness of the children's traditional knowledge. Dormitory life also attempted to take away the disciplinary powers of the children's natural parents. Aboriginals now were being managed, protected, taught and chastized like children and in this way lost much of the autonomy they formerly enjoyed.

Rita never felt that Cherbourg was her 'real' home, as she

yearned nostalgically for the days she had known in Carnarvon Gorge. A dislocated person in a sense, she was physically located at Barambah but emotionally and spiritually located in Carnarvon Gorge. Unlike an immigrant to a new country, Rita would not and could not entertain the notion that she had chosen to relinquish her place of birth for 'greener pastures'. Her soul stirred for her traditional lands. She felt an outcast, a refugee in her own country, like so many other Aboriginals in the past, present and future.

Around the age of thirteen or fourteen, the time came for girls to serve apprenticeships to train as 'worthy housekeepers': Rita remembers the expectation that all the girls, whether they were her age or younger, would fulfil the role of domestic servants. It was routine for girls to be placed in servitude as domestic servants by those in authority. The Aboriginals' Preservation and Protection Acts 1939–1946 empowered reserve superintendents to enter employment contracts on behalf of residents, to hold any funds residents might have and to control residents' spending. The then Cherbourg superintendent had arrangements with both local and distant policemen, pastoralists and farmers to supply a steady flow of workers for those in 'need'.

Rita's first job, in 1943, entailed long days from dawn until late in the evening spent in the routine of cleaning, washing, ironing, preparing food and caring for the children. She performed domestic work for many years, before and after the birth of her children. Her background and her experience of work as a domestic have, in a way, shaped her lifestyle: even today she does not feel comfortable and a 'whole' person unless she has spent the day in some kind of domestic activity, whether it be cooking or cleaning.

In 1940, when she was eighteen, Rita met Jack Huggins in Brisbane. He was a tall and handsome Aboriginal man with a Maori heritage. In the 1940s he was possibly the first Aboriginal person in queensland to hold a position in the post office. It was not until after the Second World War that Rita and Jack met again; they married in 1951. Their union produced three children—two girls and a boy. Rita already had two girls from a previous relationship. However, never fully recovering from his war injuries, Jack's life with his young family was brief. He died in 1958 of a heart attack at the age of 38.

Devastated by the loss of her husband, Rita returned to Brisbane in 1959 to the comfort of her extended family network. Hers was one of the first Aboriginal families to live in Inala, now the most densely populated Aboriginal suburb of Brisbane. As the population expanded, many Aboriginal people formed their own identifiable community groups. Rita excelled at providing a way for local Aboriginal families who were new to the city to get to know each other. She was able to operate in this manner largely under the umbrella of OPAL.

The first political organization involving Aboriginal people was the Queensland Council for the Advancement of Aborigines and Torres Strait Islanders (QCAATSI), formed on 1 October 1960 as a state branch of the existing national body known as the Federal Council for the Advancement of Aborigines and Torres Strait Islanders (FCAATSI). QCAATSI comprised largely politically rather than welfare-oriented people. Members wanted reform in the programs and legislation affecting Aboriginals in queensland. The legislation with queensland had been predominantly paternalistic and with the new interest in minorities, coming mainly from the American civil rights movement, the queensland government found itself on the defensive because of the upsurge of interest in Aboriginal rights. QCAATSI became the chief agent for attacking the policies towards Aboriginals of the queensland government.[5]

A possible reason for the evolution of OPAL was that the Country/Liberal Party government found it useful to generate an organization which could be used as a showcase of public support for government policies. Also, an atmosphere of zealous anti-communism existed in queensland in the early 1960s. QCAATSI was regarded by the queensland government and some of the media as an organization with communist membership, and thus a tool of the Communist Party. It is difficult to find objective support for the idea that QCAATSI was communist-controlled, but many involved during the breakaway period insist that there were several party members in the organization.[6] Certainly, when asked about one of the driving forces QCAATSI, Daisy Marchisotti, one of OPAL's founders, replied, 'Oh you know she was a paid-up member of the Communist Party and we were all terrified of them at the time.'[7]

OPAL was formed in 1961 in Brisbane by Mrs Muriel Langford, a former Christian missionary in India. In an effort 'to help the Aborigines', Mrs Langford organized a meeting in Brisbane on 4 July 1961 which was attended by representatives of the Anglican, Catholic, Congregational, Methodist and Presbyterian churches, Rotary, WCTU, YWCA, TocH, and the Postal Overseas Union.

The name OPAL, which stood for One People of Australia League, was adopted and incorporated under the Queensland Companies Act 1931–1960. Subsequently, the executive offered membership to the Baptist Union, Lutheran Church, Salvation Army, Presbyterian Women's Missionary Union, Queensland Temperance Union, St Joan's Alliance and the Blue Army.[8]

The main objectives of the proposed organization of OPAL
were:
1 To endeavour to solve by influence and example, the difficulties of coloured people, first in the Brisbane area, and then'
   spreading throughout the state of queensland.
2 To attract organizations and people of repute to the ranks of
   the organization.
3 To weld the coloured and white citizens of Australia into 'One
   People'.[9]

OPAL enjoyed close relations with the queensland government and
received some government funds. Indeed two members of the OPAL
board were senior public servants in the Department of Native
Affairs.

Not all organizations concerned with Aboriginal affairs had
the support of the government. QCAATSI fought continuously for
civil rights and was critical of the queensland government. It
claimed that OPAL was a government front composed of tame cats.

It was the third of OPAL's stated objectives, 'to weld the
coloured and white citizens of Australia into One People'—which
reeks of the assimilationist philosophies of the day—which led to
OPAL's immediately being viewed as a pro-government, pro-assim-
ilationist organization. In spite of these criticisms, many
Aboriginal people gained social and political confidence from
OPAL. An opportunity to work for Aboriginal welfare, outside the
political arena but encouraged by the government, was an attrac-
tive proposition for the league's early members.

The major areas of interest for all branches of OPAL, though
in varying degrees, were welfare, housing, education, employment,
socials, Badge or Tag Day activities and holiday camps. OPAL
holiday camps began as an ambitious undertaking, in the first
three years catering for groups of 50, 90 and 140 children
respectively.[10] The number of children taking part in the camps
increased, with an average of around 220 from settlements, missions and outlying regions each year from 1942 to 1972. The
reason for the holidays was to provide an opportunity for Aboriginal children, primarily from missions, reserves and settlements,
to come into contact with white children and adults.

Rita was known as the 'glamour girl' of OPAL. She was a
woman who presented herself in a dignified and commanding
manner, full of confidence and self-assurance, who defied and was
the ultimate exception to Aboriginal stereotypes existing at the
time. She knew firmly who she was and what she was and where
she stood as an Aboriginal person and a facilitator between two
cultures that were like chalk and cheese: the oppressed and the

oppressor. This is a difficult line to tread, but Rita trod it with ease and grace.

Within OPAL, a cooperative and comfortable working relationship existed with whites. Rita recalls the hours spent listening to white people speaking. She was impressed by how they conducted themselves and she learnt a great deal from these interactions. This is what essentially appealed to Rita, a great humanitarian who loves people of every colour, race and creed. She talked excitedly about her family, people and culture to those who had never encountered an Aboriginal before. First impressions may be the most lasting, and Rita has never relinquished her starring role as the Aboriginal people's ambassadress.

Aboriginals in Brisbane faced not only the usual difficulties of newcomers but also those of rural or small-town people moving into an urban area. Additionally, Aboriginals faced problems engendered by racial prejudice and discrimination. Attesting to this is the fact that Rita and her family moved house fourteen times in three years, largely because of discrimination by landlords in renting premises to Aboriginals and their intolerance of the sharing of homes with transient or homeless relatives and friends.

This did not deter Rita from helping others. She would voluntarily assist newly arrived Aboriginal people from reserves and country areas in contacting the Housing Commission, applying for benefits from Social Security, getting in touch with relations, gaining access to schools for their children, applying for employment—an overall information and access billboard.

Inala is a Brisbane suburb whose residents are of low socioeconomic status; this was particularly so in the early 1960s and it is interesting to note that the 'poor whites' in the neighbourhood also gravitated to Rita's house. She was able to assist them, always insisting that OPAL 'helps both blacks and whites in need'. Food parcels, Christmas presents and holiday camps were some of the offerings extended to many families in the Inala region. Rita thus became OPAL's official agent in the area. A former friend would joke that Rita would 'go opalling' occasionally, meaning that she would spread the good word of OPAL as far as possible, acting as a talent scout, recruiting some, and 'educating' people about the aims and objectives of OPAL.

For Rita's children, OPAL was a large and sometimes annoying part of our lives: we were constantly dragged around to dances, socials and talks on Aboriginal culture. Always displaying a deep sense of pride in her Aboriginality, Rita was able to instil this in us by talking to other people about Aboriginals for hours in the halls of OPAL. She taught not only others but also her own children to respect Aboriginal people and to recognize that they had worthy contributions to make to society.

OPAL became a meeting place where Aboriginal people could gather socially while, though many may have been unaware of it at the time, subconsciously their political identities were starting to take shape. Many well-known Aboriginal community members served their apprenticeships in OPAL, the most famous being Senator Neville Bonner. Others include Mick Miller, Lillian Holt, Michael Williams, Ted Wymara and Ron Hurley. The fact that Rita has always disliked politics and never considered herself a political person would help to explain her aversion to joining more vocal and high-profile groups like QCAATSI.

OPAL also allowed Rita's children to communicate with different groups of people from all walks of life, from politicians to traditional elders, without feeling inferior. In those days people in OPAL circles were keen to listen. We, her children, have carried through to today the ability to comfortably interact and socialize with different people and not feel 'shame'. When asked to what we attribute this, 'OPAL' is the unanimous answer from all three.

OPAL instilled a positive feeling that has had an enormous impact on Rita and her family's life. Meeting Aboriginals and empathetic non-Aboriginals has provided lasting friendships, not only for Rita's generation but for her children's. Not only did the OPAL experience equip Rita and her children with social skills, but it provided us all with a political framework from which to operate.

Yes, I too have lived through every one of Rita's stories and feelings as she related them to me. By virtue of being her daughter, and a close one at that, I possess many of her experiences.

But Rita is a product of her time, and so too am I. Some of the things she may have been obliged to accept in those days (I say obliged here, as I feel she has never simply accepted anything), particularly the blatant patronization, discrimination and subjugation, are like waving a red flag at a bull to me. Not that she never had the courage to stand up for herself; but the plain fact was that every obstacle was placed in her way, and if she objected she would have faced the barrage of insults and humiliation thrown at Aboriginal people in those days. I'm not saying this does not occur today, but the players, rules and games are different, although there isn't a level playing field yet. Aboriginal people can more easily gain access to and manipulate the system now. In those days you had to shut up and put up with things for survival's sake.

So how do 'the oppressed' write about 'the oppressed'? I was asked this question at a recent conference on autobiography and biography. I guess it's one I have to figure out for myself, but to start with, I would consider it 'the liberated' writing about 'the liberated'.

As for my mother's wishes, she wants to make the book as accessible to family and Aboriginal community members as possible. And in her words, 'This means no big words, little [conscious] politics and my story.' This is where my ego takes a bruising, because yes, it is her story, not mine. I have to constantly remind myself of that fact.

How much is 'I' the writer? It's a bit like schizophrenia, I guess. Or is it being just plain childish—always wanting to do the opposite of what you are told? If so, I think maybe someone else should have written Rita's life story, but neither she nor I could have conceded that one. I believe she has had enough tampering in her life by whites and needs no further investigation or intrusion.

Rita Huggins's biography will be typical of the new phenomenon of contemporary Aboriginal writing, whose task lies ahead, not only in addressing personal histories and life stories but in achieving a more equitable representation for Aboriginal women's history. The title of her book will be *Auntie Rita*, the term she is affectionately known by. It is not only a sign of extended family and community relations but an application given in the greatest respect to elders of our social world.

My search has been for what I can give my mother in return for her love, strength, wisdom and inspiration. I have found the answer in writing her biography. Her contribution to australia has been immense. She may not have been a public figure the way someone like Charles Perkins was, but she has been a public figure to family and Aboriginal community groups, and to her this is where it counts. She has certainly been the inspiration of my life.

Her life history is important, indeed precious, and the act of recording and publishing it is, in Aboriginal English, 'pretty deadly tidda business'—wonderful, strong Black woman stuff.

Notes

A = Aboriginal   B = Black
a = australian   w = white
e = european

'a' is for apple, agile, anger, another, address, alphabet, but not Aboriginal. It is insulting and destructive to use a small 'a'. This spelling is extremely racist, as are the biologically racist definitions of part, quarter, half-caste and full-blood Aboriginals.

It's like calling us boong, coon, nigger or abo, and is just as blatant and condescending. It is also similar to spelling a Christian name such as dianne or gail like so. Negating our identity and nationality, it lacks empathy and understanding as any Greek, Italian or Jew would understand—though they are paid the privilege of getting their names spelt with a capital.

It is indicative of notions of inferiority/superiority of Blacks and whites in Australia. On the basis of white superiority it could be presumed that the initiators of a small 'a' subconsciously act out their power games in order to further maintain their privileged positions and to keep Blacks in their 'subjugated' line. The usual excuse is that there has been a 'typo', but I have yet to see 'europeans' or 'australians' in Australian books. Why therefore does the typewriter possess an incredibly persistent disability when it comes to Aboriginal?

I note that the Black American activist, Audre Lorde, has a distinctive, consistent style in her spelling of america: 'For to survive in the mouth of this dragon we call america we have had to learn this first and most vital lesson—that we were never meant to survive' (*Sister Outsider*, 42). This establishes a principle that while the oppressed are still the oppressed, the country in which they live has been nullified by the small 'a', thus rendering it less significant. This empowers the writer and in many, if not all, of my future works I will be adopting her style as a political statement.

My political statement and preference is for the term 'Aboriginal' as both noun and adjective. While it is grammatically correct to use 'Aborigines' as a noun these are white people's rules—the good Queen's English. Are we therefore playing 'their' games in order to define ourselves? Is it better to be grammatically or politically correct?

'Aborigines' has long been a term used to classify and demean Aboriginal people by anthropologists, missionaries and government officials, particularly in the old Department of Native Affairs and Aboriginal and Islander Advancement [sic]. The word 'Aborigine' also has an unhealthy, patronising ring about it. Since the invasion, Aboriginal people's place has been described and reflected by the european winners. Only recently have we begun to name ourselves in our own terms through our struggles for equality and, basically, to be heard. This will counteract the white world view and ethnocentrism that infiltrates our movement and saps our energy.

We need to reinvent language in order to make it appropriate for our purposes. The white women's movement has certainly achieved this, e.g. the use of person. There is some debate among Aboriginal individuals themselves whether to use the term 'Aboriginal' or 'Aborigines'. In my opinion our Aboriginal words Murrie or Koorie should not be used universally either, as there are issues of protocol involved here. Only non-Aboriginal people who respect and are familiar with those terms should use them otherwise they sound like poor bastardizations of endearing terms. The key is to ask Aboriginal people what they prefer to be called.

The following biologically determined, 19th-century, outdated terms are offensive to Aboriginal people and should never be used in any context whatsoever: full-blood; part-Aboriginal; half-caste; quarter-caste; one-eighth Aboriginal; and other insulting racist definitions.

'Aboriginal descent' is another potentially offensive term as most Aboriginal people consider themselves as 'either you are or you are not'. The term, however, is still marginally used by Aboriginal people to describe themselves, but this is in no way as offensive as the above terms.

These terms were used to define Aboriginal people by europeans who attempted to divide and rule on the basis that Aboriginal people with some strands of white blood were more easily assimilated into white society than those who were not.

While some Aboriginal people may use the term 'half-caste' in their speech or writing, it is only used in an historical sense, e.g. 'my grand-parents were half-caste'. Generally, older Aboriginal people will do so more often than younger people as it was official practice to identify them in this way.

Non-Aboriginal people, particularly from British stock, are never asked to ratio out what part they are Irish, English, Scottish, etc., so neither should these types of classification apply to Aboriginals.

1 The term 'Aboriginals' will be used as a noun (as well as adjectivally), in accordance with my preference and political stance, as opposed to the word 'Aborigines', which has been used to classify and demean Aboriginal people in the repressive state in which I live, queensland. 'Aborigines' also reflects an assumption of superiority by a dominant culture. The terms 'half-caste' and 'full-blood' are biologically racist definitions which are unacceptable to most Aboriginal people today. They have been used as a divide-and-rule tactic by the colonizers.

2 N.B. Tindale, 'Distribution of Australian Tribes: A Field Survey', Transactions of the Royal Society of South Australia, vol. 64, 1940, p. 302.

3 Aboriginal word for children.

4 L. McBride, Interview with Jackie Huggins, 28 April 1989.

5 Donald E Alexander, 'A Study of the One People of Australia League: 1961–1973', unpublished MA thesis, University of Queensland, 6 May 1976, p. 6.

6 W. E. Tomasetti, 'One People of Australia League', unpublished B.A. Honours thesis, University of Queensland, May 1967, p.1.

7 Muriel Langford, Interview with Jackie Huggins, Brisbane, 23 April 1989.

8 W.E. Tomasetti, p. 1.

9 OPAL First Annual Report, Brisbane, 1963, p. 2.

10 OPAL First Annual Report, 1963 p. 3.

5 'Love me tender, love me true, never let me go . . .'[1]: A Sri Lankan reading of Tracey Moffatt's *Night Cries—A Rural Tragedy*

Laleen Jayamanne

We have been herded as people of color to mind only our own cultures. Hence, Asians will continue to make films on Asia, Africans on Africa and Euro-Americans on the world. (Trinh 1990:10)
We must assimilate all those systems we come across or admit defeat. (Shahani 1990:12)[2]

When I was in Rome several months ago, I was talking with other Chilean exiles about how the feeling of schizophrenia is becoming stronger after seven years. One recalled that he had seen himself walking down the street, another saw himself drinking a cup of coffee, and I, who normally write the dialogue for my films in a Spanish that can easily be translated into French, saw my own handwriting in French. After that I began to write in French all the time. Another was in a tailor's shop surrounded by mirrors and saw a profile he could not identify; only after several minutes did he recognize himself (Ruiz 1981:113).[3]

In framing my comments about *Night Cries* with those by these Third World filmmakers, I am not appealing to authority. I use them here because they refer in different ways to conditions necessary for work to be at all possible and they also imply ways of inventing methods. These conditions are not simply idiosyncratic needs of individual creativity (though they may be that too), but also link up with wider cultural processes in a neo-colonial and postmodern world.

An Australian friend encouraged me to do a Sri Lankan reading of *Night Cries*. What would a Sri Lankan reading be? Wrong question, you can't know what it is until you do it, because a reading is in part deciphering and in part invention in the sense of making connections. How then would I set about reading the film as a Sri Lankan, as a foreigner,[4] as one outside the cultural forces the film dramatizes in a highly distilled form? But it is not only I who am foreign. *Night Cries* itself is utterly different in look and conception from much of Australian 35mm cinema. It

can, however, be located within the 'popular culture–fiction
tradition' of Australian independent low-budget experimental
filmmaking which Adrian Martin (1989) posits in his typology of
the field. The energy of this tradition, according to Martin, lies
in an 'impulse to incorporate—in however dislocated or perverse
a way—vivid fragments of the given cultural environment (television, music and the whole 'styled' culture alongside cinema itself)'.
He further qualifies this impulse:

> The popular culture–fiction tradition differs from the
> agitational–deconstructive one in that there is less overt 'critique'
> and more emotional indulgence; and it replaces the romantic
> imagistic plundering of the strange or dark 'edges' of popular
> imagery . . . with a greater sensitivity to and awareness of original
> cultural contexts and meanings. (Martin 1989:18)

If *Night Cries* does in many ways belong here, there is also a
sense in which it doesn't. This is because it looks glossy and
breathtaking in the way big movies do. The ideology of experimental cinema, with its bias toward a rough and uncommodified
look, may declare this glossiness suspect, but I would like to
sustain a sense of strangeness in all these aspects even as I respond
to parts of the film that are more accessible than others. This
approach helps me to talk about the film, otherwise difficult,
precisely because it is a film by an Aboriginal Australian woman
filmmaker. (In the early 1980s I faced no such trepidation in
writing about, say, the work of the Belgian Chantal Akerman,
largely because her early films fitted into a feminist international
theoretical agenda where questions of cultural, regional and ethnic
specificity weren't—or didn't seem to be—relevant. But with
Moffatt's work these factors cannot be elided.)

So, to my surprise, the scenario that should have been most
accessible for feminist reasons—that of the maternal melodrama
seen from the daughter's perspective—is opaque in certain crucial
ways. Its universal aspect, the tension between the call of duty
mixed with love on the one hand and the call of desire for another
life on the other, is legible and wrenching. But it is from the film
that I learnt of the harrowing history of the assimilation policy
of forced adoption and what it means in terms of lived experience
between a 'mother' and 'daughter'.

Also, the location of this tragedy, the outback ranch, is presented in a way which is partly familiar and partly opaque. At
one level the Moffatt image is an optical image; an image that is
completely mediated by technology and therefore familiar to contemporary television and video viewers. This is interesting in the
context of 'big' Australian movies that celebrate the land and its

putative pristine otherness in a transparent cinematography. Ross
Gibson draws out the implications of this practice thus:

> The presented image of a landscape is necessarily a sign. And in
> the Australian setting, it is a sign of nature as opposed to a sign
> of a sign; Australian film culture remains 'innocent' or 'primitive',
> declining to graduate to the (post-)modernist worlds of second
> and/or third degree (re-)presentations of pre-existent social
> constructs. (Gibson 1983:49)

(He does go on to show that this seeming naivete is in the interest
of producing a product marketable elsewhere.)

In opposition to this, Moffatt's setting is the sign of a sign,
not merely an optical figuration but a specific cultural reference.
It was from the film and the discourses around it that I learnt
that its art director, Stephen Curtis, and Moffatt wanted the film
to have the colour of the painting of Albert Namatjira, the
Aboriginal artist of the Aranda watercolour school. To pursue the
implications of this decision is to explore the very terms of
Aboriginal tradition and modernity and as an outsider I can only,
with diffidence, cite a review article that seems to me to map out
lucidly the terrain of both the art historical and the cultural,
political debates. Ian Burn and Ann Stephen (1986), in their review
of a book on Namatjira, refer to some of the reasons for the
extreme popularity of Namatjira's work and for his rejection by
the art establishment. The work was related to the tourist industry;
the Aranda painters assimilated the pictorial idiom of the so-called
gum tree school of regional landscape painting which the Modernist critical establishment despised. Furthermore the use of
watercolour as a medium went against them. Burn and Stephen
make the point that

> . . . art historians would have had to qualify their Modernist
> viewpoints in order to acknowledge the significance of the art,
> particularly since the work entailed other forms of innovation in
> terms of different subject matter, new types of landscape, using
> traditional forms as a vehicle for other meanings. (Burn & Stephen
> 1986:13)

They go on to say that the kind of Aranda work that entered the
galleries in the 1950s used watercolour but in patterns that were
more 'primitive'. Geoff Batchen (1990) had referred to the cultural
similarity between Namatjira and Jimmy Little, the Aboriginal
singer who plays himself in Night Cries. (It is no accident, it seems,
that Moffatt invokes them both in her work.) I agree with Batchen
that this film 'is all about the politics of imitation and assimilation'

(Batchen 1990) but would add that it is perhaps also about an aesthetics of assimilation.

Apart from the thematic of assimilation within which the mother-daughter relationship is lived unto death, there is another sense in which Moffatt brings into play the idea of 'assimilation', which is a matter of method and also of survival—survival not in a cultural ghetto but in the market, as well as in the domains of cultural visibility and legitimacy. The *Shorter Oxford English Dictionary* defines 'assimilate' thus: 'to make like, to adapt, to absorb and incorporate, to convert into a substance of its own nature; to absorb into the system'. I also want to invoke the bodily connotations of the word, as in to assimilate food into the body, because I want to discuss how Jimmy Little performs in the film and how he in turn is performed by filmic operations such as editing and framing.

Through the performance of Jimmy Little, Moffatt both explores the violent and the fluent aspects of cultural hybridization/assimilation and taps into an Aboriginal cultural history which is neither pristinely indigenous nor completely other. The first figure to appear in the film is Jimmy Little and he also concludes it. Given that beginnings and endings are privileged moments, his presence at these points marks him as central to the concerns of the film. The song he sings unaccompanied at the opening is given in its hit version, with all the brassy trimmings, at the end. In addition to frame its events, he reappears in two crucial scenes in the body of this short, seventeen-minute film. I will discuss these two scenes in some detail presently.

In recalling Jimmy Little to our memory, Moffatt is making an enabling tradition for herself to work in. At one level, then, I see this as a 'homage' to a forgotten Aboriginal showman who had his brief place in the sun with the one hit song 'Royal Telephone' (1964). Part of the film's magic is that as one laughs at the pure cornball lyrics of 'Royal Telephone', one is nevertheless engaged by the body performing, or by the velvet texture of the voice itself and the melody of the songs. Functioning at another level is the overtly jarring effect of his songs (both heard and unheard) in the context of the tragedy between the mother and daughter. It would have been too easy to use him as a parodic figure and poke fun at his song to Jesus. This film does not work with parody, perhaps because its genre is tragedy. But what function does a singer have in a tragedy, especially a singer whose songs don't in any way set the mood but instead interrupt it? What happens in this film, however, is not a simple pitting of Jimmy Little's smoothness against the harshness of the woman's story, though this does happen once and in an interesting way.

The singer

Little reappears in the body of the film when the daughter cracks a whip outside the house while the mother, seated inside, registers each lash viscerally. There is no telling whether it is pleasure or pain or a bit of both that this aged body feels. This is a rare scene in Australian cinema for its perverse intensity. The laughter of the daughter as she cracks the whip is both utterly thrilling and chilling in its daemonic, asocial force. It is this scene that Jimmy Little interrupts, and one wonders why. He seems to function as the third term necessary to break the dyad of the mother and daughter, but his presence is not phallic although he is a man. As the whip cracks and the mother shudders, Jimmy Little is cut in. He is seen in a series of shots putting the guitar strap over his shoulder, adjusting it, then adjusting his collar in an effort to get comfortable so as to perform, and the sound here is that of static electricity. The song he then sings silently is 'Love Me Tender' (love me true, never let me go).

Moffatt certainly takes this song to heart: she will not let him go. So he returns again to the beach scene of childhood. When the little girl is tormented by her two black male playmates and is also abandoned by the mother, who just disappears, leaving her

The singer (Jimmy Little), Night Cries, *1989.*

on a rocky outcrop on a dark and hostile, thoroughly un-Australian beach, he comes back. As the little girl cries in anguish, Jimmy Little sings, in extreme close-up, a silent lullaby which fails to lull the desolate, abandoned child. In this return, the previously benign smile takes on a sinister quality. There is a need here that this figure cannot now satisfy, a register of feeling that he can not be a part of. But even so, at this critical moment too Moffatt fragments his body and in so doing, opens up multiple and contradictory zones and temporalities in it and in his voice. The seamless ease of the performance is fragmented cinematically to create tender and terrifying zones and rhythms, and Jimmy Little is refigured under the sign of cultural ambivalence.

Who is this Jimmy Little? He is a modern Aboriginal shaman/showman who sings Elvis, Harry Belafonte and country and western, that quintessential Aboriginal music, who mediates several cultural forces via his body/voice. With style and panache he embodies cultural assimilation. Here the notion of assimilation may suggest the mimicry involved in camouflage, the point of which is for others not to be able to tell if you are there or not. Now you are there, now you are not, it all depends on how you look. Ambivalent, unsettling perception becomes necessary: the performer is working in a tradition which is not his but which he sings as his own.

The mother: The daughter

There is now 'a history of feminist exploration of the mother/daughter dyad in cinema. Within that history, *Night Cries* will stand out for its completely unsentimental and yet emotionally charged exploration of this primal theme, in both its tender and murderous dimensions. *Night Cries* is a visceral film both aurally and visually. It leaves a series of sharp impressions on the viewer: the daughter biting into an apple with all the ferocity of her contained energy as she dreams of an elsewhere to escape to, the sullen, acerbic desperation of her gaze and the sensuality of her full body. Marcia Langton's daughter has a physicality and an emotional richness such as one usually associates with an Anna Magnani or Smita Patil, and rare in my experience of Australian cinema. These qualities are not 'primitive emanations' from her body (though there is a voluptuous pleasure to be had in the fragmentation of the daughter's body). They are also in part a result of the intensity of her desires, which are in fact quite modern. In opposition to the daughter's corporeal weight and voluptuousness, the maternal body is withered, just skin and bone.

The mother (Agnes Hardwick) *and daughter* (Marcia Langton) *in the homestead,* Night Cries, *1989.*

The daughter (Marcia Langton) *shuts the door on her mother,* Night Cries, *1989.*

Moffatt heightens this opposition to a point of excruciating pain by giving us close-ups of the mother's face, so that her sightless gaze seems to pierce us; the profile with the toothless mouth is held for what feels like an eternity. These images of a body's vicissitudes and traumas make me want to cry out, 'No more, no more,' and yet I watch in horror. This visual insistence is shocking in our culture (Australian) where death, old age and bodily decrepitude hardly figure so forcefully in the cinema.

Something, however, changes this opposition when the daughter washes the mother's feet soon after the whipping scene. One can't quite forget the sound of the whip when looking at the twisted and gnarled feet in extreme close-up. But the soft sound of the water pouring over the feet and the gentle gesture of the daughter washing them creates a new mood, which is again shifted in the next scene when they both sing 'Onward Christian Soldiers'. This continual shifting of emotional tone and register in such a short film has a lot to do with the suggestive power of a minimalist use of sound and colour. A paring down in order to intensify works strongly for the tableau compositions as well.

A black void[5]

Night Cries' rural tragedy begins with an emblematic sound of modernity, that of a train, almost imperceptibly becoming a cry. This doubling and forking of the sound lacerates a black void which the title then emphatically stamps and causes to vanish. A black space mediates between this shot with the title and the first appearance of Jimmy Little, seeming to function as a momentary pause. We hear his song over this blackness before we see him. Because the formal presence of the black space marks the entire film, it may be thought of as a fluid matrix. Jimmy Little emerges from it, often positioned on the left side of this generously empty black space. The two tableaux of the mother and daughter consoling each other are also placed in this black void, though positioned differently. They seem to be set within it (a function of screen position and lighting), while Jimmy Little seems to be more on the surface. The daughter lamenting the mother's death recedes into the black space's vast expanse after being held by a tiny iris-in shot. Finally, the credits roll up the side of it, leaving a moment of empty space where Little was a moment before.

This black void is not just black leader, not just a bit of empty time. It has the weight of duration and a fluidity of movement because of the way sounds are played across its immeasurable form. Its contours change invisibly through the sounds that cut across it or play on it or in it (these transformations depend on the sounds and how we hear them). So the black void is not a nothing and is not an empty space. It is the flexibility with which it is used that makes it formally possible for Moffatt to bring a 'residual'[6] figure like Jimmy Little from the forgotten past of 1950s pop culture into a filmic economy of modernist rigour.

If the act of 'reviving' Jimmy Little may seem anachronistic in such a context, the sense of 'time lag' or 'historical belatedness'[7] that marks the figure does not, however, function as a sign of retardation. This is because he is reinscribed or performed by the filmic operations. The framing fragments his body just as the montage between the voice and body puts them out of sync. His opening address to us is oblique: he is singing to someone else-where, not to us, the audience of the film. He is made to negotiate the other scene of this film before he can address us 'directly'. But even when he does so finally, his hit song is post-dubbed—he only lip-syncs it. So Jimmy Little 'mimics' his own song in a hybridizing gesture which assimilates its own history and performs its dual temporality (1964 and 1989) which is now shot through and through with the 'unspeakable' historical tragedy he has witnessed and helped to signify.

A film that can cut from the sweetness of a music-box sound to a whiplash and laughter, then to Jimmy Little singing 'Love Me

The daughter (Marcia Langton) *at night waits for her mother,* Night Cries, *1989.*

Tender', and not use one to parody the other signals the presence of a certain unusual daring in Australian cinema. From her first work as a still photographer, through her numerous video works and *Nice Coloured Girls*, to *Night Cries,* Moffatt emerges even more clearly as a fascinating, sophisticated talent in Australian cinema today. As a Sri Lankan working here[8] I can only hope that the monocultural blandness of much of Australian cinema will be transformed by the force of hybrid forms.[9]

Night Cries—A Rural Tragedy

Daughter	Marcia Langton
Old mother	Agnes Hardwick
Singer	Jimmy Little
Director/writer	Tracey Moffatt
Producer	Penny McDonald
Cinematographer	John Whitteron
Editor	Phillippa Harvey
Art director	Stephen Curtis
Original sounds	Debra Petrovich

Produced with the assistance of the Creative Development Branch of the Australian Film Commission and the Department of Aboriginal Affairs.

Notes

1 Song by Elvis Presley, sung silently by Jimmy Little in *Night Cries*. I wish to thank Madeline Preston for pointing out to me that this is indeed what he is singing.
2 Shahani 1990. The context of this statement is a discussion of the necessity for innovation within a classical Indian tradition of music perceived to be hermetic, 'seemingly self-contained in its completeness, it even gives the impression that there is no need for a renovating of the tradition'.
3 I wish to add a personal anecdote here for its methodological implications. About three years into my stay in the US, a friend who had bought a tape recorder asked me to speak into it to test it. When the sound was replayed, I failed to recognise my voice. About 10 years later, after coming to Australia, I was able to use that sense of displacement and loss as a method for organizing the sound track of a film I made there called *A Song of Ceylon* (1985).
4 Though some of the early publicity around *Night Cries* drew a connection between it and Chauvel's 1950s film *Jedda*, I won't take my cue from it. My feeling is that to address the problematic of *Jedda* as *Night Cries'* intertext is perhaps a 'white man's burden' and as such has been discharged as far as seems rewarding by Ingrid Perez's piece on *Night Cries* for *Film News*, August 1990. I bring this up here

because my failure to discuss this putative relationship aroused considerable discontent when I presented this essay recently in Fremantle (June 1991) at a cultural studies conference. I for my part, felt discontented with Perez's article because it did not mention, let alone discuss, the function of Jimmy Little in *Night Cries*. This essay is in a way a response to that omission

5 An earlier version of this essay was published in *Framework*, July 1992, without this section. 'A black void' is in fact a response to the discussion on the film held at a Power Institute public education forum with Homi Bhabha and myself. I wish to thank Homi Bhabha, Geoff Batchen, Bette Mifsud and Eloise Lindsay in particular for their contributions to the discussion which has helped me rethink aspects of the film.

6 'Residual'—Homi Bhabha has used this term from Raymond Williams in his paper.

7 This concept is Homi Bhabha's; I use it here because it seems appropriate to the work on time in the film.

8 I wish to thank Meaghan Morris for suggesting that I do a Sri Lankan reading of this film, for in so doing I have come to realise how hybrid that identity has become precisely because of working here in Australia.

9 Bette Mifsud asked me what I meant by an 'aesthetic of assimilation' at the Power Institute forum. I 'coined' the term heuristically. I could not use 'appropriation' as it has been theorized in current postmodern debates because of the specific history being dealt with in this film. 'Assimilation' felt right because it denotes a violent history but also has enabling connotations. It suggests ways of turning horrific situations and making them do something other than terrify. This ambivalence, I thought, was appropriate to what the film was doing. I don't think it would be productive to describe 'assimilation' as a set of aesthetic devices in the way the political modernism of the 1970s did. This would severely delimit what can happen in processes of hybridization and one would want to be surprised at the very least by such processes. Also, the ideas of hybridization/assimilation work very differently from the earlier notions of 'cultural decolonization', 'where forms of indigenous practices and institutions that prevailed before conquest are restored as the dominant cultural practice' (Vivien Johnson, cited by Julie Ewington 1991). An aesthetic of assimilation acknowledges the modern and tries with a sort of cunning to continually redefine its terms so as to prevent the erasure of memory and of our capacity to remember. An image from *Night Cries* that I have not spoken of now haunts me—the photograph of the white mother as a young woman, her expression of unusual pathos, affect. Is it sorrow? What is it? The little photo of the black daughter as a child is blurred in the background and the young white mother is foregrounded for us as well as in the mature daughter's memory. This is a generous figuring of the (white) mother who wasn't really her mother. What of her hopes and wishes and sorrows? That look suggests a whole history.

References

Batchen, Geoff (1990) 'Complicities', in *ARTFUL*, College of Fine Arts Student Association, University of New South Wales, October (unpaginated).

Burn, Ian & Stephen, Ann (1986) 'Traditional Painter: The Transfiguration of Albert Namatjira', *Age Monthly Review*, 6. 7, November, pp. 11–14.

Ewington, Julie (1991) 'An Essay: The Future of Aboriginal Art', catalogue essay for the exhibition *The Concept of Country* at Ivan Dougherty Gallery, 1–29 June.

Gibson, Ross (1983) 'Camera Natura: Landscape in Australian Feature Films', *Framework*, 22/23, Autumn, pp. 47–51.

Martin, Adrian (1989) 'Indefinite Objects: Independent Film and Video', in *Australian Screen*, eds. Albert Moran & Tom O'Regan, Penguin, Ringwood, pp. 172–190.

Ruiz, Raul (1981) 'Between Institutions: Interview with Raul Ruiz', Ian Christie & Malcolm Coad, *Afterimage* No. 10, Autumn, p. 113.

Shahani, Kumar (1990) 'Interrogating Internationalism', *Journal of Arts and Ideas*, no. 19, May, p. 12.

Trinh, T. Minh-ha (1990) 'Why a Fish Pond? Fiction at the Heart of Documentation', interview with L. Jayamanne and Anne Rutherford, *Film News*, 20.10 November, pp. 10–13.

6 Changing contexts: Globalization, migration and feminism in New Zealand

Wendy Larner

The lives of New Zealand women are becoming more diverse. There is an increasing polarization between a growing number of professional and managerial women with secure jobs, and women who are underpaid and overexploited in the workforce. Currently two women, one of whom has assets worth more than $1 million, are presiding over the demise of the welfare state.[1] Yet at the same time other women have found themselves excluded from any opportunity to participate in paid work, and levels of female poverty are on the increase.

Ethnic differences are more apparent. The relationships between indigenous groups (Maori) and colonizing settlers (Pakeha)[2] have been placed firmly on the political agenda. At the same time that strategies of biculturalism (power sharing) and Te Tino Rangatiratanga (Maori self-determination) generate considerable discussion, other forms of ethnic difference are receiving attention. The growing politicization of more recent settlers is reflected in the involvement of women of Pacific Islander descent in local government and community organizations. In the past five years the small but long-established New Zealand Asian communities have experienced rapid growth as a result of changing migration patterns. This growth has been accompanied by considerable discussion about the relationships between migration and economic development.

Inevitably, these economic and ethnic differences articulate with issues of sexuality, family, community and place in a myriad of ways. As a Pakeha feminist working on issues of globalization, migration and changes in women's work, it has become evident to me that any notion of a unified female experience in New Zealand must be treated extremely cautiously in the early 1990s.

While recognition of the complexity and variety of women's lives is beginning to influence feminist scholarship (cf. Novitz 1989), by and large, New Zealand feminists of all political persuasions have been loath to recognize the importance of these differences for theorization. Although in the wake of schisms within the women's movement assertions of 'sisterhood' ring hollow, notions of women's common experience are still used as the basis for theorizing. Attempts to introduce 'difference' into analyses usually involve distinguishing between Maori and Pakeha women (and then treating both as homogeneous blocs), or the rhetorical use of concepts such as 'triple oppression' or 'white capitalist patriarchy', in which the categories are abstracted and monolithic.

Elsewhere feminist theorists have begun to question the utility of such concepts. Influenced by developments in poststructuralist theory, writers have begun to rethink the unitary category of 'women'. Confronting the diverse experiences contained within this category has led a number of theorists to reject the idea that 'women' form a relatively stable or unified female subject defined by consciousness of gender oppression, in favour of thinking about women as 'subjects who are multiply organised across positionalities, across several axes and across mutually contradictory discourses and practices' (de Lauretis 1988:136).

This is not, unmediated relativism. Some differences are more significant than others, particularly those that find their root in the 'terrible historical experiences of patriarchy, colonialism, racism and capitalism' (Haraway 1990:197). In this literature, however, gender, colonial status, ethnicity, race and class are no longer seen as 'natural' identities. Rather, they are identities that are being constantly renegotiated and transformed in relation to shifting contexts made up of economic and social conditions, cultural and political institutions and ideologies (Alcoff 1988:433). Further, these multiple identities are seen as intersecting, mutually determining and sometimes contradictory. As Teresa de Lauretis (1986:14) says, 'Difference is not only sexual, or only racial, economic or cultural, but all these together and often at odds with one another.'

The politics that arises from such a position is that of affinity (Haraway 1990). Because the subject of feminism is considered to be multiply organized, unstable and historically discontinuous, it is accepted that there can be no single feminist standpoint, or even standpoints. Thus, rather than seeking to find a common identity that can form a basis for action, the task is to find connections that will enable a woman to join with others without pretending to be those others. The result? A joining of 'partial views and halting voices' into the collective subject position of 'women' (Haraway 1988:586–590).

In New Zealand, it has become crucial that the implications of adopting such an approach be explored. For as Donna Haraway (1990:203) has argued, these changes in feminist politics are rooted in 'fundamental changes in the nature of race, class and gender in an emerging world order analogous in its novelty and scope to that created by industrial capitalism'. This theme has recently been considered in a controversial article by a group of New Zealand feminists. They argue that the emergence of a 'more complex and chaotic set of feminist conceptions' was an inevitable response to, and product of, 'the developments in Western capitalism often referred to as "New Times", a British left term for the major contemporary historical shifts in social, political and cultural life' (Guy *et al.* 1990:8). While rejecting their uncritical acceptance of the relevance of the 'New Times' label to the New Zealand context, I generally agree that something significant has happened to the way that capitalism works and that this has profound implications for feminist politics.

This is not to lapse into some form of crude economic determinism, but rather to reflect on Elizabeth Wilson's recent comment that 'we may have been premature to refuse a connection between economic developments and changing ideologies' (Wilson 1990:198). Wilson suggests that while experiences of rapid economic change and upheaval may be disconcerting and seem to fragment lives, an underlying rationality from the point of view of capital can be seen. What is occurring is the globalization of the world economy; a 'totalizing capitalism' for which a 'totalizing account' remains useful (Wilson 1990:197–199).

The globalization of capitalism

Contemporary transformations in the nature of capitalism have generated a huge body of literature. Researchers working in the area have shown that as capital has become increasingly footloose, multinational companies have begun to rove the world seeking out the most advantageous place to locate their activities. The result is that individuals, companies and governments are being linked into production, trading and financial networks outside of the particular country in which they are located (Callister 1990).

Capital, goods, services, information and workers are now circulated in a transnational space.

Associated with the globalization of capitalism have been major changes in the directions and volumes of international labour migrations. Literature on the political economy of labour migration shows that the demand for labour that arises in the capitalist production process is a major precondition of migration both within and into capitalist societies (Cohen 1987, Miles 1990, Sassen 1988). During different phases of capitalist development, capital has found labour reserves in different places and through different mechanisms. The migrations that have been generated as a result of the globalization of capitalism include those population movements associated with accelerating industrialization in developing countries, increased flows of highly skilled migrants, new migrations of unskilled workers to developed countries, and burgeoning numbers of refugees (Sassen 1988, Miles and Satzewich 1990).

I will argue that the extreme mobility of capital and labour that characterizes the global economy will result in the emergence of new collectivities and the weakening of familiar groups in New Zealand. There will be increasing complexity within and between categories of race, ethnicity, colonial status, gender and class in the 1990s. Consequently it will become crucial to begin to explore the partial and contingent connections that can be developed between differently positioned women.

Postwar labour migrations

In order to develop these themes, it is useful to provide a background for discussion by demonstrating how, in New Zealand, changes in migration flows have been integrally connected to the changing nature of capitalism, and how the combined effects of these have already provided the context for complex articulations of sexual and racial oppressions and particular forms of feminist politics. There are a range of opinions about the starting point for such an analysis (Cohen 1987, Sassen 1988). This discussion will not deal with colonizing migrations, rather its focus will be on those migrations that occurred once the world economic system was consolidated: on particular patterns of labour migration since the end of the Second World War. During this period there were massive labour migrations from peripheral regions into core regions. While these migrations share a number of general traits with earlier migration phases, they were also predicated upon specific conditions that rose from the nature of capitalist development. More specifically, these migrations were integrally connected with the need for unskilled and semi-skilled labour associated with the wave of capitalist expansion in the postwar years.

These developments affected New Zealand in a specific way because of the country's position in the structure of world production and trade. Before 1945, the development of capitalism in New Zealand had been based on pastoralism. It was not until the Second World War, when the disruption in world trade necessitated an increase in domestic industrial production, that sustained industrial development was able to take place (Jesson 1987). The dramatic growth in manufacturing, in particular vehicle assembly, the processing of primary products (e.g. frozen and canned food production, newsprint and carpet manufacture) and the production of certain consumer durables, generated a substantial increase in the demand for labour. This demand was not just the result of quantitative expansion, but also of the move towards mass production techniques. New jobs created were often dirty, monotonous, unhealthy and unpleasant. The need for labour was satisfied predominantly through migration, although at the same time increasing numbers of urban Pakeha women also entered the labour force as levels of part-time work increased and opportunities for employment in the service sector expanded.

Labour migration took a variety of forms. First, there were internal migrations. For Pakeha, economic expansion merely accentuated a rural drift to the cities that had started well before the Second World War, but for Maori the change was abrupt (Pearson 1990). In 1945, three-quarters of the Maori population were living in rural areas. This figure was still two-thirds in 1956, yet by 1966 62 per cent of Maori people were urban (Pool 1991:153). Second, there was international migration from various Pacific islands that had been in colonial relationships with New Zealand earlier in the twentieth century. These were classic chain migrations in that intending migrants, who were both men and women, usually obtained their first jobs in New Zealand through friends or family who had already migrated. The result was that Pacific Islander populations in New Zealand were concentrated in urban centres, in particular Auckland but also Wellington and Christchurch. Finally, migration from western Europe was also encouraged in order to expand the skilled workforce. The majority of these migrants were from the traditional British source, although labour shortages were such that other migrations were also encouraged. With the exception of a small number of Dutch migrants from the Netherlands and Indonesia, however, the numbers of non-British European migrants were relatively small. One study suggests that 85 per cent of all migrants who arrived in New Zealand between 1947 and 1958 were of British origin (Pearson 1990:114).

While the expansion of capitalism provided the catalyst for these labour migrations, outcomes depended on the ways in which economic relations articulate with other sets of social relations, including those of gender and race. Not only did new workers enter a labour market in which there was a clear distinction between men's work and women's work, but they performed specific tasks within these categories. Both Maori and Pacific Islander women were incorporated into a narrow range of manufacturing positions that were characterized by lower wages, poorer conditions, less security and fewer opportunities for advancement than those occupied by many Pakeha women (Ongley 1991). European migrants, on the other hand, tended to take up skilled positions and were more occupationally dispersed.

Changing patterns of reproduction, sexuality, culture, consumption and production were generated as a result of the interactions of once geographically and socially distinct groups of people. With the emergence of the second wave of feminism in the early 1970s it was inevitable that understandings of what it was to be 'women' in New Zealand would be contested. Pakeha feminists were forced by Maori and Pacific Islander feminists to recognize that too often their analyses were both class and race specific, and that the experience of being female in New Zealand was more diverse than many participants in the women's movement had initially understood. Increasingly ethnicity, racism and colonization were seen as critical issues for feminism.

The debates around these issues have taken specific forms in the New Zealand context as a result of a bipolar frame of reference arising from the distinctive history of settler colonialism and the relative homogeneity of subsequent migration flows. Overwhelmingly, the focus has been on the relationship between indigenous people and descendants of British migrants. With remarkably few exceptions, people who are neither Maori or Pakeha have either been ignored or had their experiences submerged within the Maori–Pakeha bifurcation (Jagose 1988, Max 1991).[3]

The relationship between Maori and Pakeha has a legal foundation in the Treaty of Waitangi, signed in 1840 by representatives of Maori and the British Crown. Contemporary interpretations of the Treaty involve a model of two peoples within one nation, each with rights and obligations to each other. Biculturalism, based on the understanding that resources should be equally distributed between Maori and Pakeha, dominates discussions of social justice in New Zealand (Sharp 1990). Te Tino Rangatiratanga, Maori sovereignty or self-determination, is a more controversial strategy involving tribal authority over human, natural and economic resources (Awatere 1984, Kelsey 1991). Land, and an attachment to place, are pivots around which debates revolve. Maori assert that by right of prior occupation they have a unique place in New Zealand. Cultural identity as *tangata whenua* (people of the land) is established through a spiritual connection with the natural environment. Despite the controversy and confusion that surrounds the notion of Pakeha, as distinct from European or some general 'whiteness', a bond with the land is also crucial to an emergent postcolonial Pakeha identity (cf. Dann 1991, King 1991).

Relationships between Maori and Pakeha women have been central to feminist politics during the 1980s. Throughout this period, Maori and Pakeha have usually been constructed as separate social categories, often in conflict with each other (Sharp 1990). Similarly, men and women were seen as separate groupings, women as sisters in oppression, men as the enemy (Guy *et al.* 1990). Feminist responses to the recognition of differing experiences among women have usually involved a split and regrouping according to a redefined 'natural' unity. The experience of living in a Pakeha-dominated political and economic system led Maori and Pacific Islander women to organize the first National Black Women's Hui held in 1980. By 1983 Maori and Pacific Islander women were holding separate meetings as differences resulting from Maori women's status as *tangata whenua* and Pacific women's experiences as migrants were recognized. In turn, Pakeha women began to explore their own ethnicity, a move that involved the questioning of the appropriateness of Anglo-American debates in the New Zealand context. Implicit in all these developments was the assumption that there are discrete, coherent and separate identities based on absolute divisions between various sexual, racial and ethnic identities (Martin & Mohanty 1986).

Into the 1990s

Among commentators on the global capitalist economy there is widespread consensus that the 1980s saw events that signal major discontinuities with previous developments. Many writers have begun to speculate that capitalism is moving into a new phase, resulting in increasingly complex social and spatial relationships. Existing notions of community in New Zealand are likely to be problematized by the new capital and migration flows which emerge. In the 1990s more diverse groups of people will come into daily contact with each other and as a result new tensions will be generated. Global changes will articulate with local struggles to generate complex, and as yet unknown, outcomes.

There are two divergent hypotheses about contemporary changes (Gordon 1988). The literature on the 'new international division of labour' focuses on the movement of capital from the developed countries of the core to the newly industrializing countries (NICs) of the periphery. In this literature the availability of a large low-cost, politically malleable, feminized labour force, accompanied by political stability and a well-developed infrastructure, is seen as encouraging capital to move 'offshore' from developed countries into the NICs, including South Korea, Taiwan, and more recently Malaysia and the Philippines. The most distinctive feature of the 'new international division of labour' is that manufacturing has been relocated in countries of the periphery and core countries have moved towards specialized service industries.

The literature on the 'globalisation of production' does not emphasize the core-periphery divide as dramatically as that on the new international division of labour. Instead it argues that, as a result of the mobility of capital, production is decentralizing throughout both developed and developing countries, and that this is being accompanied by the increasing centralization of control and coordination by multinational corporations, often with their headquarters in the burgeoning 'global cities' of the world. The result has been international interdependence and enhanced multinational leverage over governments (Gordon 1988:27).

Despite differences in emphasis, the logic in both sets of literature is much the same. Advances in telecommunications, transportation technologies and materials, together with flexible manufacturing processes, have enabled capital and resources to be more easily moved around the world. Consequently, the markets for capital, goods, services and labour are no longer nationally based. This has encouraged the growth of multinational companies and undermined the power of both governments and workers. Higher-level functions requiring skilled labour are now concentrated in certain privileged locations, while unskilled assembly functions are scattered over more varied locations (Knox & Agnew 1989). The polarization of skill structures, and changing global and regional divisions of labour, have articulated with existing social and spatial divisions of labour to create highly differentiated global labour forces.

Over the past ten years New Zealand has been increasingly linked into the global economy. As the result of a series of government-initiated reforms, involving deregulation of the financial sector and reduced levels of protection and industry assistance, the New Zealand economy has moved from being one of the most highly regulated economies in the world to one of the least regulated. Economic liberalization and emphasis on a market-driven economy have forced New Zealand primary producers and manufacturers to compete internationally. The state sector has also been reorganized: many government departments have been corporatized and are now required to run on a commercial basis. A program of asset sales, introduced in an attempt to reduce New Zealand's overseas debt, has seen a number of these corporations fully privatized. In both private and public sectors, New Zealand enterprises have been forced to become more responsive to the vagaries of the global market.

Globalization of the New Zealand economy has led to dramatic changes in patterns of capital flows in and out of the country. Britton (1991:7-15) identifies four elements in these new, highly dynamic flows. First, New Zealand–based capital has expanded offshore. Large domestic companies, for example Fletcher Challenge and the NZ Dairy Board, have expanded overseas in attempts to become multinational corporations. At the same time many subsidiary branches of international companies involved in New Zealand have also moved offshore in order to take advantage of new opportunities, such as the export processing zones of South-East Asia and Fiji. This has been most common among those import-substitution industries that were once highly protected. Small investors have also contributed to outward capital flows. Individuals and trusts are transferring funds out of New Zealand, particularly to Australia, often in response to adverse economic and social conditions.

Second, capital flows into New Zealand have increased. Deregulation has enabled new competitors to enter once-protected markets, particularly in the business services and finance industries. International speculative investment has increased and shareholdings of major New Zealand companies are increasingly controlled by foreign interests; in 1989 the Stock Exchange reported that approximately 30 per cent of company stock was purchased from overseas owners (Britton 1991:10). Privatisation of many former government functions, including telecommunications, banking and transport, has encouraged increases in foreign ownership. The New Zealand telecommunications industry, for example, was sold to American interests after privatization.

The third significant change in capital flows has resulted from reductions in border protection. Plant closures and redundancies have affected companies unable to compete with increased levels of imported products. Those companies which have survived have

had to make major changes to their operations, including techno-
logical innovation and organizational changes. Trade liberalization
has also been integral to the final set of changes; those resulting
from Closer Economic Relations. CER is a free-trade agreement
between New Zealand and Australia designed to strengthen economic relations between the two countries. Second only to the
European Community agreement in the range of measures covered,
CER has resulted in substantial capital movement and production
reorganization between New Zealand and Australia. The 1992
review of the agreement is likely to result in further economic
harmonization, allowing levels of trans-Tasman trade and investment to continue to increase (Lloyd 1991).

In sum, New Zealand in the early 1990s has been transformed
into a small open economy dominated by large-scale investors.
The variables determining conditions of domestic production no
longer reflect the actions of the state, but rather those of the
money market, large corporations and international speculators.
Globalization means that the economic and social character of
New Zealand is increasingly shaped by overseas agents and international capital with no particular commitment to the country.
Castells and Henderson (1987:7) have described this phenomenon
as the 'space of flows', in which the dynamics of territorial
development are increasingly placeless from the point of view of
dominant organizations and social actors.

One of the most significant consequences of increasing links
into the global economy has been the reconstitution of the New
Zealand labour market. There has been a shift in the composition
of employment opportunities away from the primary sector and
manufacturing towards services. Between 1978 and 1988 employment in the primary sector declined by 11.5 per cent and in
manufacturing by 9 per cent, while in the same period employment
in the service sector increased by 13 per cent (Haines 1989:96).
Further, there has been an overall substantial reduction in employment opportunities. Unemployment figures are now at their
highest levels in 50 years, and are expected to increase well into
the mid-1990s. These high levels of unemployment have had
different effects on the various ethnic groups. Recent figures
suggest that the rate of unemployment for Pacific Islanders is more
than 30 per cent, three times that for Pakeha (*New Zealand*
Herald 1/2/92).

Associated with the reconstitution of employment opportunities is an increased fragmentation of the labour market. The
current trend is to reduce the number of full-time workers and
rely increasingly on a 'flexible' workforce that can be drawn on
when needed and laid off when times get bad. Thus while numbers

of full-time workers declined after 1985, levels of part time employment have continued to grow. There has also been an increase in the number of self-employed people, many of whom are likely to be women engaged in outwork (Armstrong 1991). Both increased levels of part-time work and self-employment are explicitly identified as allowing employers increasing flexibility, and as having displaced full-time positions (Haines 1989:98). Important shifts in industrial organization have accompanied these labour market changes. The number of small businesses is increasing rapidly (Haines 1991). Many of these are linked into subcontracting arrangements with larger organizations. The rapid growth of the 'black' or 'informal' sector seems likely to continue and will give rise to complex linkages extending well beyond the traditional sphere of 'production', including linkages into the home.

Commentators have begun to speculate about the 'feminization' of the labour force, not only because women's job losses have been fewer than men's,[4] but also because it seems likely that more workers, both men and women, will be employed in peripheral, part-time and insecure positions. The trend towards fragmentation has been exacerbated by radical reform of labour relations legislation. The Employment Contracts Act (1991), which shifts employment relations away from collective agreements towards individual contracts, is designed to 'free up' the labour market. It has allowed employers to push for more flexible work regimes and individual labour contracts.

Labour migrations have also been affected by changes associated with globalization. The general assumption is that with the end of the expansionary boom in the 1970s, the era of large-scale labour migration from the periphery to the centre gradually came to an end. Certainly in New Zealand, stricter control over immigration and settlement from the Pacific had, by the early 1990s, reversed a long-established trend. Migration to New Zealand from all Pacific Island countries except Fiji declined dramatically.[5] The process of migration, however, is not a simple economic process where demand and supply fortuitously coincide (Munck 1988); rather, it is a contradictory process which engenders complex outcomes. By the 1990s international migrant workers of the 1960s and 1970s had become settler populations. A second generation, and often now a third generation, of young Pacific Islanders born in New Zealand, and often with only a secondhand knowledge of the country of their parents and grandparents, form an increasingly significant proportion of the Pacific Islander community in New Zealand. While Pacific Islander and Maori workers have borne the brunt of the displacement and unemployment resulting from the changing structure of employment, to argue that Pacific Islander workers should return 'home' once their labour is no longer required is to fundamentally misunderstand the nature of migration. Where is home for a young woman born in New Zealand, with a Samoan mother and a Rarotongan father, off to search for work in Australia because there are no jobs for her here?

Further, the current reorganization of the global economy has stimulated new migrations which will result in more complex patterns of ethnic segregation. Overall levels of international migration into New Zealand increased dramatically in the 1980s. Bedford (1990) has shown how the composition of migration flows changed during these years. Particularly significant has been the removal of the traditional source bias towards Europe and relatively large increases in migrations from Asia. In the early 1980s migration from Europe comprized nearly one-third of total net migration; in the second half of the decade there was a substantial net loss of European citizens. Migration from Asian countries, on the other hand increased from 21 per cent to 67 per cent of total net migration. There are a number of aspects to these new migrations.

Globalization has resulted in the increasing movement not only of capital but of the agents of capital. This label refers to both those who own and control capital directly and those who manage in various ways the use of capital (Miles 1990). Since 1986 significant attempts have been made to market New Zealand as a destination for wealthy Asian entrepreneurs and their investment capital. Although there are some doubts about the future success of this scheme, increased levels of 'business migration', from Taiwan and Hong Kong in particular, have resulted. Further, a new migration policy, based on a points scheme, targets people with those technical and professional skills that are increasingly in demand as the New Zealand economy is restructured. The migration of skilled non-manual workers will be an important aspect of labour migrations to New Zealand in the 1990s. While the source countries for these latter migrations are as yet unknown, they are likely to be more disparate than those traditionally associated with New Zealand.

Closer examination of recent migration figures raises further issues. Both business and professional migrants can be accompanied by 'dependents' who do not have their skills assessed. Migration research from a diverse range of countries confirms that a very high proportion of women who migrate as 'dependents' enter the labour market. The question of where and how remains to be explored in the New Zealand context, although the increasing importance of small businesses and self-employment may be significant, given declining opportunities in the core labour force. Already there are marked differences in the involvement of New Zealand-born and migrant populations in self-employment; Asian and continental European groups in particular have long been overrepresented in this labour force category (Haines 1991:23). Further, it seems highly likely that a number of different experiences are being conflated in analyses of new Asian migrations. While images from the media are of wealthy Taiwanese businessmen, at least two of the new migrations (from the Philippines and Singapore) are female-dominated. The causes of feminized migration streams from these countries to New Zealand have yet to be explored.

The point is that population movements into New Zealand in the 1990s are both volatile and complex. There is little understanding of how new labour migrations will articulate with changing economic structures. Even if the proposed net annual gains of 20 000 migrants are not reached, it seems inevitable that the articulation of gender, economic and ethnic differences in New Zealand will become more pronounced. Different groups will be incorporated into the New Zealand labour market in complex and contradictory ways as the implications of fundamental structural changes in the New Zealand economy emerge.

Conclusion

The forms of feminist politics that develop in New Zealand in the 1990s will be the outcome of the interplay between global forces on one hand and historically produced forms of community on the other. On one hand, the globalization of production and associated changes in migration patterns have created a context in which the economic and social characteristics of New Zealand will be increasingly influenced by large-scale internationalized capital and overseas interests. Many of these actors are linked into networks that do not depend on the characteristics of any particular place for the fulfilment of their requirements. On the other hand, an attachment to place is central to contemporary feminist politics in New Zealand. The challenge for the 1990s will be to articulate familiar struggles based on local interests into the 'space of flows'.

For many New Zealand feminists, both Maori and Pakeha, the most obvious response may be to retreat further into forms of identity politics based on territorial integrity. One observer has suggested, for example, that the struggle for New Zealand's national and economic sovereignty could provide a source of common interest between Maori and Pakeha (Kelsey 1991:47). Recent responses to global/local tensions suggest, however, that the outcomes of such political practice may be unpredictable. A self-appointed 'Maori immigration office', concerned about the lack of consultation over changes to New Zealand's migration laws, has been advocating 'cultural and environmental sensitivity tests' for prospective migrants, which involve swearing an oath of allegiance to the Treaty of Waitangi. The first Pakeha to sign for the 'citizenship papers' issued by the office was a prospective National Party politician, who used the opportunity to argue that New Zealand should have a closed-door immigration policy (*Sunday Star* 15/12/91).

When arguments about territorial integrity and cultural homogeneity are made by a conservative male Pakeha politician, it is clear that they are being used to foreclose discussions about a more democratic future in New Zealand. But when these same arguments emerge from radical Maori groups, feminists and others on the 'left', the implications are more elusive. On one hand, attempts to defend a coherent Maori identity and further develop a sense of Pakeha identity based on commitment to place can be seen as precisely the form in which democratic aspirations have been articulated both within feminism and in New Zealand as a whole. The recognition of 'difference' and the emergence of distinctive forms of identity politics have been crucial developments in this respect. On the other hand, the fact that such strategies can be interpellated into positions on the right suggests that identity politics cannot be guaranteed always to have progressive results (see also Mercer 1992).

Contemporary developments seem likely to further problematize forms of feminist politics based on assumptions about absolute divisions between 'natural' identities that are dealt with one at a time. The globalization of capitalism and associated changes in migration patterns will result in the increasing complexity of relations within and between the categories of race, ethnicity, colonial status, class and gender. As a result it will become difficult to sustain fixed notions of identity and coalitions built out of 'summing and subsuming parts' (Haraway 1988). First, increasing heterogeneity will disrupt the Maori–Pakeha dichotomy assumed to structure the experiences of women in New Zealand. Relationships between Maori women and Pakeha women are likely to be complicated by the emergence of a 'deterritorialized diaspora' (Ram 1991) made up not only of unskilled workers but also increasingly of middle-class professional and highly skilled women from a wide range of ethnic and cultural backgrounds. More complex patterns of labour force segmentation and ethnicity mean that contradictions are more likely to arise both within and between various groups. As a result it seems inevitable that the increasing diversity of experiences within the category of 'women' in New Zealand will strengthen the demand for conceptualizations which examine difference in more complex ways than has been the case until now (cf. Guy *et al.* 1990).

Further, globalization will also mean that New Zealand feminists are more likely to come into contact with their counterparts elsewhere. Many of these women will have positionalities inflected by very different political understandings from those that currently predominate in New Zealand. As CER is strengthened, for example, and economic linkages between Australia and New Zealand become more pronounced, feminists in both places will need to develop a sustained dialogue. The contrasts between New Zealand feminisms based on biculturalism and Australian feminisms premised on multiculturalism are striking. The point is reinforced if New Zealand's place on the emergent Pacific Rim is considered. Effective attempts to develop oppositional coalitions that can act regionally will require the negotiation of enormous differences in language, as well as political, social and cultural 'traditions' (Morris 1992). Common identity and a single feminist standpoint, or even standpoints, cannot be used as a basis for action in this context.

Contemporary versions of feminist politics in New Zealand face profound challenges. Consequently, it is crucial that the implications of new theoretical frameworks and alternative forms of politics be explored. Feminist theorists who draw from poststructural debates to discuss the ways in which situated actors construct multiple and shifting identities in relation to specific historical conditions may provide the basis for such an alternative. If the construction of identities is seen as an ongoing process of struggle that has no 'natural' outcome, the conflicts and contradictions in relations within and between political actors can be integrated into the analysis rather ignored. The adoption of these theoretical understandings would facilitate the emergence of new forms of political practice both within feminism, and between feminism and other social movements. The politics of affinity is based on shared purpose rather than common identity. In a context where there is a proliferation of different identities within the category of 'women', the implications of such an approach must be explored.

In a recent radio interview, Meaghan Morris emphasized this point. She suggested that there is a new era involving a multi-centred world. She pointed out that available political discourses have tended to be based on binary themes: the discussions have been about capital/labour, men/women, black/white. Morris concluded by saying that 'because there are strands within feminist theory that have at least started to think about the complexity of the relationships between gender, race, class, ethnicity and the environment, it has acquired at least a set of skills that will enable us to think about these questions. If any kind of new political practice is going to come about in the next few years, it's going to be from that direction' (Morris 1991:16).

Notes

This paper was first presented in a School of Social Sciences Seminar Series at the University of Waikato convened by Anna Yeatman on the theme of *The Politics of Representation*. Anna's ongoing encouragement, support and advice have been invaluable. Don Kerr and Lorna Weir have also made helpful comments.

1 The ministers of Finance and Social Welfare are both women.
2 'Pakeha' is a highly contested term. It is used in this paper to describe New Zealanders of European descent whose cultural values have been primarily formed by the experience of being a member of the dominant ethnic group in New Zealand (Spoonley 1988).
3 According to the New Zealand Census of Population and Dwellings (1986), 12.5 per cent of New Zealanders were Maori and 3.9 per cent Pacific Island Polynesian. With the exception of small Chinese (0.6 per cent), Indian (0.2 per cent) and Other (0.4 per cent) categories the remaining population was classified as 'European'.
4 Figures published recently in the *New Zealand Herald* (14/2/92) put the level of unemployment for men at 11.6 per cent. While the figure for women is likely to obscure considerable levels of hidden unemployment, at 9.4 per cent it is considerably lower than the male rate.
5 In the year from April 1989 to March 1990 there was a net loss of Western Samoan citizens for the first time since 1962, and Tongan citizens for the first time since the mid 1970s (New Population Monitoring Group 1991). The relatively high levels of Indo-Fijian migration from Fiji to New Zealand are an ongoing consequence of the 1987 coups in that country.

References

Alcoff, Linda (1988), 'Cultural Feminism versus Poststructuralism: The Identity Crisis in Feminist Theory', *Signs* 13(3), 405–436.
Armstrong, Nicola (1991), 'Women Outworkers in New Zealand'. Paper presented at the Women and Work Conference, Massey University, 17 August 1991.
Awatere, Donna (1984), *Maori Sovereignty*, Broadsheet Publications, Auckland.
Bedford, Richard (1990), 'Ethnicity, Birthplace and Nationality Dimen-

sions of Cultural Diversity', *New Zealand Population Review* 16(2), 34–56.

Britton, Stephen (1991), 'Recent Trends in the Internationalisation of the New Zealand Economy', *Australian Geographical Studies* 29(1), 3–25.

Callister, Paul (1991), *Expanding Our Horizons: New Zealand in the Global Economy*, New Zealand Planning Council, Wellington.

Cohen, Robin (1987), *The New Helots: Migrants in the International Division of Labour*, Avebury, Aldershot.

Dann, Christine (1991), 'In Love with the Land', in Michael King (ed) *Pakeha: The Quest for Identity*.

de Lauretis, Teresa (1986), *Feminist Studies/Critical Studies*, Indiana University Press, Bloomington.

——(1988), 'Displacing Hegemonic Discourses: Reflections on Feminist Theory in the 1980s', *Inscriptions* 3/4,127–144.

Gordon, David (1988), 'The Global Economy: New Edifice or Crumbling Foundations', *New Left Review* 168, 24–65.

Guy, Camille, Jones, Alison & Simpkin, Gay (1990), 'From Piha to Post Feminism: Radical Feminism in New Zealand', *Sites* 20, 7–19.

Haines, Lesley (1989), *Work Today: Employment Trends to 1989*, New Zealand Planning Council, Wellington.

——(1991), *Small Business Is Big Business*, New Zealand Planning Council, Wellington.

Haraway, Donna (1988), 'Situated Knowledges: The Science Question in Feminism and the Privilege of Partial Perspectives', *Feminist Studies*, 14(3), 575–599.

——(1990), 'A Manifesto for Cyborgs: Science, Technology and Socialist Feminism in the 1980s', in Linda Nicholson (ed), *Feminism/Postmodernism*, Routledge, London.

Henderson, Jeffrey & Castells, Manuel (1987), *Global Restructuring and Territorial Development*, Sage, London.

Horsfield, Anne (1988), *Women in the Economy*, Ministry of Women's Affairs, Wellington.

Jagose, Annamarie (1988), 'The W(hole) Story: Lesbians of Colour in Aoteoroa', *Broadsheet*, September, 30–32.

Jesson, Bruce (1987), *Behind the Mirror Glass: The Growth of Wealth and Power in New Zealand in the Eighties*, Penguin, Auckland.

Kelsey, Jane (1991), 'Tino Rangatiratanga in the 1990s', *Race Gender Class*, 11/12, 42–47.

Knox, Paul & Agnew, John (1989), *The Geography of the World Economy*, Edward Arnold, London.

Lloyd, Peter J. (1991), *The Future of CER: A Single Market for Australia and New Zealand*, Victoria University Press, Wellington.

Martin, Biddy & Mohanty, Chandra Talpade (1986), 'Feminist Politics: What's Home Got To Do With It?', in Teresa de Lauretis, *Feminist Studies/Critical Studies*.

Max, Lesley (1991), 'Having It All: The Kibbutznik and the Powhiri', in Michael King (ed.) *Pakeha: The Quest for Identity*.

Mercer, Kobena (1992) '1968: Periodizing Postmodern Politics and

Identity', in Lawrence Grossberg, Cary Nelson & Paula Treichler (eds) *Cultural Studies*, Routledge, London.

Miles, Robert (1990), 'Whatever happened to the Sociology of Migration', *Work, Employment and Society* 4(2), 281–298.

Miles, Robert & Satzewich, Victor (1990), 'Migration, Racism and "Postmodern" Capitalism', *Economy and Society* 19(3), 334–358.

Morris, Meaghan (1991), 'Multipolar Feminism', *Australian Left Review*, August 1991, 14–15.

——(1992), 'On the Beach', in Lawrence Grossberg *et al.* (eds) *Cultural Studies*.

Munck, Ronaldo (1988), *The New International Labour Studies: An Introduction*, Zed Books, London.

NACEW (1990), *Beyond the Barriers: The State, The Economy and Women's Employment 1984–1990*, National Advisory Council on the Employment of Women, Wellington.

Novitz, Rosemary (1989), 'Women: Weaving an Identity', in David Novitz & Bill Willmott (eds), *Culture and Identity in New Zealand*, G.P. Books, Wellington.

Ongley, Patrick (1991), 'Pacific Islands Migration and the New Zealand Labour Market', in Paul Spoonley, David Pearson & Cluny Macpherson (eds) *Nga Take: Ethnic Relations and Racism in Aotearoa/New Zealand*, Dunmore Press, Palmerston North.

Pearson, David (1990), *A Dream Deferred: The Origins of Ethnic Conflict in New Zealand*, Allen & Unwin/Port Nicholson Press, Wellington.

Phizacklea, Annie & Miles, Robert (1980), *Labour and Racism*, Routledge, London.

Pool, Ian (1991), *Te Iwi Maori: A New Zealand Population, Past, Present and Projected*, Auckland University Press, Auckland.

Population Monitoring Group (1991), *On the Move: Migration and Population—Trends and Policies*, New Zealand Planning Council, Wellington.

Ram, Kalpana (1991), ' "First" and "Third" World Feminisms: A New Perspective?', *Asian Studies Review* 15(1), 91–95.

Sassen, Saskia (1988), *The Mobility of Labour and Capital: A Study in International Investment and Labour Flow*, Cambridge University Press, Cambridge.

Sharp, Andrew (1990), *Justice and the Maori*, Oxford University Press, Auckland.

Spoonley, Paul (1988), *Racism and Ethnicity*, Oxford University Press, Auckland.

——(1991), 'Debates and Issues', in Paul Spoonley *et al.* (eds) *Nga Take*.

Wilson, Elizabeth (1988), *Hallucinations: Life in the Post-modern City*, Radius, London.

7

Colonizing women: The maternal body and empire
Margaret Jolly

This paper struggles to make a fertile conjunction between two approaches to colonizing women. The first is the recent feminist literature which deals with white women in colonial history, from the viewpoint of a realist, even empiricist, history, sociology or anthropology. The second is a novel and prolific literature on colonial discourse, which tends by contrast to be preoccupied with fictions, be they stories or other cultural products constructed as part of a collective imaginary.

I am discontented with both these approaches, the first because it tends to be too zealously preoccupied with the historical minutiae of behaviour in certain times and places, with depicting the real conditions of white wom*en* as they pertained in the colonies of Fiji and Nigeria, for instance, as against the ideological constructions of white wom*an* perpetrated by white men. As Jane Haggis (1990) has cogently argued, white women are on the one hand recuperated as actors in the colonies, but simultaneously seen as the victims of colonial ideologies, which appear to be exclusively authored by men. This is problematic not so much because it absolves women from the burden of past colonial associations, and elides their authorial voices in creating colonial culture, but because it obscures the particular ways in which white women were colonial actors and authors of myths, fictions, and colonial discourses.

Such fictions are, of course, the particular province of theorists of colonial discourse, including Gayatri Spivak (1986, 1987, 1988) and Homi Bhabha (1986a, 1986b). My discontent with this approach is rather different, focusing on the way in which it detaches texts from historical contexts.[1] It separates texts from both authors and readers as complicit agents in colonialism and tends to overgeneralize the logic of alterity. This writing often seems imprisoned by the binary terms of what it analyses—black and white, male and female, self and other—evoking a state of 'Manichean delirium' (Bhabha 1989:137). I have chosen the term 'colonizing women' partly to destabilize this terrain of binary exclusions. In discussions of the 'other', there is often a confluence between the other as woman and as colonized. There is an undoubted affinity between the ways in which the hierarchical and encompassing logics of race and sex have operated. But the logics are not segregated. There is no apartheid between the relations, either as logical terms in a discourse or as standing for real historical agents. They intersect. And it is the specificity of the way they intersect for women that interests me (cf. Spivak 1986, 1987, 1988; Trinh Minh-ha 1989).

Later, I will consider this specificity through a reading of the lives and texts of two colonizing women in the Pacific: Charlotte Geddie, Presbyterian missionary wife, dedicated to a project of rehabilitating Pacific women, remoulding them as good mothers; Beatrice Grimshaw, lady traveller, journalist and novelist, who was inclined rather to see Pacific women as beyond rescue, and their sexuality and maternity as ruinous of white civilization. In very different ways for these two women, the maternal body is central to their relationship to indigenous women. Pacific women's maternity was an object of their work and maternalism a key trope in their writings.

Although this essay tries to effect a conjunction of these historical and theoretical literatures, my interest in colonizing women is not just theoretical or historical. It is also personal and political. Colonizing women concern me because they are a contemporary presence and not an ancient absence. Colonialism may have ended as a formal historical relation, but it persists in political/discursive practices (Mani 1989; Said 1989). The persistence that troubles me is within the sphere of internationalist feminism. Despite some optimistic hopes for a 'one world women's movement' (e.g. Bulbeck 1988), a disconcerting maternalism persists both in the contexts of academic theory and the practical politics of forging international alliances (see Amos & Parmar 1984; Haggis 1987; Hooks 1981, 1984; Mohanty 1986; cf. Jolly 1991a). Perhaps, we (white/colonizing women) have not relinquished our embrace of the maternal body even if the Empire has receded from our grasp.

No place for a white woman: *Boys' Own*, memsahibs and ruinous racism

Let me start with a critical consideration of some empirical writing on white women in the colonies. From this huge literature[2] I select two texts, Claudia Knapman's *White Women in Fiji, 1835–1930: The ruin of Empire?* (1986) and Helen Callaway's *Gender, Culture and Empire: European Women in Colonial Nigeria* (1987). I select these because they are the finest feminist reappraisals of colonizing women, and because these texts echo each other. They appeared within a year of each other and developed rather similar arguments independently for two remote parts of the British Empire. Both criticize the prior representation of white women in a masculinist colonial history and develop a feminist reappraisal. In my reading of these two texts, I must acknowledge a debt to Jane Haggis's (1990) review of them, provocatively entitled 'Gendering Colonialism or Colonizing Gender' (1990).

Both books oppose the orthodox treatment of white women in colonial history, which has either rendered white women invisible or seen them in terms of the gross stereotype of the memsahib. In the first view the Empire envisaged is Boys' Own, not just a masculinist possession of other places, but a portrayal of that possession in terms of adventure, of derring-do and pluck (see Mackenzie 1988). Many recent writers have commented on the phallic imagery of early colonialism as penetration of virgin territories, daring exploration of the dark continent.[3]

In such views of Empire, there was little symbolic or actual space for the colonizing woman. This 'being out of place' is evoked by the titles of many of the memoirs of such women— wives of colonial administrators, nurses, teachers, or, in the later colonial period, minor colonial officials. This was not just a matter of difficult terrain, 'threatening natives', and the masculine character of imperial adventure: there were also tight exclusions appropriate to both the office and the club.

In the second variant of masculinist colonial history, women are not invisible or marginal, but present as a gross stereotype. The image both Callaway and Knapman evoke is taken from India or rather the fictional India of Kipling and Orwell.[4] It is the memsahib. Be they 'haughty and venal' or 'frothy and silly', English women are seen as the source of snobbishness and racism and are ultimately blamed for the loss of Empire, witness this comment from a historian of India:

> It has often been said that all the worst faults of the Raj—its petty
> intolerance, its prejudices and snobberies, its coldhearted

arrogance—stemmed from the memsahib (Allen 1977:18, cited in Callaway 1987:27).

Knapman cites equally compelling examples on the part of Pacific historians. In his otherwise consummate study of colonial land policy in Fiji, Peter France proclaimed: 'As in the rest of the Empire, the final and irrevocable estrangement from native society came with the arrival of the European lady' (France 1969:40, cited in Knapman 1986:7).[5] However, Knapman's best examples from the Pacific are two literary gentlemen: Geoffrey Dutton and James MacAuley. In Dutton's novel *Queen Emma of the South Seas*, one of the characters speaks with what Knapman hears as Dutton's own voice:

> Into this free and natural society, comes a poker-backed white woman, all whipped up in whale bone, and in no time she is trying to persuade everyone that the Samoans are naked, immoral savages, and those who cohabit with Samoan women are living in sin (1976:17, cited in Knapman 1986:9).

James MacAuley reflected on the sterility of Australia's colonial project in Papua New Guinea: 'nothing seems to take deep root and nothing flowers . . . Why? the simple answer is: the white woman' (1975:172–3, cited in Knapman 1986:9).

Such gross stereotypes of white women in the colonies typically condense three features: the idea that women were idle; the idea that they were preoccupied with petty gossip, rivalry and sexual jealousies; and the idea that they were to blame for the stricter racial segregation and the conflicts of the later colonial period. Both Callaway and Knapman treat such stereotypes as male myths and, through the details of their historical sociology, aspire to present the true picture of what white women's lives were like. Knapman suggests that we have taken novelistic fictions and male myths of the white woman for 'accurate depictions of real lives' (1976:176). Knapman presents her work as restorative realism:

> By telling their story I hope to have restored in some measure the integrity of white women who crossed the seas, loved and endured living with their husbands, bore and wept for their babies, worked, relaxed, laughed, suffered, and died—ordinary women (1986:177).

The correctives, the real stories told by both Knapman and Callaway, challenge all three aspects of the male myths.

First, they insist that white women in the colonies were not idle or bored creatures. They worked hard, they struggled to produce and reproduce under horrific conditions, but their work was typically elided by male mythic constructions and effaced by bourgeois ideals of the 'lady'. Knapman provides exhaustive documentation of the hard labour white women in Fiji expended giving birth to children, bringing them up, and contributing to economic enterprises on the plantation, on the farm or in town.[6] Their birthing and nurturing of children was construed as important not just for themselves and their families, but to reproduce the race.[7] In less prosperous families, white women did most of the domestic duties and child care and even where Indian or Fijian women were employed as domestic servants and nannies, they often maintained some direct involvement in the nursing, feeding and medical care of their children. Some were heavily engaged in work beyond the home as nurses, teachers, dressmakers, milliners, hoteliers, barmaids and businesswomen, and later as clerks, secretaries and telephonists. Many worked as unpaid partners in family enterprises—tending the angora goats, packing the bananas, scalding the vanilla pods, weeding the pineapples, helping out in the store.

Callaway portrays similar industry in the lives of white women in Nigeria, although here this more often occurred within the colonial bureaucracy. Women were heavily involved in health care, as both nurses and 'lady medical officers': in education, especially teaching girls and women; and finally after the Second World War as junior administrative officers in the Colonial Service. For those who were married, there was the work of being an 'incorporated wife', supporting the husband's career, offering hospitality to streams of visitors, and maintaining the intense social relations which were a central part of colonial culture (cf. Callan & Ardener 1984). After the Second World War, when children were allowed to remain with their parents, the work of mothering was added.

Second, in dealing with daily lives and leisure both Callaway and Knapman challenge the view that these women were preoccupied with petty gossip, sexual affairs and rivalry. White women in early Fiji seem preoccupied rather with trying to make homes in flimsy shanties. Later their pleasures seem canonically domestic—family picnics, Christmas parties, reading, writing, sketching, and later family photography with a box Brownie. In Suva, tennis, hockey, club dances, dinners, balls and *meke* (Fijian dances) were all popular pursuits. Although such social functions were segregated according to colour and class, women were not more segregationist than men, and class divisions between Europeans could override racial barriers. Upper-class English ladies often made friends with high-ranking Fijian women. Thus Lady Gordon wrote of Adi Kuila, 'She is such a lady,' and 'Nurse can't understand it at all, she thinks we are silly about natives and looks down on them as an inferior race. I don't like to tell her that these ladies are my equal and she is not' (Knapman 1986:111).

The perception was mutual—Adi Kuila wrote to Lady Gordon requesting some lace, with the words 'You are a lady like me' (ibid.).

Callaway concedes more to the status rivalry of white women, particularly in the later colonial period when, as Sylvia Leith-Ross observed, 'rugged pioneer' conditions gave way to a competitive spiral of ostentation in Lagos society—from silver coffee pot to silver salver to silver tray. But some women (like Leith-Ross, who wrote an ethnography of the Igbo and the 'women's war') were very interested in indigenous society, spoke vernacular languages fluently, and perhaps because they were engaged more in service to than in surveillance over local people, were appreciated, admired and even loved by them.

Third, both Callaway and Knapman challenge the view that white women were responsible for the racial segregration of the late colonial period and indeed for the loss of Empire. In the writings of many white male historians such as Memmi (1965), Mannoni (1956) and others, white women are portrayed as more racist than men, and as responsible for the institution of racial segregation in the later colonial period. This claim is usually linked to sexuality: in the early colonial period racial harmony is deduced from sexual relations between white men and colonized women, and increasing strictures on such liaisons are seen as the result of white women's sexual jealousy and intolerance. Both Callaway and Knapman do much to undo this misogynist chain of reasoning. First, although both concede that white women were racist, there is no persuasive evidence that they were *more* racist than men. Indeed women, because of their structural location, were more likely to sustain close friendships with locals. Second, they challenge the extraordinary presumption that sexuality between white men and colonized women was indicative of racial harmony.[8] Even when such sexual relations did not constitute rape, and when indigenous women voluntarily embraced a sexual or love relationship with colonizing men, there was still an element of conquest: sexual access to local women legitimized the colonial relationship. Sexual relations between white women and 'men of colour' on the contrary betrayed the imperial accumulations of the power of race, class and sex.

Thus Knapman and Callaway argue that it was not so much women's sexual jealousy of the 'woman of colour' as men's sexual fear of the 'man of colour' that was behind the institution of stricter racial segregations in the later colonial period. They argue that men rather than women had the power to enact such codes— the most spectacular being the Papuan White Women's Protection Ordinance of 1926. Despite scant evidence of the sexual menace of black men, this ordinance was enacted, with extremely punitive sanctions, namely the death penalty for rape or attempted rape of any European woman or girl (Inglis 1974). This coincided with an intensification of white settler interests and of exacerbated racial conflicts over land and labour.[9] The arrival of large numbers of white women was often part of such expansive periods. The 'rush in Fiji', the extensions of plantations and colonial control in Papua, *these* precipitated racial conflicts, resistance and strikes, not the racism of white women.

Important as this realist corrective is, like Jane Haggis I have problems with the way in which these books are written and the presumed identification between the white women talked about, the white woman as author and the white woman as imagined reader. Both texts work to establish an identification with colonizing women—and to portray both the people of the place and the colonial system itself as merely background to their epic heroic endeavours. Knapman conjures up an image of Fiji in which the troubles with local Fijians and conflicts with Indian workers are reduced to a threatening background, akin to hurricanes, tidal waves or earthquakes (1986:86–87). She expressly excludes any consideration of Fijians or Indians, but sometimes uncritically represents them, through the eyes of white women, as cannibalistic, widow-strangling savages or untrustworthy and ungrateful coolies.

My problem with Callaway is both similar and different. Although her work deals more closely with the relationship between European and indigenous women, she uncritically endorses the benevolent aspects of colonialism—nursing, teaching, women's service for the Empire. Her final chapter establishes a contrast between the nasty male characteristics of Empire—the dispossession of landowners, the economic exploitation, the racial segregation and violence, and the nice feminine forms of benevolent service, of conferring the gifts of civilization, of racial intimacy and of harmony.

> That 'the women lost us the Empire' might be seen then in a more positive way . . . that the women contributed to the loss of Empire by helping to gain the Commonwealth. The masculine ethos of the imperial era—characterised by hierarchy, authority, control and paternalism—had to be replaced by what might be seen as more 'feminine' modes required for 'the family of nations'—sympathetic understanding, egalitarian rather than authoritarian relations, diplomacy and flexibility (Callaway 1987:244).

Less racist and more humane intentions still served British cultural imperialism; feminine 'service', through the missions of medicine and education, still legitimated the overall project of colonialism. In Fiji and in Nigeria, the impact of white women cannot be analysed merely through their own lives, words and representations of their relations with other races. White women presented an image of the 'lady', which Fijian, Indian and Nigerian women were encouraged to emulate. The project of female improvement had a profound impact on them, even if they resisted as well as accommodated it.

Callaway and Knapman tend to see white women as simply the victims of male myths, be it as 'angels in the house' or 'devilish destructors of Empire'. But women were also involved in the creation and perpetuation of such myths. Below, I examine a rather spectacular example of this: Beatrice Grimshaw, propagandist for Empire and prolific novelist, whose journalism and romances perpetrate strong images of colonizing and colonized women. Even women who were not such prolific authors of colonial discourses more likely colluded with male myths of white women than challenged them. They were, perhaps, consoling fictions. Thus, the approach adopted in both these texts is recuperative—recovering white women as decent actors in colonialism, but exempting them from association with its indecencies by portraying them as victims of male projects and discourses.

Colonial discourses

In contrast to the realist recuperation of white women in the colonies, I now turn to a genre of writing which expressly deals with imperial fictions—colonial discourse theory. Earlier I lamented the facts that writers in this genre refuse to situate texts within historical contexts and are preoccupied with theoretical problems in the logic of alterity or difference. The documents of colonial officials, the memoirs of missionaries, the romances of fiction, the writings and photographs of travellers are read as examples of colonial discourse, but often with dedicated disregard of the 'scene of writing', the colonial agency of writers and readers, and the ways such texts circulated among audiences, empowering colonialism through words and pictures, both in the imperial outposts and in the metropolis.

Let me take as an example Gayatri Spivak's essay 'Three Women's Texts and a Critique of Imperialism' (1986). This is vintage Spivak. She expressly selects texts which are celebrated within the European feminist canon—Charlotte Bronte's *Jane Eyre*, Jean Rhys's *Wide Sargasso Sea* and Mary Shelley's *Frankenstein*— all of them celebrated 'women's books'. The first in particular she sees as inflected by the high feminist norm of the isolated and autonomous female subject. Spivak claims here as elsewhere (1987, 1988) that the constitution of female subjectivity in Europe is predicated on the 'othering' of women in the 'Third World'. She proposes that the imperial female subject is composed on two registers: on the one hand, she is created through the cathexis of companionate love, the romance of marriage and of sexual reproduction, while on the other she is constituted through devotion to a social mission, and especially the imperial project of female service. But this construction of a female individualist in the metropolis is predicated on the exclusion of the 'native female' or, in more contemporary guise, the 'Third World woman' (see also Mohanty 1986: Trinh Minh-ha 1989:79–114). So in *Jane Eyre*, the constitution of Jane as the unique individual is predicated on the othering of Bertha Mason, the Jamaican creole. Spivak's reading of all three texts is scintillating in its insistence on the imperial context and its consideration of the various ways in which the subjectivity of colonizing women is celebrated at the expense of the subjectivity of the colonized woman.

What I find problematic in Spivak's work is the way in which the subjectivity of the European woman is imagined as constantly interpellated against an unchanging background of imperialism, regardless of epoch and of the agencies of writer and reader. I crave consideration of *Jane Eyre* and *Frankenstein* in the context not so much of the life of Charlotte Bronte or Mary Shelley, but of their place in the imperial moments in which they lived. In relation to *Jane Eyre*, Spivak insists that she is studying the book, and not the author. She admits that a rigorously deconstructive approach would 'loosen the binding', undo the binary oppositions of book and author, individual and history, and allow the seamless 'scene of writing' whereby the text and the named subject Charlotte Bronte constitute each other. She refrains from considering Bronte's life, with the rather mysterious excuse that that 'would be too risky here' (1986:263). And yet she claims that the self-immolation of Bertha Mason as 'good wife' must be read in the context of the 'archives of imperial governance', 'the history of the legal manipulation of widow sacrifice in the entitlement of the British government in India' (1986:278). So it seems that not all contexts are risky and that some incautions are imperative.

Spivak's analysis of the relationship between the female imperial subject and the 'other woman' in literary texts and in the discourses of Indian colonial government was path-breaking. But her evocation of 'imperialism' elides the historical shifts in colonial and postcolonial relations, the variety of ways in which colonial discourses have authored the 'other woman', and how colonizing

women were situated as authors of such discourses. Here I return
to the Pacific to consider two colonizing women of different
epochs, engaged in very different colonial projects, and the contrasting ways in which they authored their relations with Pacific
women.

Embracing and denying the maternal body

I said at the start that I wanted to effect a fertile conjunction
between these two approaches to colonizing women. My dissatis-
factions with both have perhaps rendered the coupling infertile,
or aborted the baby. But let me now try to unite them in a
consideration of two colonizing women whom I have encountered
in the colonial history of Vanuatu.[10] I choose these women both
because we know something about their lives and because they
were both prolific authors of colonial discourses. But I also choose
them because of their difference from each other—they represent
quite different epochs and agencies in the colonial process. Charlotte Geddie was a Presbyterian missionary working with her
husband in Vanuatu from 1848 to 1872. Beatrice Grimshaw was
a single woman—a traveller, a journalist, and later a settler in
Papua from 1907 to 1934—who promoted the economic interests
of settlers and planters and was highly critical of missionary
endeavour. The maternal body is crucial in the way both of them
conceive and represent their relationship to Melanesian women.
But I counterpose the maternalism of the missionary woman
dedicated to the improvement of heathen 'girls' on the model of
the European mother with that of the promoter of white planter
interests convinced that Melanesians were dying out, that Melanesian women were beyond rehabilitation, that miscegenation meant
degeneration, and that the fertile romance of the white woman
and the white man was the future hope of repeopling the Pacific.

Charlotte Geddie: remoulding the maternal body

Elsewhere, I have examined in some empirical detail how Presbyterian missionaries in the south of Vanuatu represented and related
to local women, and the centrality of their ideals of domesticity
and mothering to their projects of 'raising them up' (Jolly 1991b).
Like Callaway and Knapman, I recuperated the stories of white
women. Here, I focus on how maternalism as a trope recurs in
the writings of these missionary women, in particular in the letters
of Charlotte Geddie (1908). These were not just private correspondence but propaganda instruments for Presbyterian

proselytization. Such texts of missionary lives were immensely popular, abetting both the ideological and the financial promotion of missionary efforts in the Pacific.

Charlotte Geddie came with her husband, John, from Nova Scotia in 1848 as missionaries of the Reform Presbyterian Church. Like most of the white missionaries to Vanuatu in this period, she came from a comfortable middle-class family (her father was a doctor), organized around Christian devotion and the mother as 'angel of the house', dedicated to her children and domestic duties. Charlotte married at seventeen and seemed equally ready to 'bury herself in the quiet duties of a country manse or go afar off to the heathen' (1908:14). Just as her husband prepared himself by learning how to build and plaster, print and administer medicines, Charlotte's vocational preparation was domestic training. Domesticity, the ideal of the emergent and often evangelical middle class (see Davidoff & Hall 1987) was presented as *the* European model to which other women should aspire. To impart this domestic model to heathen women was patently Charlotte Geddie's project from the time she arrived on Aneityum (southern Vanuatu) till her departure in 1872. Throughout her writing there is a pronounced tension between her perceived racial distance from local women and her potential identification as a woman. This tension is, I suggest, negotiated through the symbolic construction of a maternal relationship.

Charlotte Geddie shared the prevailing view of ni-Vanuatu as degraded savages. Degradation was apparent in primitive tools and houses, scanty attire, incessant warfare, worship of ancestral spirits, abnormal familial relations and especially in the position of women. They were habitually depicted as 'down-trodden' or 'debased' by being 'beasts of burden', by the horrors of male violence, female infanticide and widow strangulation. Such degradation was not thought to be an innate racial characteristic, since the very purpose of the missionary project was predicated on their potential for salvation. The division of labour whereby women worked to convert women was not so much because their husbands were unable to get close to them, but because as women they were thought to evince a natural sympathy. So we are told by Charlotte Geddie's daughter that 'Our dear lady's heart ached for the condition of the women' (1908:14) and that Jessie Inglis, another Presbyterian missionary, welcomed those Aneitymese women 'who came to her to explain all their ailments and embosom all their griefs and sorrows' (Inglis 1887:270–271).

Aching hearts and cushioning bosoms are strong bodily metaphors of sympathy and identity as woman, but also metaphors constitutive of a maternal relationship. The first contacts they had with local women suggest that *they* were less certain of such shared identity. So Margaret Whitecross Paton reports of her arrival on Futuna:

> I believe we were the first white women who ever landed on Futuna. The *ladies* were in consequence very curious to have us examined properly and they went about it in a business-like way as I can testify from the pokes and thumps received. They always felt themselves at the same time to see how far we were alike. Poor things they had yet to learn that we were sisters, resting under the same penalty and equally in need of and entitled to the same Saviour. (Paton 1894:27, emphasis in the original)

Arguably, rather than sisters, these missionary women were in their knowing condescension casting themselves more as mothers (cf. Haggis 1989; Ramusack 1990).

Throughout their letters, diaries and autobiographies, missionary women describe female children, adolescents and adult women alike as 'girls'. Thus Charlotte Geddie depicts the women who came to her school to learn the domestic arts, or who stayed in her employ as domestic servants, as 'girls'. The language she uses is throughout matronizing and infantilizing. Like other missionary wives, she believed that she should guide indigenous women as if they were her own children.

Herein lies an interesting irony. These women stressed the remoulding of local women as mothers. They saw indigenous mothering as incompetent, and although their interventions did not actually extend to forcibly removing children from their mother's care (as occurred in Australia), they did forcibly reshape the maternal relationship—the forms of reproductive control, the character and length of breastfeeding, how infants were weaned and fed, the patterns of care and discipline of children.[11] But they themselves were typically deprived of their own children, through either death or separation. Past infancy, most missionary children in this epoch were despatched to schools in Australia, Canada or England, because of the perceived risks of exposure to disease and to sin and savagery. Many missionary women mourned this as the hardest burden of the mission field (e.g. Paton 189:16). The maternal relationship Charlotte established with local women is often acknowledged as a consolation, even surrogacy, for her own maternal deprivation. Thus Charlotte Geddie was to say of her intimate friend, Mary, who died in the measles epidemic on Aneityum in 1861, '[S]he was an affectionate daughter to me' (1908:52).

The relation constructed with Mary is typical; I call it maternalism (cf. Haggis 1989; Ramusack 1990). This is not merely substituting a new female-centred term, maternalism, for the old male-centred term paternalism, privileging the place of the mother over the place of the father in the familial romance of colonialism. Maternalism was a different construction and the mother–daughter relationship a very different relationship to that which is commonly imagined between white man as father to black man as son. It is not the difference between soft feminine intimacy and harsh masculine distance, which Callaway posits in the transition to the 'family of nations'. Rather, I stress the different way in which race, sex and class intersected for women. The terms of hierarchical subordination for white men in the colonies were usually in alignment: their race, their sex, their class were all constitutive of their place as 'the father'. For white women, although race and class might intersect to accumulate her power, her sex did not. The symbolic constitution of the relationship between colonizing women and colonized women in the familial mode as that between mother and daughter was a poignant but strategic expression of the tension between superordination and identification, between detachment and agonized intimacy, between other and self.[12]

Beatrice Grimshaw: The New Woman of the Pacific?

This kind of maternalist sympathy for ni-Vanuatu women seems vastly different from the way in which Beatrice Grimshaw's racist distance suppresses her potential identification with ni-Vanuatu women. Beatrice Grimshaw was a canonical New Woman of the early twentieth century—lady traveller and later settler, journalist, novelist. She has acquired a place in Australian literary history and in the history of women's liberation, or as Gardner expresses it, 'release', in the colonies (Gardner 1977, 1987–88). Yet in a way that Spivak would relish, this autonomous, freewheeling, even cavalier individualist constitutes herself in oppositional relation to the savage woman as bestial and oppressed. Her propaganda for white settler interests in the Pacific not only reflected but helped create the gendered and erotic basis of racial segregation in the Pacific.

Beatrice Grimshaw was born of 'good Irish stock' and grew up in a country manor in County Antrim and then in Belfast. Her father was a linen merchant there (his great-grandfather had set up the first Irish cotton mill). Her mother, as was appropriate to her time and class, concentrated her energies on domesticity, bringing up eight children including Beatrice. But, as the Laracys observed (1977:155), young Beatrice was never one to 'sew a fine seam'. She was well educated, first by private tutors and then at school successively in Normandy, Bedford College in London and Queen's College, Belfast (although she never took out a degree). She has been cast as a model New Woman of the 1890s, enjoying both the benefits of higher education and a bicycle, an important sign of liberation for women of this class and period, as both the means and the icon of escape from chaperones (Laracy & Laracy 1977:156).[13] She disappointed her parents in their hope that she might become a lecturer in classics, but combined her talents for writing and mobility in a career of travel journalism. After writing advertising material for travel firms and shipping lines in Dublin and London, she received a commission from the *Daily Graphic* to write promotional literature in return for free travel passes to the 'South Seas' (Gardner 1977:13). Later she worked as a freelance journalist propagandizing for British and Australian commercial and settler interests. She was on occasion employed by Hubert Murray (governor of Papua) and Alfred Deakin (prime minister of Australia) to write in a semi-official capacity in support of British and more especially Australian imperial interests. In 1907 she went to Papua, ostensibly on a short visit; she stayed till 1934. During this period she wrote many journalistic works and novels. She never married or had children, although she was engaged to William Little, a miner and later government tax collector in Papua.[14] She was an intimate friend, often a houseguest (but never, it seems, a lover) of Governor Murray. After leaving Papua, she enjoyed a few more Pacific adventures before moving to her brother's farm at Bathurst, where she died in 1953.

As well as producing an enormous number of newspaper and magazine articles, Beatrice Grimshaw was the author of 50 books, both fiction and non-fiction, with titles like *When the Red Gods Call, Sorcerer's Stone, Beach of Terror, South Sea Sarah* and *Murder in Paradise*. Her fictions are, in the words of Eugenie and Hugh Laracy, 'escapist out of door romances with exotic, titillatingly dangerous Pacific settings' (1977:5). Critical opinion about her differs. James Michener called her the 'Queen of Gush', others have dubbed her the Kipling of the Pacific. The Laracys portray her as the laureate of 'a dusty lower middle class Australian version of the British Raj' (Wolfers 1975:54, cited in Laracy & Laracy 1977:154). The Laracys stress how racism saturates both her fictions and journalism,[15] but given her preference for hyperbole and embellishing the facts, it is often hard to tell the difference—romance and realism merge imperceptibly.

What I consider here is not the enormous corpus of novels and travel writing, which has been dealt with by the Laracys (1977), Gardner (1977, 1987–88) and Hunter (n.d.). I will briefly allude to some of these, but I concentrate on a journalistic text about Vanuatu, Life in the New Hebrides, published in *The Sydney Morning Herald* (1905–1906), a text which combines the genres of travel writing and political reportage. I am concerned with the way in which this operates as an incitement to Australian colonialism and the way in which Grimshaw's representation of and relationship to local women is an intimate part of this.

As in much earlier travel writing about the New Hebrides, enthusiastic depictions of the beauty of the place are combined with derogatory descriptions of the ugliness of its inhabitants. Port Vila is 'loveliness itself . . . dozing in a nest of lemon-flowered hibiscus and plumy cocoa-palm . . . The natives, however, strike an ugly note' (25/11/1905:6). Grimshaw depicts Efate as a fortress isle with omnipresent guns and latent violence, between white settlers and their labourers and between British and French settlers. She opposes the latter, lamenting the recent demographic and cultural preponderance of the French, the subsitution of 'bottles of thin claret' for the 'Britannic pint of beer' (ibid.).

But this is ancillary to her broader project of defending *all* colonial interests against the interests of the indigenous inhabitants. Local men are portrayed as ugly, stupid and always spoiling for a fight. Their bestiality is especially apparent to Grimshaw in their treatment of women. Local women are depicted as ugly, oppressed by overwork, and the objects of male exchange. She describes Malekulan women as 'bent and misshapen with the enormous loads they are obliged to carry' and 'with expressions, if possible, more degraded than that of the men' (16/12/1905:6). For her, the practice of giving bride wealth is patently a simple business of women being sold as commodities. She concocts this conversation between Malekulan women who are co-wives:

> 'I cost 12 pigs' Mrs. Frizzyhead No. 1 boasts to Mrs Frizzy Head No. 4, who is a new acquisition, and inclined to be cheeky. No. 4, who is painting her forehead black with burnt cocoanut and drawing a line of red ochre down her nose, pauses in her toilet to say, contemptuously 'I cost fifteen' . . . The Frizzyhead ladies subside, and wait till they can catch young Mrs. Blackleg coming up from the yam plantations, with a baby in her arms and a hundred weight of yams on her back, to revenge themselves by telling her that she only cost ten pigs and is a low creature anyhow. (ibid., cf. Grimshaw 1907b:159)

Given that Grimshaw did not understand even *bislama* (ni-Vanuatu pidgin), let alone any of the Malekulan languages, and that by her own report Malekulan women fled from her in terror, there is little doubt that this is Grimshaw's fecund imagination and not reportage. But her racist distance from the 'savage' Malekulan women cannot restrain her from flagrant and absurd acts of maternalism when she is finally able to make contact with one of them.

> I shall never forget the face of a bushwoman (who came down to the mission house some days later from another village, carrying yams for her husband to sell) when I gave her a pink ribbon and tied it around her neck. A sort of sacred joy seemed to flow from her whole countenance, and lift her far above the things of common earth. She seemed to feel ennobled and enriched by this wonderful thing that had happened to her. That she should have had something given to her—she, a woman!—and that it should be this marvellous piece of loveliness, this nameless thing of beauty! Surely the skies were going to fall! She was all one ecstatic grin until she went away, evidently treading on air and feeling six inches taller; and I was glad to know that her husband could not take the treasure away from her, as anything worn by a woman might never afterwards be allowed to disgrace the form of the superior sex. (16/12/1905:6)

Grimshaw the arch-racist remodels herself as a kind of fairy godmother, raising the stature of this Malekulan woman, both literally and symbolically, by the mere act of conferring on her a cheap pink ribbon. The gift of beauty and civility is much more effortless than the decades of instruction which Charlotte Geddie undertook, and yet briefly a similar relationship to local women is constituted—a lament about their savage state, a project of 'lifting up', and a condescending maternalism. But for the most part Grimshaw saw Malekulan women, like all Melanesian women, as beyond rescue, as degraded because of their race.

Beatrice, the New Woman, did not extend the boundaries of her own individual liberation to embrace all women. She did not even extend much sympathy to Presbyterian missionary women, engaging in a farcical satire of their fertility.[16] She speculates that the Presbyterian baby must be the principal product of the islands, in advance of copra or coffee (9/12/1905:6). Here she takes up in a fanciful way what she was deadly serious about, the necessity of promoting white settler and planter interests rather than missionary endeavours, and the necessity for whites to populate these islands.

A eugenic argument and a plea for white settlers also structure the romance of her fictions. This is most obvious in *When the Red Gods Call*. Stephanie, the daughter of the governor of Papua, marries the planter Hugh Lynch but discovers he was previously wed to a Papuan girl. She returns to England. Only when he repents of his folly does she return to Papua to remake their divinely ordained union. Stephanie is like many a Grimshaw heroine, 'a blade of steel in a silken scabbard'; Hugh like many a hero, taciturnly masculine. If white men succumb to the charms of black women, they become 'living ghosts of men', outcasts from civilization. If they father half-caste children, these are monstrous abominations. Only the white woman can redeem the white man from such ruin, although if she becomes stepmother to his children, there is always the question of how and when 'the dark drop' will show.[17]

It is clear from her writings that Beatrice was no feminist. She satirized what she called 'the equality brigade', and the fact that she was single was more the result of individual choice and later personal tragedy (William Little died in 1920) than of any opposition on her part to the conventions of heterosexual romance and marriage. Indeed, her entire romantic corpus can be read as advocating the higher and nobler qualities of the union of White Woman and White Man.

How, then, is Grimshaw read by feminists today? In the writings of Susan Gardner, I find a recuperative relation to Grimshaw, rather parallel to that which both Knapman and Callaway display towards their white women subjects. Gardner does not deny Grimshaw's racism (though this is seen to be a contextual and shifting quality in her work). She does not elide her influence both over colonial policy-makers and in the 'colouring of the popular imaginations about race' for readers in the Pacific, England and the United States. Indeed, she sees her as an important mediating link between scientific theories and popular notions of race (1977:17). But in her fanciful depiction of her own adventures in Ireland and in Bathurst, chasing up Grimshaw's origins, death and destiny, Gardner summons up a sympathy for her much-maligned subject. The photograph of the family home at County Antrim, kept crumpled close to her person, Grimshaw's ring (from William) passed eventually to Gardner herself—these are artifacts of her memory delivered to us with irony, but nostalgic sentiment nevertheless. By telling us how she commissioned the monumental mason to erect a headstone over Grimshaw's pauper's grave, Gardner literally recuperates and restores her subject. We are told that she will really 'rest in peace' when her books are republished, at Gardner's behest. But I wonder what summoning up our sympathies for Grimshaw accomplished for white feminist readers of *Hecate* in the bicentennial year of Australian white settlement.

Gardner interprets Grimshaw not as liberated in a feminist sense, but as 'released' from the oppressive patriarchal environment, class confinements and racial divisions of that first English colony, Ireland. There is evidence that Grimshaw experienced a relief in 'breaking away' (the title of her first novel), although whether she would have depicted her confinement in Gardner's terms is debatable. But we also need to ponder how her new-found Pacific freedom is enhanced by imprisoning Melanesian women within the confines of her colonial imagination, which cast them as oppressed and yet complicit in that oppression, as ugly and yet seductive, as innocent and yet the ruin of the white man. It is not a question of exoneration or of blame, but of the politics of identification of interpreting colonizing women today. We may stress the colonizing woman's racism in order to elide our own. We may also stress her liberation in order to celebrate our own, and, like her, set it against that archetypical victim, the 'native female' or the Third World woman.

Conclusion

It may be suggested that my attempt at forging this conjunction between two approaches to colonizing women has only demonstrated how far apart they are. Yet in texts dealing with the historical contexts of imperial lives, colonizing women appear as something other than the victims of male myths or the ciphers of colonial dicourse. In both ways of approaching colonizing women, however, we have the same problem of how our contemporary politics of identification inflects our stories. By stressing how lived experience and discourses relate, and how the changing character of colonialism shapes the imperialist practices of women, I am not attempting to deny the contemporaneity of colonizing women— just the reverse, in fact. But our lives and our discourses are also importantly different from those of these dubious ancestresses of the nineteenth and early twentieth centuries, even if we do not yet inhabit the promised land of postcoloniality.

Notes

1 Let me qualify this criticism. I do not implicate all theorists of colonial discourse. For example, there is a different approach in Edward Said's *Orientalism* (1978) and his later work, the works of Ranajit Guha and the Subaltern Studies scholars (e.g. 1989), Henry Gates (1986) Sander Gilman (1986) Tzevetan Todorov (1986) and Hazel Carby (1982, 1986). The tendencies I criticize are most pronounced in the writings of Homi Bhabha and Gayatri Spivak. See also the recent criticisms by Gates (1991), Dirks (1992) and Thomas (n.d.).
2 A few other recent texts might be alluded to here: Hunter's study of American missionary women in China (1981), Grimshaw's in Hawaii

(1989) and Langmore's in Papua (1989). A special issue of Women's Studies International Forum was dedicated to the theme in 1990, and the editors of that collection propose another collection on European women and imperialism. Ann Stoler has published a number of papers which deal with the intersections of gender, race, sexuality and reproduction in the colonies, particularly the Dutch East Indies and French Indochina. Stoler (1991) is a superb overview of these processes. One of the most blatant examples of the recuperative genre is the survey by Joanna Trollope (1983) who, *The Times*' reviewer tells us on the dustjacket, is 'well known as a historical novelist' and who has used 'a vast range of sources to produce a panoramic picture of the countless women, from penniless pioneers to governor's wives, whose strength, support and heroic contributions helped to build and sustain the Empire.'

3   Sander Gilman (1986) notes that this term came to signify not just Africa, but all places inhabited by dark colonized others and, even before Freud, the shrouded mysteries of the sexed female body and psyche which defied masculine Enlightenment.

4   Note that these are stereotypes, derived from such novels and perhaps later cinematic representations, and do not necessarily reflect the range of characterizations in either Kipling or Orwell. Knapman alludes to two characters, specifically Mrs Hauksbee from Kipling's *Plain Tales from the Hills* (1965) and Elizabeth Lackersteen from Orwell's *Burmese Days*. Lucy Hauksbee confides to her bosom friend Mrs Mallowe about her life in Simla, 'I will act, dance, ride, frivol, talk, scandal, dine out and appropriate the legitimate captive of any woman I choose, until I d-r-r-op' (Kipling 1951:13, cited in Knapman 1986:13). She notes that Hauksbee is a 'more complicated lady' than the stereotype based on her and admits that Kipling's representations of white women are quite diverse. Orwell's Elizabeth Lackersteen is perhaps less complex: she wants to talk of nothing but 'gramophone records, dogs and tennis racquets', and her husband, who loves Burma, laments that she looks on it 'with the dull, incurious eyes of a memsahib!' (Orwell 1967:111–112, cited in Knapman 1986:14). As Tinzar Lwyn has recently noted, the images of Elizabeth the colonizing woman and Ma Hla May the colonized Burmese woman are complicit oppositions. Flory's earlier Burmese mistress, Ma Hla May, is portrayed as 'grotesquely beautiful' at first, but then, when she reveals their affair to the English community, and is seen to manipulate Flory and take revenge for abandonment, she is cast as a 'screaming hag of the bazaar' (1991:29).

5   See also John Young's study of the white frontier society of the 1860s and 1870s in Fiji in which he adjudges 'It was not then the attitude of the male settlers, nor the Fijian authorities, but the arrival in Fiji of an influential number of European women which led to developing racial antagonism' (1968:338, cited in Knapman 1986:4–6).

6   There is a gap between Knapman's insistence on supplanting the mythic representation of white women with the facts of their lives, and her dealing only with the mythic representations by white women

of Indians as coolies and Fijians as cannibals (1986:88–91). Her justification for not counterposing myth to the facts is that her subject is white women, not Fijians or Indians (1986:88). But as Haggis (1990) points out, it is the effect of such a definition of the subject from the viewpoint of white women that effectively 'others' women and men of different races in the colonial encounter.

7 As Davin (1978) and de Lepervanche (1989) have pointed out, maternal bodies and imperialism were intimately associated. White women were enjoined to reproduce, while colonized women were either encouraged not to or else seen to be such incompetent mothers that their race was dying out (Fiji), or that their children should be taken from them into white families or institutions (Australia). See Jolly (n.d.) for a consideration of the reproductive and eugenic arguments echoing between the metropolis and the colonies. Class was as important as race in these debates.

8 Long ago, in critique of Mannoni's view of the free sexuality between French soldiers and the young women of Madagascar, Fanon presented this stunning riposte. When a soldier of the conquering army went to bed with a young Malagasy girl, there was undoubtedly no tendency on his part to respect her entity as another person. The racial conflicts did not come later, they coexisted. The fact that Algerian colonists went to bed with their fourteen-year-old housemaids in no way demonstrates a lack of racial conflicts in Algeria (1968:46).

9 Similarly, Knapman's (and Ralston's) analysis of the increased racial segration in Fiji during the period of 'the Fiji rush' is that although this coincided with the arrival of many more white women, these segregationist codes were not their creations nor indeed instituted at their urging (Knapman 1986:136–149; Ralston 1971, 1977: Knapman and Ralston 1989).

10 Vanuatu was declared an independent nation in 1980. This archipelago of Pacific islands was previously a joint colony of Britain and France, when it was known as New Hebrides/ Nouvelles Hebrides.

11 See Jolly (n.d.) for a consideration of how this notion of maternal insouciance persisted in the later debates about depopulation.

12 Compare Ramusack's consideration of five British women activists in India, 1865–1945, and the tension between constructing themselves as 'mothers' or 'sisters' of Indian women, between maternal cultural imperialism and feminist political alliances (1990; cf. Haggis 1989). In the Indian situation this familial construction sometimes originated from local women, but not all colonized women admitted a familial construction of their situation. Indeed in another context Cock has noted how although white women employers in South Africa conceived of their black female servants as 'one of the family', as daughters or sisters, their maids vigorously eschewed such constructions (Cock 1980; see also Gaitskell 1982).

13 Grimshaw helped edit a cycling magazine; there is, however, conjecture about whether she set a record in a women's 24-hour cycling race as she later claimed! (Laracy 1977:157).

14 Hank Nelson notes that Little was well loved by other colonists, as

is witnessed by the memorial on his headstone in Port Moresby cemetery: 'William John Little died 26 Oct 1920, aged 57 years BRAVE PIONEER, TRUE MATE, UNIVERSALLY LOVED (personal communication, December 1991). His appointment as a tax collector in 1919 was a sort of invalid pension, Nelson suggests; he had previously been a pioneer prospector and a Legislative Councillor.

15 In defence of Grimshaw, Susan Gardner (1987–88) observes that her racism was fluid and changing. She contrasts the romance about the Pacific which characterises her book *In the Strange South Seas* with the tone of the book from the latter part of the same journey, *From Fiji to the Cannibal Islands*. The difference is patent, yet it seems to reflect not so much a generalized ambiguity in her attitude to Pacific peoples but that persistent European predisposition to partition the Pacific into its positive Polynesian and negative Melanesian aspects. Her different attitudes to them is stated directly at several points, as both Gardner herself (1977:14) and the Laracys (1977:161–162) have noted. Witness this quote:

> East of Fiji, life is one long lotus-eating dream stirred only by
> occasional parties of pleasure, feasting, love-making, dancing and very
> little cultivating work. Music is the soul of the people, beauty of face
> and movement is more the rule than the exception, and friendliness to
> strangers is almost carried to excess. Westward of the Fijis, lie the
> dark, wicked cannibal groups of the Solomons, Banks and New
> Hebrides, where life is more like a nightmare . . . murder stalks
> openly in broad daylight, the people are nearer to monkeys than to
> human beings in aspect, and music and dancing are little practised,
> and in the rudest possible state. (Grimshaw 1907b:7)

Fiji, as in many such contrasts, is liminal (Thomas 1989); Grimshaw describes the civilized patina over the cannibal as only 'varnish deep' in Fiji (Laracy & Laracy 1977:162). However, perhaps Gardner is right that the hard racism of her 1906–07 writings softened in the later years in Papua, perhaps under the influence of Murray's protectionist policies towards the 'natives'.

16 'It rained Presbyterian babies throughout the whole tour. They lay on saloon sofas, sucking bottles, they flopped on smoking room seats chewing bananas, they toddled up and down perilous unprotected decks, and attempted to commit suicide over precipitous rails, and wiped their small hands on newly painted ventilators, and cleaned it off on officers white and gold coats, and held noisy synods of their own in private cabins, with boxes of lollies representing the missies funds' (9/12/1905:6, cf. Grimshaw 1907b:156).

17 Her differential attitude to Polynesians is again manifest in her portrayal of Vaiti, central character of *Vaiti of the Islands* and *Queen Vaiti*. She is of 'mixed blood', daughter of a Cook Islands princess and a disgraced English nobleman. She is both beautiful and brave. In the first novel she marries a Tongan king. In the second he dies, and she encounters the presciently named Tempest, a British naval officer, with whom she had had an affair in the first novel. But this second generation of mixing is thwarted, their future ruin avoided by

their dying at sea as an underwater volcano erupts over their schooner (see Laracy & Laracy 1977:166–167).

References

Allen, Charles (1977) *Raj: A Scrapbook of British India* 1877–1947, Andre Deutsch, London.

Amos, Valerie & Pratibha, P. (1984) 'Challenging Imperialist Feminism', *Feminist Review* 17:3–20.

Bhabha, Homi (1986a) 'Rembering Fanon: Self, Psyche and the Colonial Condition', in Barbara Kruger & Phil Mariani (eds) *Remaking History*, Dia Art Foundation, Discussions in Contemporary Culture, No. 4, Bay Press, Seattle pp. 131–148.

——(1986b) 'Difference, Discrimination, and the Discourse of Colonialism', in Francis Barker *et al.* (eds) *Literature, Politics and Theory*, Methuen, London.

Bulbeck, Chilla (1988) *One World Women's Movement*, Pluto Press, London.

Callan, H. & Ardener, S. (eds) (1984) *The Incorporated Wife*, Croom Helm, London.

Callaway, Helen (1987) *Gender, Culture and Empire: European Women in Colonial Nigeria*, St Antony's College, Oxford/ Macmillan, London.

Carby, Hazel (1982) 'White Woman Listen! Black Feminism and the Boundaries of Sisterhood', in Centre for Contemporary Cultural Studies *The Empire Strikes Back: Race and Racism in 70s Britain*, Hutchinson, London, pp. 212–235.

——(1986) ' "On the Threshold of Woman's Era": Lynching, Empire and Sexuality in Black Feminist Theory', in Henry Louis Gates (ed.) *'Race', Writing and Difference*, University of Chicago Press, Chicago, pp. 301–316.

Cock, Jacklyn (1980) *Maids and Madams: A Study in the Politics of Exploitation*, Ravan Press, Johannesburg.

Davidoff, Leonore & Hall, Catherine (1987) *Family Fortunes: Men and Women of the English Middle Class*, Macmillan, London.

Davin, Anna (1978) 'Imperialism and Motherhood', *History Workshop* 5:9–65.

de Lepervanche, Marie (1988) 'Racism and Sexism in Australian National Life', in G. Bottomley & M. de Lepervanche (eds) *The Cultural Construction of Race*, Sydney Studies in Society and Culture No. 4 Sydney Association for Studies in Society and Culture, Sydney, pp. 80–89.

Dirks, Nicholas B. (1992) 'From Little King to Landlord: Colonial Discourse and Colonial Rule', Nicholas B. Dirks (ed) *Colonialism and Culture*, University of Michigan Press, Ann Arbor.

Dutton, Geoffrey (1976) *Queen Emma of the South Seas*, Macmillan, Melbourne.

Fanon, Frantz (1968) *Black Skin, White Masks*, trans. by Charles Lam Markmann, MacGibbon and Kee, London.

France, Peter (1969) *The Charter of the Land: Custom and Colonization in Fiji*, Oxford University Press, Melbourne.
Gaitskell, Deborah (1982) 'Are Servants Ever Sisters?' *Hecate* 8(1):102–112.
Gardner, Susan (1987–88) 'A "'vert to Australianism": Beatrice Grimshaw and the Bicentenary', *Hecate* 13 (2):31–68.
——(1977) 'For Love and Money: Early Writings of Beatrice Grimshaw Colonial Papua's Woman of Letters', *New Literature Review* 1:10–36.
Gates, Henry Louis (1986) 'Writing "Race" and the Difference It Makes', in Henry Louis Gates (ed.) *'Race', Writing and Difference*.
——(1991) 'Critical Fanonism', *Critical Inquiry* 17(8):457–470.
Geddie, Charlotte (1908) *Letters of Charlotte Geddie and Charlotte Geddie Harrington*, privately printed, Truro, Canada.
Gilman, Sander (1986) 'Black Bodies, White Bodies : Toward an Iconography of Female Sexuality in Late Nineteenth Century Art, Medicine and Literature', In Henry Louis Gates (ed.) *'Race', Writing and Difference*.
Grimshaw, Beatrice (1905–06) 'Life in the New Hebrides', *Sydney Morning Herald*, November 25, December 2, 9, 16, 23, 30, 1905 and January 6, 1906.
——(1907a) *In the Strange South Seas*, Hutchinson, London.
——(1907b) *From Fiji to the Cannibal Islands*, Hutchinson, London.
Grimshaw, Patricia (1989) *Paths of Duty: American Missionary Wives in Early Nineteenth Century Hawaii*, University of Hawaii Press, Honululu.
Guha, Ranajit (1989) (ed.) *Subaltern Studies VI: Writings on South Asian History and Society*, Oxford University Press, Delhi.
Haggis, Jane (1987) 'Women and Colonialism: Untold Stories and Conceptual Absences', M.A. thesis, Economics and Social Sciences, University of Manchester.
——(1989) 'English Ladies and their Indian "Sisters": A View of Relationships from the C.E.Z.M.S. Magazine *India's Women*, 1880–1900', paper presented to conference on Women, Colonialism and Commonwealth, Institute of Commonwealth Studies, University of London, March.
——(1990) 'Gendering Colonialism or Colonising Gender?: Recent Women's Studies Approaches to White Women and the History of British Colonialism', *Women's Studies International Forum* 13 (1–2):105–115.
Hooks, bell (1981) *Ain't I a Woman? Black Women and Feminism*, Pluto Press, London.
——(1984) *Feminist Theory: From Margin to Center*, South End Press, Boston.
Hunter, Anne (n.d.) B.A. Hons. thesis proposal for 'The romance fiction and travel accounts of Beatrice Grimshaw', Sociology, La Trobe University.
Hunter, Jane (1981) *The Gospel of Gentility: American Women Missionaries in Turn of the Century China*, Yale University Press, New Haven.

Inglis, Amirah (1974) ' "Not a White Woman Safe": Sexual Anxiety and Politics in Port Moresby, 1920–1934', ANU Press, Canberra.
Inglis, John (1887) *In the New Hebrides . . . 1850–1877* Nelson, London.
Jeffries, C. (1949) *Partners for Progress: The Men and Women of the Colonial Service*, Harrap, London.
Jolly, Margaret (1991a) 'The Politics of Difference: Feminism, Colonialism and Decolonization in Vanuatu', in G. Bottomley, M. de Lepervanche & J. Martin (eds) *Intersexions*, Allen & Unwin, Sydney, pp. 52–74.
——(1991b) ' "To Save the Girls for Brighter and Better Lives": Presbyterian Missions and Women in the South of Vanuatu, 1848–1870', *Journal of Pacific History* 26(1):27–48.
——(n.d.) 'Other Mothers: Maternal "Insouciance" and the Depopulation Debate in Fiji and Vanuatu 1890–1930', in M. Jolly & K. Ram (eds) *Maternities, Colonial and Post Colonial in Asia and the Pacific*.
Kipling, Rudyard (1951) *Wee Willie Winkie, Under the Deodars, The Phantom Rickshaw and Other Stories*, Macmillan, London.
——(1965) *Plain Tales from the Hills*, Macmillan, London.
Knapman, Claudia (1986) *White Women in Fiji 1835–1930: The Ruin of Empire?*, Allen & Unwin, Sydney.
Knapman, Claudia & Ralston, Caroline (1989) 'Historical Patchwork: A Reply to John Young's Race and Sex in Fiji Re-visited', *Journal of Pacific History* 24(2):221–224.
Langmore, Diane (1989) *Missionary Lives: Papua 1874–1914*, Pacific Islands Monograph Series No. 6, University of Hawaii Press, Honolulu.
Laracy, Eugenie & Hugh (1977) 'Beatrice Grimshaw: Pride and Prejudice in Papua', *Journal of Pacific History* 12 (3):154–175.
Lwyn, Tinzar (1991) 'Close Encounters: Colonial Discourse on Gender, Ethnicity and the Politics of Burma', B.A. Hons. thesis Women's Studies, Macquarie University.
McAuley, James (1975) 'My New Guinea', in *The Grammar of the Real: Selected Prose 1959–1974*, Oxford University Press, Melbourne.
Mackenzie, John (1988) *The Empire of Nature*, Manchester University Press, Manchester.
Mani, Lata (1989) 'Multiple Mediations: Feminist Scholarship in the Age of Multinational Reception', *Inscriptions* 5:1–23.
Memmi, Albert (1965) *The Colonizer and the Colonized*, trans. Howard Greenfield, Souvenir Press, New York
Mannoni, Octavio (1956) *Prospero and Caliban: The Psychology of Colonization*, trans. P. Powesland, Methuen, London.
Mohanty, Chandra Talpade (1988) 'Under Western Eyes: Feminist Scholarship and Colonial Discourses', *Feminist Review*, 30:61–88.
Paton, Margaret Whitecross (1894) *Letters and Sketches from the New Hebrides*, ed. James Paton, Hodder & Stoughton, London.
Orwell, George (1967) *Burmese Days*, Penguin, Harmondsworth.
Ralston, C. (1971) 'The Pattern of Race Relations in 19th Century Pacific Port Towns', *Journal of Pacific History*, 6:39–59.
——(1977) *Grass Huts and Warehouses: Pacific Beach Communities of the Nineteenth Century*, ANU Press, Canberra.

Ramusack, B. (1990) 'Cultural Missionaries, Maternal Imperialists, Feminist Allies: British Activists in India, 1865–1945', *Women's Studies International Forum*, 13(4):309–321.
Said, Edward (1978) *Orientalism*, Penguin, Harmondsworth.
——(1989) 'Representing the Colonized: Anthropology's Interlocutors', *Critical Inquiry* 15(2):205–225.
Spivak, Gayatri Chakravorty (1986) 'Three Women's Texts and a Critique of Imperialism', Henry Louis Gates (ed) *'Race', Writing and Difference*.
——(1987) *In Other Worlds: Essays in Cultural Politics*, Methuen, New York.
——(1988) 'Can the Subaltern Speak?' G. Nelson & L. Grossberg (eds) *Marxism and the Interpretation of Culture*, University of Illinois Press, Urbana.
Stoler, Ann Laura (1991) 'Carnal Knowledge and Imperial Power: Gender, Race and Morality in Colonial Asia', M. di Leonardo (ed) *Gender at the Crossroads of Knowledge: Feminist Anthropology in the Postmodern Era*, University of California Press, Berkeley.
Thomas, Nicholas (1989) 'The Force of Ethnology: Origins and Significance of the Melanesia/Polynesia Distinction', *Current Anthropology* 30:27–41.
——(n.d.) *Colonialism's Culture: Readings in Anthropology, Travel and Government*, forthcoming, Polity Press, Cambridge.
Trollope, Joanna (1983) *Britannia's Daughters: Women of the British Empire*, Century Hutchinson, London.
Todorov, Tzevetan (1984) *The Conquest of America: the Question of the Other*, trans. Richard Howard, Harper & Row, New York.
Trinh, Minh-ha (1989) *Woman, Native, Other: Writing, Postcoloniality and Feminism*, Indiana University Press, Bloomington.
Young, John (1968) 'Frontier Society in Fiji', Ph.D thesis, University of Adelaide.

8 Timing differences and investing in futures in multicultural (women's) writing
Efi Hatzimanolis

The category 'multicultural writing' has not yet passed the test of time to enter the disinterested and disembodied (liberal) realm of quality, and as such it is implicitly and commonly defined in Australia as a racist embodiment, a sort of throwback in literature. But in resisting liberal calls for self-improvement, which often operate through ideas of quality and function to produce the counterparts the migrant success story and the migrant as the problem, the term multicultural writing can be useful in disrupting individualist ideas of difference that conceal their own material production according to the dyads same/other and success/problem. In other words, the 'throwback' of multicultural writing represents an intervention, albeit ambivalent, in unequal relations of power through which dominant ideas of the other function to fetishize and infantilize migrant and non-Anglo-Celtic Australians as products of the past. Timing others as the embodiment of the past is, of course, a way of keeping 'them' out while simultaneously suggesting that 'we' gain access to 'our' past through 'them' in ways that enable 'us' to predict their future as our present and to imagine our own future as more of the same. Bhikhu Parekh puts it succinctly: 'Liberalism has always remained assimilationist: others must become like us, my present is your future' (Parekh 1989:27). Similarly, Trinh Minh-ha describes the anxiety in one-way assimilationism: 'Just be "like" [us] and bear the chameleon's fate, never infecting *us* but only yourselves.' (Trinh 1989:52). Liberalism's assimilationist rhetoric, produced around individualist ideas of a linear, progress-based narrative of subjectivity and history, implicitly defines the (liberal's) future as perpetually inaccessible to others, and conceals prevailing anxieties about the other's in/authenticity. Trinh's use of the chameleon image is telling in this context. It points to the ways dominant groups displace their fear and insecurity about their own identity and power onto paranoid ideas of the other's sinister power to appear 'same' while 'deep down' remaining unchanged. Similarly, ideas of others' (in)authenticity are often represented through racist ideas of their traitorousness and shiftiness.

For example, recent debate in Australia around multicultural writing has tellingly shown how the other's body, specifically that of the migrant theoretician/critic, is discursively inscribed as in/authentic through just such liberal fears and fantasies about 'ethnic identity' and power reversal. In an article exemplifying prevailing liberal anxieties around issues of authenticity and authority (Dessaix 1991), critics like Sneja Gunew and Nikos Papastergiadis who theorize cultural differences in writing are deemed to have forfeited their right to speak about multicultural writing because they are making an academic career out of fostering bad writing under the guise of espousing cultural differences; their desire to institutionalize multicultural writing is suspect because they have been corrupted (the migrant success story becomes the migrant as the problem—in Gunew's terms, the assimilated guest becomes the parasite), unlike the author of the article himself, who is speaking in the name of quality. According to the article, such critics are also suspect because they use obscurantist French theory; more insidiously, their linguistic competence and theorizing about migrant writing inauthenticated their arguments because migrant writing, after all, is plain, undemanding storytelling (Gunew 1991a). The implication is that the migrant critic's sophisticated linguistic competence and engagement in bourgeois institutions render her inauthentic, a traitor to her ethnic origins and migrant background. She is pretentious and unnatural, oppressive to herself and to the migrant writing she promotes. In other words, the proper migrant writer/critic should not be conspicuously clever. The explicit 'divide and conquer' tactics informing the article's anti-feminist, anti-intellectual politics are an attempt to silence the confrontational voices of race, class and gender differences by tying ideas of quality to ideas of 'native Australian English' (Dessaix's term) in literature, for which should be read authentic, authoritative writing. These attempts are anxiously fraught with the desire to re-secure authority in one disembodied and abstract voice whose very disinterestedness assures 'us' that our personal/professional investments in differences are misguided and divisive. The anxiety here about the migrant critic's theoretical language also operates as an anxiety about free speech insofar as 'plain speech' is a displaced incarnation of (patriarchal bourgeois) ideals of free speech. So not only is 'obscure' language un-Australian, it is also, significantly, undemocratic. Ideas of democracy and free/plain speech here are linked to the tradition of Anglo-Celtic Australian masculine mateship (Morris 1991). These sentiments are a reminder that 'we' ungratefuls live in a tolerant society (Gunew 1991b:11; Hage 1991).

In a partly sympathetic reply to Dessaix's article, Maria Lewitt revealingly raises these issues of authority and authenticity around ideas of the multiculturalists' exposed bodies (Lewitt 1991). Her letter begins by applauding Dessaix's courage in exposing the vested interests of the 'ethnocrats', characterizing him as the brave boy who exposes the emperor's new clothes. What is significant about this characterization is the way it aligns ideas of the migrant critic's body with ideas of the crude self-serving investments represented by Dessaix's 'multicultural professionals'. Dessaix's body, which remains well concealed by that magic mantle called quality, represents the sort of subject engendered as time-less, abstract and unified, *and as authoritative because neutral*—like the child in the fairy tale, it is innocent of power relations and therefore (and this is the contradiction) can see through them. Presumably, Dessaix has no vested interests except to promote quality in writing regardless of the race, class and gender differences which inform that writing. Promoting writing precisely because of the cultural differences, for example, which inform its production threatens the supposed neutrality of purveyors of quality, but it also upsets some migrant writers who, like Lewitt, understandably want to resist what they see as the stereotyping and ghettoizing of their work as examples of the 'migrant experience'. However, very little of their work is published or taught in educational institutions, and the reasons for this are due largely to the very bourgeois patriarchal assumptions about quality as neutral and timeless which Lewitt champions, and which inform the differential and unequal access to literary production experienced by marginalized groups in Australia.

Meaghan Morris has argued that the panic being generated around multiculturalism in Australia—exemplified by the recent Australian reprinting of and sympathetic engagement with American anti-multicultural debates on pedagogy and 'political correctness' (Kimball 1991; Taylor 1991; Schama 1991), together with Dessaix's article—is an anxiety about history, the mixing of temporalities and (free) speech, at the heart of which is anti-affirmative-action sentiment informed by economic rationalist discourse (Morris 1991). In the literary debates around multi-culturalism in Australia, as Gunew has shown, this is intimately related to opposition to anthologies/bibliographies of multicultural writing which attempt to clear cultural spaces for writers whose access to the material conditions of literary production are marginal. The strategies central to this opposition are aimed at reinforcing ideas of the dependent and insecure status of migrant writers—the migrant ghetto—by constructing a slippage between ideas of social welfare groups and ideas of other writing, that is, between ideas of multiculturalism as a policy tied to social welfare and multicultural writing, an opposition which Gunew has criticized in terms of the host and guest/parasite relationship constructed by and operating according to dominant ideas of Australian literature and migrant writing (Gunew 1991b).

Moreover, opposition to multiculturalism has engendered some curious and spurious identifications by its conservative critics around the issues of authority, authenticity and history. For example, an article published in *Quadrant* in 1989 equates multiculturalism with both 19th-century English colonialism and contemporary feminism, suggesting that the Anglo-Celtic Australian male is marginalized and oppressed in much the same way as Aborigines are (O'Reilly 1989; Hatzimanolis 1990). In other words, the article capitalizes on Aboriginal oppression in order to construct and authenticate an idea of Anglo-Celtic aboriginality so as to reclaim Australia from migrants and from feminists.

In this context one wonders to what extent Dessaix's call for 'native Australian English' in writing is yet another displaced anxiety about feminism and about white Australia's racist colonial history operating through the equation/identification of multi-culturalism with British colonialism. John Docker similarly capitalizes on this spurious equation, implying, in effect, that the category migrant writing, especially as it is used by Gunew in an early essay, is an extension of colonialism in this country (Docker 1991). Multicultural writing for these critics seems to violently invoke/represent Australian literature's unexorcised and repressed other—its uncanny double, English literature. These displacements may be exposed usefully to estrange Australian literature's (repressed) investments in the type of universalism represented for so long by notions of English literature, but they rarely are. Sneja Gunew argues

> . . . that everything we currently term Australian Literature may productively be reread—for example, by means of nostalgia (as a means of liberating the uncanny)—from positions currently outside that literature, constructed in non-Anglo-Celtic Australian writings.

This renders uncanny the traditional renditions of the
home/mother/land for which the referent is arguably an Australia
always mediated by somewhere else—the shadow of England,
Ireland and so on. (Gunew, 1990:28)

I have argued elsewhere (Hatzimanolis 1992) that what is also
significant about Docker's argument is a type of repressed sentimental romanticism informing his use of the term victim to describe
Aborigines rather than migrants, as if the status of victim were an
enviable one worth competing for, and as though acknowledgment
of the fact that European immigrants have been/are victims of
racism would release a flood of sympathy for their (illegitimate)
claims to Australia. Like Dessaix, Docker employs an argument
replete with fears and fantasies about power reversal through which
he repositions readers to perceive the feminist migrant writer/critic
as problem. Historically, notions of power reversal have been used
against feminists and working-class, black and gay activists, for
example. Feminist desires to change unequal relations of power in
order to empower women have often been conveniently misconstrued as a hunger for power, particularly where these same
feminists in their demands for equality refuse to reproduce patriarchal notions of women as victims. Similarly, the feminist migrant
writer/critic who refuses to comply with this positioning (of victim)
becomes a threat who must be recontained according to the couplet
victim/victimizer. In other words, if she cannot be sentimentalized
as a victim, and thereby categorized as being needy of (paternalistic)
protection (that is, silenced and excluded), she may then be defined
according to the second term, victimizer.

Anne Cranny-Francis has noted that sentimentalism is a substitute for caring and a displaced fear of mutuality engendered by
and engendering patriarchal relations of power (Cranny-Francis
1992). According to these terms, the protectiveness extended by
patriarchal subjects towards powerless subjects/groups operates as
a type of possessiveness which disempowers the latter. Moreover,
official multiculturalism, as Ghassan Hage has argued, operates in
similar ways through its prevailing rhetoric of tolerance:

The person asked to be tolerant is by definition someone who
retains the power to be intolerant, but is invited not to exercise it.
In being tolerant, Anglo-Australians can experience both the joy of
'extending their tolerance' and the security lying in the implicit
capacity to retract it. (Hage 1991:12–13)

Far from questioning unequal relations of power, the rhetoric
of tolerance discursively positions and engenders migrant and
non-Anglo-Celtic Australian subjects as *insecure* dependents, and
hence addresses them both as potential traitors (Hage points out

that the Gulf War was used against Arab Australians in this way) and as victims, disempowering them in ways closely related to the liberal opposition to the term multicultural writing I discussed above.

The cover of a publication by the Office of Multicultural Affairs (OMA) titled 'Sharing our Future'.

Moreover, the slippage from 'victim' to 'dependent' that Hage also describes is exemplified by the ways tolerance and sentimentalism in the above terms operate discursively and are realized textually in the cover of a booklet distributed by the Office for Multicultural Affairs in 1989 through major metropolitan newspapers like *The Sydney Morning Herald*. The booklet was just one part of a major federal government campaign to promote and clarify the term multiculturalism and the policies to which it is linked.

In one sense the booklet cover appears to be an example of how the fear and insecurity embodied by patriarchal liberal authority may be addressed in non-confrontational terms, but its rhetoric of mutuality and tolerance is underpinned by sentimentality in ways that operate to reproduce implicitly oppositional ideas of the dystopian, divisive time of the past, of the other. Multiculturalism, according to the cover, signals a unified, synchronized future of the nation, a nation that is represented as innocent of social relations of power by the cover photograph, which positions the reader to look down benignly on a multi-ethnic group of children cheerfully huddled together against a green background beneath the eyecatching yellow words 'The People of Australia' at the top of the page. Although Australian nationalism and patriotism are signified through the green and gold colour scheme, significantly, the nominalization 'People of Australia' together with the image of the children functions to suppress the exclusionary term 'Australians' which commonly signifies adult, usually male, Anglo-Celtic Australians, 'typical' Australians. However, the oblique view of the children positions them as vulnerable and dependent—they look up to 'us', and 'we' look down at them—producing a patriarchal viewing position which sentimentalizes the notion of multicultural Australia (read for this the ethnics) as dependent rather than sharing. Moreover, the slogan 'Sharing our Future' is at the bottom of the page in smaller, less emphasized white print. Whose tolerance and acceptance is sought and constructed through the cover design? More to the point, whose anxieties about (sharing) power are anticipated and displaced by the image of a non-threatening 'rainbow' coalition/group of children who are 'our' hope for a unified future?

The cover appeals to and produces a paternalistic idea of Australia through the relationship of dependency constructed around a disembodied (paternal) gaze. In this way, it implicitly contradicts the rhetoric of sharing, and suggests that the more centrally visible and hence more powerful image is addressing the fears and insecurities of a patriarchal Anglo-Celtic Australian audience. That is, it discursively reproduces the normative social relations of power in and by which 'ethnic' and migrant subjects are infantilized: the stereotype of the migrant as dependent (child)/victim. *Moreover, it does this by re-envisioning and re-embodying the suppressed term 'Australian' through the bourgeois patriarchal reading/viewing position of the text.* What is significant about this viewing position together with the image of the children is that it obfuscates racist discourses, through displaced childist discourses, promulgating a sentimental and therefore possessive view of the future in which power and authority lie, in Hage's terms, with the 'tolerator'. And this 'tolerator' is specifically engendered in and by the text as the bourgeois patriarchal Anglo-Celtic Australian (the sort most likely to read *The Sydney Morning Herald*?) This is the unified subject of liberalism implicitly represented as unconstrained by the body; a body which is both 'absent' from the photograph and 'above' it all. But as many feminists have shown, this idea of subjectivity, far from being disinterested, is the embodiment of the white bourgeois male naturalized as the neutral, universal norm.

Despite its utopian slogan, 'Sharing Our Future', which appeals to notions of 'time-sharing' in a mutually accessible future, the cover as a whole is a far cry from the more reformist rallying call 'It's Time' used by the Australian Labor Party in its successful federal election campaign in 1972 the same year in which it introduced multiculturalism as an official policy. Historically, the urgency of this call was in response to an endemic racism institutionalized in the policies of assimilationism and integrationism. But the slogan 'Sharing our Future' reveals an anxiety about the past in the form of insecurity about whether the present is the right time to change social practices which foster inequality. In this sense, the cover as a whole implicitly acknowledges and disavows Anglo-Celtic Australian resistance to multiculturalism in Australia. The history of multiculturalism is displaced through the appeal to a mutually accessible future; a future not contaminated by the past and present historical moment of multiculturalism. In disavowing its history, the cover also recognizes and acknowledges the fear and insecurity which have informed conservative criticism of multiculturalism since its introduction, producing debates which have fuelled ideas of it as divisive, as a repository of migrant pasts and other cultural identities in opposition to a 'native' Australian identity, for which should be read Anglo-Celtic Australian history and culture. The image of the children suggests also an anxiety about history, displaced anxiety about the past as a burden that the next generation will redeem through a synchronization of cultural differences named cultural diversity. Such pluralism, however, as I have been arguing, is a displaced form of paternalism constitutive of those patriarchal ideas of tolerance commonly associated with revealing cliches like 'forgetting our differences' (read for this forget your identity) and 'burying the past' (whose past?). The price of this sort of tolerance under the sentimental guise of future 'time-sharing' is the suppression of migrant memories and the obfuscation of racism.

This idea of 'tolerance' is not so different from the fear and anxiety expressed by some literary critics around the term multicultural writing. It is an insecurity constructed around the fear that they will be marginalized if they can no longer speak for the other. As such, voices of cultural differences are misconstrued all too often in oppositional terms. What is significant about much of this fear and insecurity is that it is a fantasy about power reversal wherein those in relative positions of power claim the position of marginality for themselves, thereby re-enacting their desire for the other. For example, Ted O'Reilly's implied Anglo-Celtic aboriginal (O'Reilly 1989) is one inflection of this insecurity. In the terms adopted by these critics, equality and mutuality are produced through their patriarchal authority to sentimentalize the other, a type of *possessive* identification, rather than recognition, which depends on and maintains the other's silence. And their fear is that mutuality and equality entail the loss of history, and that the bourgeois patriarchal Anglo Australian subject will be rendered homeless. The desire for the other circulates together with the fear of the loss of history. What is really disturbing about all of this is that those who desire to voice their cultural differences in terms of social relations of power are often either positioned as oppressors reproducing racist bloodlines and/or inciting racial hatred or sentimentalized in ways that reposition them as dependent and hence as potential victims. In the latter case, the other's body is frequently inscribed as potential victim through the proprietary paternalism informing sentimental notions of caring, and this is reciprocally linked to definitions and descriptions of the former as ungrateful, as potential traitors and/or victimizers.

The OMA booklet cover also suggests a coming-of-age narrative of the people of Australia. This is the sort of linear, progress-based narrative that informs ideas of assimilation as self-improvement and through which ideas of the migrant success story and of the enlightened, migrant individualist operate as counterparts to the idea of the migrant as the problem. Accordingly, the migrant other must practise some form of self-overcoming in order to gain access to a future defined as the liberal's present. That this may also engender self-hatred in migrants is hardly surprising; it is useful too in maintaining their complicity in ideas of the migrant success story (self-defining future) and its counterpart, the migrant as the problem (self-constraining past). Middle-class ideas of upward mobility and future success here depend in part on individualist ideas of self-improvement in which migrants' personal 'inadequacies' are defined as the inevitable result of their past, their cultural otherness.

These displacements both obscure and reinforce unequal social relations of power, and also their own production in these relations. They do this partly by reproducing liberal ideas of a self-identical and disembodied subjectivity, the individualist subject who has passed the test of time. As Parekh's description of liberalism quoted above, suggestively implies, in assimilationist terms 'The Future' is inaccessible to the other but the other makes the past accessible to the liberal. Ideas of the implied timelessness of individualism here operate as a heavily invested idea of the future as more of the same, and the implied epithet 'their future is in our hands' reproduced through the OMA booklet cover is a continuation of this.

In the same year that OMA produced its booklet (1989), Anna

Couani and Peter Lyssiotis published *The Harbour Breathes*. Couani's written text (Lyssiotis produced the photomontages) signifies the desire for a different future and narrative authority from that which I have discussed above; a narrative authority which is more fragmented but which, like OMA, addresses the mixing of temporalities in contemporary Australia. Couani relates this to questions of the past and personal history in narrative and to the ways non-Anglo-Celtic Australian women's writing negotiates ideological assumptions about class, sex/gender, race and cultural differences. Indeed, the fragmented narrative and the mixing of prose and poetry in *The Harbour Breathes* operate as a way of disrupting ideas and representations of the individualist subject together with the public/private division informing official narratives of history. The text engages with ideas of different experiences of temporality in the formation of subjectivity, embodied through dreams and memories, through the past and through what Gunew has called the 'unimaginable future'. Its ideas of fragmented subjectivity, narrative and history neither reproduce the self-identical body which improves over time nor defuse the radical politics of difference by reconstituting a substitute repository of others where difference is equated with the working class, women, blacks and migrants.

In 'Another Engagement' and 'Parramatta Sestina', for example, Couani reworks the sestina in prose form so that stanzas look like paragraphs. The mixing of poetry and prose here draws attention to the spatial organization of the narrative's development in ways that eschew a linear temporal unfolding. This is exemplified in part by the two texts' repetition of six key words: clear, invisible, attraction, Chinatown, reoriented and engagement in 'Another Engagement'; and ancient, city, like, track, days and Parramatta in 'Parramatta Sestina'.

The significance of these textual practices poses the question crucial to debates around cultural difference in writing, namely, who has access to the conditions of writing? For example, the relationship between memory, place, the past and present, writing and subjectivity is developed by Couani's narrative in terms of the desire to map other temporalities and to reclaim (past) places in the present as a decentring narrative strategy, that is, as an intervention in official bourgeois Anglo-Australian maps of the city, narrative and history. In mapping her relationship to the city, the narrator also negotiates the different subject positions produced through her memories of her relationship to her parents' racial and cultural differences, to their memories of the city, and to the ways in which she is discursively positioned by different generic conventions in writing about personal memories of cultural differences.

In addressing this temporal, racial and cultural mix, the text is fraught with the aesthetic/political tensions involved in representing personal experiences of cultural differences in terms other than what Couani calls 'that personal approach to writing' which conventionally defines and delimits the space to which women's writing and migrant writing is assigned and suppressed as autobiographical and confessional. So, while 'that personal approach to writing' signifies the text's concerns with the types of narrative strategies available to non-Anglo-Celtic Australian women writers, it is also a refusal to reconstruct the self-centered, self-regarding Western quest narrative whose individualist techniques are commonly valued most, but which conceal insecurity about others' temporality.

Moreover, migrant and non-Anglo-Celtic Australian women's voices are under a similar pressure to that described by Trinh in her experience of the liberal politics of difference through which questions of the authenticity of others function as a diversionary tactic aimed at silencing those who interrogate unequal social relations of power (Trinh 1989:88). In these terms, as Hage and Cranny-Francis also implicitly recognize, a liberal politics of difference functions as a patriarchal form of possessiveness and acquisitiveness masquerading as protectiveness and genuine interest, and this is particularly virulent in relation to ideas of authenticity where 'that voice of difference [is] likely to bring us *what we can't have* and to divert us from the monotony of the same' (Trinh 1989:88). Like the childist discourses operating through OMA's booklet cover discussed above, ideas of 'authentic' migrant writing function to deny the *inter*dependence of social relations, and this is informed by prevailing anxieties about the mixing of temporalities and the fear of the future as the end of history which Morris has discussed (Morris 1991).

''Parramatta Sestina' also challenges ideas of migrant writing implicitly produced according to primitivist ideas of the other's predictive role in history—a sort of going back to an Anglo-Australian future via migrant memory while remembering to forget the migrant's past—and in this sense, Gunew's description of *The Harbour Breathes* on the book's back cover is significant:

> Beneath this representative Sydney lies another city in which past and future surface as a dream landscape of displaced legacies converging to spawn an unimaginable future.

Gunew's use of the term 'unimaginable future' here hints at the mostly conservative fear of a (multicultural) future as the end of history. But the idea of an 'unimaginable future' is also indicative of an utopian space of resistance to narratives naively informed

by individualist discourses through which ideas of the future are
produced as predictable, that is, determined as more of the same
disavowal, both of the interdependence of social relations and of
migrant and non-Anglo-Celtic Australian memories.

In the poem 'The Fold', for example, ideas of memory not
only represent a nostalgia for community but also suggest the
desire for narrative forms which are more 'folding' than
'unfolding', that is, forms which do not subsume the interdependence of social relations through teleological narrative techniques.
In these terms, 'The Harbour Breathes' engages with and constructs ideas of memory as a form of anticipation in the present
rather than as a way of looking back from a fixed present to a
fixed past. Experience 'as it was happening' becomes the anticipation of the memory of the experience. Memory, in other words,
is not only linked to a type of self-conscious decentred subjectivity
but is also the desire for a future linked to the past in unpredictable and discontinuous ways. And, most significantly, memory in
these terms is related to ideas of community in which community
is defined against homogenizing geopolitical maps and narratives
of the city through which interdependent social relations and
histories informed by race and cultural differences are silenced. In
'The Fold', Couani writes:

> everything swept aside and away
> by the anglo elite
> submerging people like us
>
> eliminating the differences
> any disturbance or challenge
> like cutting out our tongues
>
> the city is different
> it folds us in
> opens up a space to rest
> . . .
>
> Those years we shared that space
> it wasn't just geography
> our lives were softly colliding

Couani's writing here, as elsewhere, is informed by the desire
to remap official public/political terrains in personal/political ways
in order to claim narrative spaces for those intersections between
race, class and gender differences subsumed not only by 'big
capital' but also by 'leftist and alternative groups' which naively
'persist in maintaining hierarchical structures which duplicate
those of the establishment'. 'The Tunnel', for example, criticizes
the liberal notions of excellence and quality used to promote both

literary star systems and politically naive, complacent and oppressive assumptions about how equal access to institutions like publishing may be brought about by new, supposedly insuppressible individual talent.

Similarly, 'The Harbour Breathes' relates the discursive positioning of others within the personal sphere to inner-city redevelopment and gentrification, likening the depopulating of inner-city spaces to the disempowering of the body through invasive medical technologies. The disempowering of community groups, and particularly women, through the increasing privatization of the city is represented as another realization of the public/personal distinction according to which narrative and city spaces available to marginalized groups to engage in collective political/aesthetic change are both severely constricted and paranoically policed: 'I feel stuck in the alien world of the personal. Woman's world. I have a map of it.'

The Harbour Breathes' aesthetic investments in representational practices and place, and its feminist politics' desire to redefine the significance of the 'personal' in terms of women's desires for political change, are also addressed in the poem 'The Decade, The Street'. Desire here is not defined in phallocentric terms of lack but as a type of expanding and uncontainable temporality of feeling, the excess of cumulative investments of memory and experience over time imbuing place with a special significance:

> a feeling
> a feeling of the fullness of decades
> the multiplication of experiences, connections
> getting fuller, can't be contained.

But the text's representations of the street through images of intimate familiarity in which feelings are embodied and given aesthetic significance through the landscape and its architecture are followed by the final lines:

> football crowds suddenly stream down the street from the station
> for them, the streets are hard, for walking on
> everything's like an action diagram
> man gets ball, man runs with ball
> he is strong, I cower before him.

Ideas of the street as a site of sexual politics where women's struggle to (re)claim public spaces intersects with their desire for aesthetic space (the 'not just "for walking on" street') form a major part of the significance of *The Harbour Breathes* and are produced through its insistence on examining the implied Anglo feminist slogan 'the personal is the political' in terms of other, subsumed race and cultural differences. Hence, when the text asks: 'Is my city your city, and the city your body like it's my body' it signifies more than either the expression of the narrator's intimate familiarity with the city or ideas of the city as organic. The body here also represents other types of knowledge—neither neutral/ized nor timeless personal/political/aesthetic investments and interventions in public cultural spaces, whether those spaces are categorized as History, the Future, the Nation, Narrative, Poetry, or as Sydney, the main focus of the 1988 'Celebration of a Nation' and a major site of 'official bicentennial self-congratulation' (Arthur 1991). But, as *The Harbour Breathes* recognizes, ideas of the city as a fragmented site of discursive contestation and potential social and aesthetic change need to be specified (whose city?) to take into account the ways sexual politics intersect with class, race and cultural differences in the production of social agents and their narratives. Examining the material production of subjectivity in these terms is an important way of critiquing and changing the ways in which 'ethnic identity' is discursively produced as an essentialist category—through which others' experiences of and desires to negotiate their temporal dislocation and fragmented subjectivity in terms of the dominant culture are commonly perceived as disruptive, unstable, shifty and opportunistic (the sinister chameleon) and prevented, as Trinh puts it, 'from infecting us' (Trinh 1989:52).

References

Arthur, K.O. (1991) 'Recasting History: Australian Bicentennial Writing', *Journal of Narrative Technique*, vol. 21 no.1, Winter, pp. 52–59.

Couani, A. & Lyssiotis, P. (1989) *The Harbour Breathes*, Sea Cruise Books and Masterthief Enterprises, Sydney and Melbourne.

Cranny-Francis, A. (1992) *Engendered Fiction*, University of New South Wales Press, Sydney.

Dessaix, R. (1991) 'Nice Work If You Can Get It', *Australian Book Review*, Feb/March, no. 128, pp. 22–28.

Docker, J. (1991) 'The Temperament of Editors and a New Multicultural Orthodoxy', *Island*, 8, Spring, pp. 50–55.

Gunew, S. (1991a) 'Response', *Australian Book Review*, no.29, April, pp. 6–7.

——(1991b) 'Against Multiculturalism: Rhetorical Images', *Typereader* 7, Centre for Studies in Literary Education, Deakin University, Melbourne, pp. 28–43.

——(1990) 'PostModern Tensions: Reading for (Multi)Cultural Difference' *Meanjin*, vol. 9, no. 1, Autumn, pp. 21–33.

Hage, G. (1991) 'Racism, Multiculturalism and the Gulf War' *Arena*, 96, Spring.

142   FEMINISM AND THE POLITICS OF DIFFERENCE

Hatzimanolis, E. (1990) 'The Politics of Nostalgia: Community and Difference in Migrant Writing', *Hecate*, vol. 16, nos 1/2, pp. 120–127.
——(1992) 'Forum: Victims and Victimisers', in *Typereader* 7, Centre for Studies in Literary Education, Deakin University, Melbourne, pp. 24–25.
Kimball, R. (1991) 'Multiculturalism and the American University', reprinted in *Quadrant*, July–August, pp. 22–31.
Lewitt, M. (1991) Letter, *Australian Book Review*, no.129, April, p. 8.
Morris, M. (1991) 'White Panic or Max and the Sublime (The "Costs" of Multiculturalism)', The Mari Kuttna Lecture on Film delivered September 17, University of Sydney (unpublished).
Office for Multicultural Affairs (1989) *The People of Australia: Sharing Our Future—A Special Report*.
O'Reilly, T.D. (1989) 'Alienation: Embracing the Destroyer', *Quadrant*, May.
Parekh, B. (1989) 'Identities on Parade: A Conversation,' *Marxism Today*, June.
Schama, S. (1991) 'No Future For History Without Its Stories', *The Sydney Morning Herald* , November 18, p. 13.
Taylor, J. (1991) 'Up Against The New McCarthyism', *The Sydney Morning Herald*, April 2, p. 13.
Trinh T. Minh-ha (1989) *Woman, Native, Other*, Indiana University Press, Bloomington.

9 Of black angels and melancholy lovers: Ethnicity and writing in Canada

Smaro Kamboureli

A word without destiny, an unpronounceable name was the floral ornament of our page. (Edmond Jabès)

The story always begins long ago. It is already old by the time we try to tell it. It is older than its teller, older than the silence it dissolves, older than the language it is spoken through. As American writer Trinh Minh-ha says, 'the story never really begins or ends, even though there is a beginning and an end to every story' (Trinh 1989:2). It may be built on difference, but it remains relentlessly vigilant as to where it comes from: the recesses of the self.

There is no apocalypse in this story, only a subtle recognition, often nothing more than a gnawing feeling, a gut instinct, that what we encounter in the story is dangerously familiar, or, as the case may be, soothingly pleasing. We live by a series of encounters—with friends, lovers, books, places—but every encounter, as Jacques Derrida says, is 'separation,' a 'contradiction of logic' (Derrida 1978:74) in that it signals an encounter with something other than ourselves, a long-felt absence, that element of difference that breaks the illusory unity of the self. For the story—and this is why I am shying away from the plural—is always already about the foreigner in ourselves.

This foreigner is a black angel: black because the message she delivers is a cipher, a message veiled by layers and layers of deferred meaning. Most of the time we don't bother taking a peek at what lies behind this veil. We would be content if that otherness inside us were to remain silenced, forever furled up neatly. For when this angel surfaces, she bears, more often than not, unsettling news; and we bruise her by burying her even more deeply inside

143

the self. The black angel, then, takes the shape of exiled speech. This is where the adventure of the story begins. The story as 'weed, as outlaw' (Kristeva 1991:67); the story as that absence—bruised memories—marking the distance of the wandering foreigners that we are, unbeknown to ourselves. But when the story is written, the black angel is lost by being pronounced. She flies away, she disappears, leaving inside us a secret wound, the seed of nostalgia. And we spend our lives pining after that stranger, desiring what we have worked so hard to exorcise. It is this stifling of the other's voice inside us, this negation of our condition as foreigners, that initiates the frenzy with which we set out towards language.

It is, perhaps, this incessant search for the foreigner we exile from within the self that incites us to frame the foreigners outside ourselves with a vengeance. And this is also, perhaps, why we become foreigners ourselves. As Julia Kristeva says, we 'recognize that one becomes a foreigner in another country because one is already a foreigner from within' (Kristeva 1991:14). We seek to avenge that black angel, to reverse the process of visitation, to make amends, to disentangle the mysteries of humanity. Some of us begin and end this series of displacements as tourists; we come and go, we dare to be adventurous, secure in our knowledge of origin. Our departures and arrivals share the same home base. And we must be prepared to know how to handle our bodies under the rule of a foreign text. The tourist, in her watchfulness, must revise herself, confront her own exiled demon. If she's lucky, she will hear among the strange voices around her the purloined speech of the black angel, that harbinger of her own otherness, of her barbarism. She has to practise the sophistication her own culture affords her. And she must have stories to tell upon her return. As Trinh says, stories circulate like gifts (Trinh 1989:2).

When Homer invented the word *barbaraphone*, he had in mind those wandering non-Greeks who fought alongside the Greek army in Asia Minor, who swarmed into the Greek city-states. As Kristeva says, he 'seems to have coined the term on the basis of such onomatopoeia as *bla-bla, barabara,* inarticulate or incomprehensible mumblings. As late as the fifth century, the term is applied to *both Greeks and non-Greeks* having a slow, thick, or improper speech' (Kristeva 1991:51). Strabo, a historian and geographer of the seventh century BC, wrote that 'the barbarians are all those whose pronunciation is clumsy and coarse' (Strabo cited in Kristeva ibid.). This clumsiness, these infelicities of language that make us all barbarians mark, however, a momentary condition. The tourist reserves the right to come and go as she pleases: she can cease to be a barbarian in a foreign land; she can always go back home. In doing so, the tourist can retrace her meandering route on the white pages of the story waiting to be told. She professes the prerogative of the self to declare itself its sovereign source, to configure her as the source of language. The result is a kind of story that speaks not of the barbarians we become away from home, but of the otherness we import upon our return home. When we translate into our mother tongue the foreign images we appropriate as tourists, we see the story of the self run amok, for it asserts itself as being independent of all foundations while claiming to be the origin and law of everything. This kind of story often reeks of appropriation. 'Foreigners,' Kristeva tells us, 'could recover their identities only if they recognized themselves as dependent on a same heterogeneity that divides them within themselves, on a same wandering flesh and spirit' (Kristeva 1991:82). In other words, in the stories we tell of others, we might find inscribed the castaway voice of the black angel.

But there is also another kind of foreigner, another kind of barbarian, who moves so far from her origin that she has no home to go back to: she then becomes a stranger to her mother (country). This foreigner does not travel with a camera hung around her neck. She doesn't have to revise herself. Instead, she must reinvent herself. I'm talking about those foreigners we have come by a twist of syntax to call ethnics. All it takes is changing the position of the word *ethnic* from that of adjective to that of noun. We all have ethnic origins, but only she is an ethnic. Sometimes called members of minority groups, or immigrants, or migrants, ethnics are condemned, or blessedly allowed, depending on one's point of view, never to lose their barbarity. They are 'never completely true nor completely false' (Kristeva 1991:8). They become the supplement to our Canadian culture, the excess element to our otherwise bland identity. In other words, they are very useful. We need their foreignness to measure our own otherness. The ethnic as an other to us determines, tests, the economy of our tolerance, the subtleties of our speech, the elasticity of Canadian identity.

When multiculturalism was introduced as an official federal policy in 1971, it was offered as an acknowledgment of otherness, a celebration of plenitude. More than that, however, it was meant to frame otherness inside the two official languages and so-called heritage groups. In asserting that cultural and linguistic diversity was an integral part of Canadian society, multiculturalism disclosed the master narrative of Canadian identity to be a myth, and began grafting onto it, albeit in an overdetermined fashion, the politics of Canada's cultural disparity. From the illusory cer-

tainties of modernism, then, to the indeterminacies of postmodernism. From two solitudes to many.

The decentred Canadian subjectivity conjured up by
postmodernism, however, did not eliminate the marginal position
of what was thought to be foreign to Canadian identity. By
legislating on otherness, by legitimizing the foreign, by assimilating
barbarism in the guise of cosmopolitanism, multiculturalism
became a host to the virus of appropriation, posited itself as that
kind of postmodernism that retreats from the political 'through
pastiche and schizophrenia' (Gunew 1990:22).

Thou shalt be ethnic, our legislators say; thou shalt honour
thy mother tongue; thou shalt celebrate thy difference in folk
festivals; and thou shalt receive monies to write about thy difference (providing thou art a member of an ethnic organization that
sponsors thy application). And we have responded to that call,
ethnics and non-ethnics alike; we have responded by discovering
that difference is sexy.

Yet the story of multiculturalism, like any other story, began
long before it reached the House of Commons, long before the
secretary of State allocated funds to the promotion of ethnic
programs, long before ethnic writers discovered the aesthetics and
marketability of their ethnicity. Before it begins functioning as a
corrective gesture, multiculturalism operates as an affirmation of
the strategies of marginalization. Multiculturalism pre-empts any
attempt the foreigner might make at ceasing to be a foreigner. It
appeases racial and cultural discrimination, but it does so by
segregating difference. It recognizes only the difference it itself
elicits. Yes, it wants ethnics to be domesticated, but it wants them
domesticated as ethnics. In this country, the ethnic has privileges
only insofar as she remains ethnic.

Even though my foreignness is inscribed in my name, even
though my speech bears the signs of my own barbarism, I have,
with a great sense of intent, and, I should add, irony, assumed,
so far, a position of comfort: I've approached my topic by taking
the normative position to this other. This positioning is in itself
a paradoxical gesture, for it speaks of a postmodernism that
articulates the 'provisional and fragile construction' (Gunew
1990:22) of minority identity. By bracketing my ethnicity, while
still speaking in an accented voice, I wish to articulate the hybrid
position of an ethnic who, without seeking to abscond from her
origins, seeks to blend together the foreign within and the foreign
outside. The displacement of an immigrant does not necessarily
have to be a negative experience. It becomes that only when the
immigrant considers herself to be a kind of tourist in the host
country, only when she longs for a past whose conditions were

what sent her away from home in the first place. Displacement, after all, is not the prerogative of ethnics alone. As Mark Krupnick says, displacement 'sums up the spirit of the present age' (Krupnick 1987:3–4); it is 'a constant' in contemporary experience, 'the one certitude you can count on amidst the dissemination that unsettles everything' (Krupnick 1987:4). Displacement is potentially an enabling condition, for it mediates the immigrant's new life as she crosses over from familiar territory to an unfamiliar mode of existence. We are, then, all 'strangers to ourselves' (Kristeva 1991). Our otherness is irreducible, for it speaks of our indefinite incompleteness as humans.

When this kind of stranger is a storyteller, when this storyteller longs for the cultural and geographical origins of the self, she more often than not configures her foreignness in the shape of a melancholy lover. The foreigner exists, survives within her, precisely because she falls in love with her estrangement, falls into that geographical, cultural, and linguistic gap that separates her from her origins. Her melancholy is the outcome of her nostalgia for the homeland, the abandoned family, the trunk of memories she left behind. She locates her marginalization and her power as ethnic writer in that same history of relations that has blackened her black angel. And if her melancholy, sponsored as it is by multiculturalism, is shaped in the established mode of realism, if it speaks of ethnicity in the ways in which ethnicity has been so far understood, then she might be lucky enough to reap the results of literary success.

It rarely happens that a book by a Canadian author other than Margaret Atwood, Robertson Davies or Alice Munro makes the Canadian bestseller list. But recently, Nino Ricci's novel *Lives of the Saints* found a place for five weeks at the top of that list. And even more recently Rohinton Mistry's novel *Such a Long Journey*, nominated for the coveted Booker Prize in Great Britain, also made that list. *Lives of the Saints*, a first novel, won the Governor-General's Award in 1990, and Mistry's novel, also a first novel, was the winner in 1991.

What is the secret of these novels' immediate success, so rarely granted to first books, especially to first books by so-called ethnic authors? One can only speculate. Without intending to diminish or doubt the success of these novels, I would like to argue that one of the main reasons for the high profile these books have achieved is the fact that, seen within the context in which they were published and within which their authors live, they assert the image of the foreign. *Lives of the Saints* takes place exclusively in Italy, with only its last few pages set in Canada. In it, we read of invisible characters who emigrated to Canada, presumably the setting of the novels that will complete the trilogy Ricci plans to write. The journey in *Such a Long Journey* takes place in India, with Canada referred to only through a minor character who contemplates immigration. Both novels thematize not the foreignness of ethnics in Canada but the concept of the foreign itself imaged *as* Canada. This reversal, however, is not without consequences. By writing about their origins without contaminating them with any elements of Canadianness, by importing otherness into Canadian literature as otherness, Ricci and Mistry exemplify the expectations multiculturalism has generated from ethnic writing. Paradoxically, although their novels are examples of traditional realism, the authors exemplify ideologically the postmodern condition of the Canadian ethnic writer: they inscribe the image of the foreign in foreign terms.

But how does an ethnic text embody its difference: How do we author ourselves as melancholy lovers?

Lives of the Saints is told from the point of view of Vittorio, whose mother, Christina, is the protagonist of the novel. Although at the time of the story's telling Vittorio is a mature man, the perspective he assumes as narrator is that of a child; he thus endows the novel with a certain kind of innocence, wonderment and superstition that are the keys to the story. The story begins on a hot July day in 1960. But the 1960s that we see depicted in this novel have nothing in common with the frenzy of sexual liberation, drugs, and human rights and anti-war movements of the 1960s in North America. Instead, we delve into a past that is exotic to the North American reader by virtue of the superstitiousness of the Italian village where the novel's action is set. Although a world that has long lost its innocence, it is offered to the Canadian reader as having almost a pristine charm. This feigned innocence, this primitiveness that we are supposed to understand only as metaphor, is what we often expect from ethnic writing. And Ricci admirably fulfils this expectation.

So the story begins with a 'muffled shout . . . [that] sounded like a man's' (Ricci 1990:10), which young Vittorio hears coming from the direction of the stable. Many pages later, we find out that the man who cried out in the stable upon seeing the snake that bites Christina is Christina's lover. He is, in fact, one of the key characters in the novel, but a character who never quite manifests himself. He is a fascinating instance of character construction: he exists by virtue of his absence. He becomes a metonymy, named and defined by a series of signs that are woven in and out of the story.

Originally, he is a pair of blue eyes, and a pair of tinted glasses abandoned in the stable; later on, his presence is indicated by yet another pair of tinted glasses, this time found on the ground of the cave where young Vittorio is taken by Christina for a swim; he is also evoked metonymically, longingly, by Christina's naked body, its nakedness speaking of her secret assignations with that absent lover in this very cave; his presence is also intimated by the letter Christina receives, a letter young Vittorio knows not to be written in his father's 'violent scribble' (Ricci 1990:8). The father, by the way, is also absent as an emigrant to Canada. This blue-eyed lover who keeps losing his glasses (another sign of his flawed, uncertain vision) also appears in the idle but often malicious gossip of the villagers about Christina. The nameless, faceless man is fated to remain forever the other. His foreignness is further reinforced by the fact that he is indeed a foreigner; he is a German, a former soldier. He is forced to lead a clandestine life because the village has carefully insulated itself from any intrusions by the foreign.

Young Vittorio tries on the tinted glasses that he finds: he bends their thin wire arms tightly around his ears and stares into his mother's mirror. What he sees there is 'a strange figure' (Ricci 1990:32). Vittorio, who by the end of the novel will arrive in Canada, is fascinated by the tinted world these glasses reveal to him: the 'glasses . . . showed a world, when I stared out through them from my mother's balcony, that was tinted a heady bluish-green' (Ricci 1990:33). This new vision is at once one of revelation and concealment: it distorts reality at the same time that it manifests a reality of another order. The glasses reveal to him the process of estrangement, so necessary to the formation of the self.

In keeping with the temptation to submerge the black angel inside us, young Vittorio hides the glasses under his mattress, only to find them shattered against the bedsprings the following morning. Then he goes out to the pasture, digs a hole, and buries the remains of the glasses (Ricci 1990:34). This burial, Vittorio concealing a secret he barely comprehends himself, authors the dissimulation the foreign subject is bound to undergo if it is to enter a process of otherment, of transformation from the strange to the familiar.

It is no coincidence that Christina is the only one in the village to welcome, in fact embrace, the otherness her German lover embodies. She is an other herself, as she does not fit the familiar image of motherhood in the village. 'Mothers in Valle del Sole', Vittorio tells us, 'formed a class: ruddy, swollen hands, thick skirts of homespun wool, hair short and tucked under a kerchief, round bellies protected with aprons of burlap or grey linen, like sacks of wheat. They moved with a slow, elephantine gait, arms akimbo, all the movement coming from the hips' (Ricci 1990:8–9). In

contrast, Christina has a slim, sleek figure; she speaks better
Italian than the other women in the village; she doesn't drag her
son out into the fields at the crack of dawn as the other mothers
do; and she doesn't share the villagers' superstitions. When the
village begins to shun Christina, she 'withdraw[s] into a shadowy
silence . . . the passing days brought only a growing awkwardness,
as if my mother and I had suddenly become strangers, with no
words now to bridge the silence between us' (Ricci 1990:74). What
the villagers cannot abide in Christina is what they have buried
deep inside themselves: her defiance, her silence, speaks the voice
of the foreigner who is within all. Against all odds, against the
villagers' common sense, Christina lets her black angel author her
future.

She becomes a melancholy lover, desiring absence. When, after
a series of events, she boards a boat with Vittorio to emigrate to
Canada, she leaves her silence behind in Valle del Sole. On board,
at sea, she releases her otherness into articulation. On our side of
the Atlantic, Christina intends to meet the black angel of love—not
her abusive husband, but her blue-eyed lover.

This lover and foreigner, absent but surreptitiously present, is
emblematic, I think, of the condition of the ethnic. He exists by
effacing himself. Ricci shows in this novel how the foreign beckons
us but also how it can take the form of a taunting image, the
seductive promise of a dream. Christina dies in childbirth. The
blue-eyed lover, the father of Vittorio's baby sister, appears one
last time at the end of the novel, as one of the two visitors Vittorio
sees while lying sick in a Canadian hospital. 'I had seen him only
once before, and then only fleetingly, but his eyes, blue flames,
had burned themselves into my memory then, and I recognized
him at once when he came to stand over my bed . . . But I was
only just coming out of the delirium of my fever then; and
afterwards I could not say for certain whether he had actually
stood over me, or whether I had merely imagined him' (Ricci
1990:233-234). When the blue-eyed lover appears in Canada,
whether in flesh or in dream, he is no longer the foreigner he was
before. Paradoxically, Vittorio recognizes the image of the foreign
in the figure of someone else: his second visitor at the hospital is
'a stranger who was my father' (Ricci 1990:234). It is this man,
this familiar stranger, who walks away from the hospital with
Vittorio and with Christina's baby in his arms.

Lives of the Saints, feigning to be ethnic discourse, feigning a
certain innocence, feigning to be in the margins as ethnic literature, reveals the centre of the self to be a gaping hole. Although
the novel has virtually nothing to do with Canada, although its
author is Canadian-born, *Lives of the Saints* succeeds in reinscrib-

ing the signature of ethnicity, but it does so by addressing the strangers we are within rather than the foreigners we become in a strange country. It is a narrative that pretends that the self exists in and for itself, that identity is independent of ideology. It is not a coincidence, then, that its most interesting character, Christina, dies without again embracing her absent lover, and before she becomes a foreigner in Canada.

It takes, I think, a much more daring imagination to deconstruct multiculturalism's singular vision of ethnicity. Ven Begamudré accomplishes this, and more, in his recent collection of short stories, *A Planet of Eccentrics*. The title is apt not only because many of the characters are indeed eccentric, but because almost all of them occupy ek-centric positions; they are, in other words, off centre. Their off-centredness, however, is not to be confused with marginality. Begamudré shows us that marginality—like gender, like femininity, like ethnicity—is a sociocultural construct, a 'system of representation', as Teresa de Lauretis would say, 'which assigns meaning (identity, value, prestige, location in kinship, status in the social hierarchy, etc.) to individuals within society' (de Lauretis 1987:5). He demonstrates that the meaning of the centre is differential, which suggests that the representation of ethnicity is its construction, that the ethnic is at once 'the product and the process of its representation' (de Lauretis 1987:5).

There is an abundance of what I call melancholy lovers in *A Planet of Eccentrics*. The stories in which they appear display a desire, a respect, for the unknown, thus acknowledging, surreptitiously, the spectre of black angels haunting these characters' lives. Behind the various forms in which the stories are written, behind the complex clarity of the narrating voices, behind the blending of garden and city, India and Canada, Regina and Victoria—'one queenly city for another' (Begamudré 1990:58)—there is Begamudré's constant reminder that the paradigm of human consciousness falls under the shadow of the paradigm of language; that representation—the way we present ourselves, the way we arrange characters on the page—is a performative act, an act of speech; that our struggles, the ethnics' struggles, in everyday life are nothing but 'an agonistics of language'. As Jean-François Lyotard said once, 'to speak is to fight, in the sense of playing—in the sense of having to disclose ourselves to ourselves, of having to re-create ourselves for others. Through words. Through storytelling'. (Lyotard 1984:10)

This is what happens in 'Mosaic,' one of the stories in *A Planet of Eccentrics*. Ramesh, the protagonist of this story, remains absent in an equivocal way. Although he is the central focus of all seven narrators in the story, Ramesh never speaks directly himself. His voice reaches the reader only from within quotation marks, as it is quoted by, among others, a bank teller, a cashier in a cheap restaurant, the male manager in the office who has just fired him, an Indian friend of his, and a prostitute. Through the mosaic of these voices, Ramesh is imaged as the ethnic *par excellence*. Although he speaks English impeccably and with a 'cute accent' (Begamudré 1990:110), dresses in fine clothes, and has a very good education, he doesn't fit in. He loses his job; he gets beaten up by a pimp.

Unlike the blue-eyed lover in *Lives of the Saints* who walks away in the end of the novel after he is perceived as a familiar figure, Ramesh never becomes domesticated. He cannot embody the foreign within him, because he chooses to remain a foreigner himself. He is the ethnic as envisaged by multiculturalism. He is well-bred but with a sophistication that always misses the point. He is not a character in search of a story because he has already essentialized his identity as being that of an ethnic. That is why he is the object of the narratives of others, never the subject of his own discourse. He is the product of the multicultural 'mosaic', therefore invisible. He is a character exiled in the story that contains him.

Indeed, Ramesh cannot abide the idea that he might become someone other than ethnic. When his only close friend, an assimilated Indian, advises him to go back to India after he loses his job, he declines to do so with a vehemence that shows his ethnicity to be synonymous with eccentricity: 'Go home and leave Canada to people like you? People who turn their backs on their ancestry? I will not go home.' (Begamudré 1990:123). Ramesh's claim on Canada ironically expresses his certainty that Canada ought to be a host to difference. Canada, Ramesh has learned by parroting the script of multiculturalism, needs its ethnics as much as they need it. He stays in Canada out of ethnic pride because he wants to 'show' the people at home. 'If I go back,' he muses loudly, 'people will ask me how much I am making as a foreign-returned officer. You know how they talk. They are crazy for coming to Canada or the US, any place to get away from the corruption. But I will know I did not return to earn a higher salary than my classmates. I will know I fled this place . . . I will remain in Canada. I will remain in Saskatchewan. I will remain in Regina' (Begamudré 1990:123). Not only does Ramesh reside in a Canada that is largely of his own making, but the resilience with which he survives is ill-conceived. Ramesh remains oblivious to the fact that in wanting to prove himself to the Indians of India, he proves his desire to flee from them; that by staying in Canada he further dislodges his self within himself.

In his feeble and reluctant attempts to understand the culture that envelops him, Ramesh engages himself in a process of misappropriation and mistranslation. He misinterprets, for example, a statement he overhears while standing in line in a bank: 'Can you help me out here?' (Begamudré 1990:110), a man in cowboy boots asks, pleading for help with the deposit slips. Ramesh doesn't respond; instead, he turns his back on him. The silence of his apostrophe speaks of the foreigner that he is but also of the way in which he drowns the other inside him. 'We have people like that in India,' he says to the bank teller, meaning beggars; 'they are called scheduled castes. They used to be called outcastes, but one cannot call them that any more . . . it would be discrimination . . . So now the government discriminates against good students by lowering pass marks in college so these people will get degrees. It results in mediocrity only, not equality' (Begamudré 1990:110–111). The problem is not his misunderstanding of what he hears but rather the blind confidence with which he misreads the social codes of Canada: he doesn't entertain the possibility that Canada's cultural text might not be written in Indian script; nor does he realize that in criticizing India's policies toward equality he condones his own victimization in Canada. When he is asked by the bank teller what caste he is, he is surprised: 'Is it not obvious? We are brahmins. We are lighter skinned than most South Indians . . . That fellow had no business calling me a black man' (Begamudré 1990:111). The painful irony here is that he responds to the racial slur against him by being racist and classist himself. His audacious temerity embodies a monolithic vision of his self, a vision undermined by the mosaic of contradictory voices that reconstruct his experiences in the story.

Ramesh, solipsistic in his ethnicity, not a 'team player' (Begamudré 1990:117) but 'all clean hands and genteel' (Begamudré 1990:113), is the ethnic as reader who reads by misreading because he insists that everything is readable. This is why he does not bother to read Canadian newspapers. Instead, he reads the *India–Canada Times*, an ethnic newspaper, thus invariably affirming the foreignness of his ethnicity. And he also reads—but just for the articles, he assures his friend—*Penthouse* and *Playboy*. Yet he fails as the reader of his own desires, too. When Ramesh goes to a prostitute one night, he doesn't like what he sees. As the prostitute herself says, he just 'squeezes my tit, and I look up to see him staring at me like I've hit him in the balls. He practically whines, "it is so soft. It should be firm." So I tell him, "You want melons, there's a Safeway other side of Broad" ' (Begamudré 1990:126). Ramesh, who decides to call the prostitute by the name of the secretary at his office—yet another example of misplaced and misdirected desire—rejects the prostitute because her body does not fit the pornographic depictions of the male gaze. She is too real to be desirable; too unromantic to satisfy his melancholy yearnings.

Ultimately, Ramesh is betrayed by his decorum, by his adherence to the image of ethnicity. The foreign both attracts and repels him. He covets the foreign only insofar as it might distinguish him among his own people in India. He remains unabashedly blind to the stranger that he is to himself because he prevails in Canada as that kind of tourist who neglects to revise himself, the foreigner as non-reader. He is a melancholy lover. He has forgotten how to love because he has completely shunned his own otherness. To love, for him, is neither a transitive verb nor an act of self-reflexivity. It expresses the image of the ethnic self as cultural icon.

But if Ramesh fails to author himself because of his self-imposed displacement, because he reifies his marginality, Thittu, the central character in 'Vishnu's Navel', exceeds his marginality despite his inarticulation and miserable existence. In this story, set in India, Thittu is mistaken for an idiot because he 'refuse[s] to respond [to the calling of his relatives] with anything but grunts or single words delivered hoarsely' (Begamudré 1990:10). Not a beggar, but mistaken for one, he makes his home in a bird sanctuary; not only does he learn to speak the birds' language, but he also, 'though employed by no one to do so', greets 'visitors with the mating dance of the peafowl'. He approaches the guests with 'mincing steps, then hop[s] from foot to foot', all the while making 'loud shrieks, imitations of the peafowl's warning call' (Begamudré 1990:11). This bird-like man, residing on the margins of society, on the margins of sanity, becomes an allegory of the act of representation. He is so good at imitating the calls of the most exotic of birds that he causes a cleft, a fissure between articulation and voice. In doing so, he demonstrates that mimesis—held so dear by our Western tradition, practised faithfully by Ramesh—is meaningless; he shows that meaning is dislodged when denied a context. No one pays attention to Thittu, except for a 'foreign watcher of birds' who one day point[s] a strange camera at Thittu' (Begamudré 1990:12) and gives him a Polaroid picture of himself. 'Heh, heh,' Thittu exclaims, 'click, click.' It is no coincidence that it takes a foreigner to show Thittu his own image. This Polaroid portrait, together with Thittu's response to it, reveals the 'technologies of the self' (Foucault 1988:16); it exposes the failure of mimesis as representation, and initiates a process—'Heh heh, click click'—by which Thittu is going to attain a certain happiness, a purity of soul, the very things that Ramesh lacks in his life. 'Over time the colours faded until [the photograph] became a pale yellow shadow. [Thittu] decided this happened because he had kept it; that it would have remained true to life only if the visitor had taken it away' (Begamudré 1990:12). Although threatened by his fading image, Thittu, unlike Narcissus, is not enamoured of himself: Begamudré subtly lays bare the fictionality of the Western concept of selfhood. Although homeless and socially displaced, Thittu proves that the kind of eccentricity privileged by Ramesh is yet another fiction. Thittu intuits that a solid, stable image of the self is untenable. 'Unable to bear the sight of his self fading, Thittu buried the photo near his hut. But even as he grew past manhood toward old age, so did his fear' (Begamudré 1990:12). Thittu buries away the only documentation he has of his existence. Yet his fear (fear of the lapidary self produced by the technology of construction) is what, strangely enough, keeps him free.

Thittu becomes a racket-tailed drongo, a night prowler, a shama, any bird that might attract the attention of tourists with cameras. 'If they took his photo, a memory of him would lie in their house, and he would never grow invisible' (Begamudré 1990:13). Thittu renders himself invisible by destroying the evidence of his visibility, but at the same time he wants to ensure that he remain visible. This infraction of strategies, this breach of logic sums up, I believe, the process of translation to which the ethnic subject has to surrender. Like the materiality of words which cannot be translated or carried over to another language (Derrida 1978:210), the materiality of the ethnic self, the materiality of what resides in the margins, must be relinquished in order to survive. True to the spirit of tourism, the tourists carry their cameras—'Heh heh, click click'—but no one takes Thittu's photograph again. Thitthu, caught as he is between nature (the birds) and culture (the tourists' cameras), dies a cruel death, but he is reincarnated as the bird of his choice: a crow whose cawing no one can ignore. Thittu, by becoming one with his black angel, winds up releasing the margin from its marginality.

To exceed the melancholy condition of the ethnic, we must submit our imported certainties to the unreadability of our selves. We must walk hand in hand with the strangers residing inside us. And we must take hold of the differences outside us. Only then can we release ourselves from the history of our relations and begin to write anew our stories. As long as we let multiculturalism codify ethnicity, our stories will simply endure as icons. Only when multiculturalism becomes a circuit of exchange will storytelling become circulation. Only then will our stories become the gifts they ought to be.

Note

This paper was presented as the third annual Caroline Health Lecture at the Saskatchewan Writers' Guild 1991 Annual General Meeting. It was first published in *Freelance* xxi, 5, Dec. 1991/Jan. 1992.

References

Begamudré, Ven (1990) *A Planet of Eccentrics*, Oolichan, Lantzville, B.C..
de Lauretis, Teresa (1987) *Technologies of Gender: Essays on Theory, Film, and Fiction*, Indiana University Press, Bloomington.
Derrida, Jacques (1978) *Writing and Difference*, trans. Alan Bass, University of Chicago Press, Chicago.
Foucault, Michel (1988) *Technologies of the Self*, ed. Luther H. Martin, Huck Gutman, & Patrick H. Hutton, University of Massachusetts Press, Amherst.
Gunew, Sneja (1990) 'Postmodern Tensions: Reading for (Multi) Cultural Difference', *Meanjin* 9, 1:21–33.
Kristeva, Julia (1991) *Strangers to Ourselves*, trans. Leon S. Roudiez, Columbia University Press, New York.
Krupnick, Mark (1987) 'Introduction', in *Displacement: Derrida and After*, ed. Krupnick, Indiana University Press, Bloomington.
Lyotard, Jean-François (1984) *The Postmodern Condition: A Report on Knowledge*. Trans. Geoff Bennington and Brian Massumi. Foreword by Frederic Jameson, University of Minnesota Press, Minneapolis.
Ricci, Nino (1990) *Lives of the Saints*, Cormorant, Dunvegan, Ontario.
Trinh, T. Minh-ha (1989) *Woman Native Other*, Indiana University Press, Bloomington.

10 All-owning spectatorship
Trinh T. Minh-ha

Of late, a friend's mother died. One day the family chanced to eat steamed sorghum, which was of a reddish color. A local pedant felt that while in mourning it was inappropriate to have a meal with the main course in so gay a color, so he took up this point with them, pointing out that red was always indicative of happy events, such as weddings. The friend replied: 'Well, I suppose all those people eating white rice every day are doing so because they are in mourning!' (Wit and Humor 1986:1) In classical Chinese humour, a position of indirectness is assumed; a reaction to social conditions is woven into the fabric of an anecdote; a laugh momentarily releases demonstration from its demonstrative attribute. In the world of Western film production, some would call such an opening a 'directorial trick', highly valued among feature-film makers. Others would mumble 'clumsy dramatic devices', 'poor exposition', 'muddy connectives', 'lack of clear thought'. Public opinion usually prefers immediate communication, for quantified exchange dominates in a world of reification. To have knowledge, more and more knowledge, often takes precedence over knowing. The creed constantly reads: if one has nothing, one is nothing.

A mother died. What holds the reader? What motivates the story and generates the action? A reddish colour; a family's attempt; a local pedant; a 'steamed' meal; people's white rice . . . in mourning. Red is the colour of life. Its hue is that of blood, of the ruby, of the rose. And when the world sees red, white could become the international colour of mourning. Conventionally a bridal colour in many Western societies, white is indeed the funeral colour in numerous African and Asian cultures. Passionate reds and pinks also populate the joyful decor of weddings, but they cut across the borderlines of both Western and Eastern cultural traditions. Even the bride is clad in red in the latter part of the world. Whoever has taken a stroll in Chinatown on Chinese New Year's days cannot have missed the sight of doorways vividly adorned with red scrolls and of streets thickly coated with the red refuse of firecrackers. Children are accordingly greeted with red envelopes with lucky banknotes inside and words of luck, prosperity and happiness on the outside. The return of spring is celebrated as a renewal of life, growth and emancipation. After days of intense preparation, women are allowed to enjoy five days of idleness when, to preserve good luck, they are spared the drudgery of cooking, washing and sweeping (since during this period, all such drudgery means throwing away the happy fortune). At once an unlimited and profoundly subjective colour, red can physiologically or psychologically close in as well as open up. It points to both a person's boundless inner voyage and the indeterminate outer burning of the worlds of war. Through centuries, it remains the badge of revolution.

Here is where the earth becomes blue like an orange.[1] To say red, to show red, is already to open up vistas of disagreement. Not only because red conveys different meanings in different contexts, but also because red comes in many hues, saturations and brightnesses, and no two reds are alike. In addition to the varying symbols implied, there is the unavoidable plurality of language. And, since no history can exhaust the meaning of red, such plurality is not a mere matter of a relativist approach to the ever-shifting mores of the individual moment and of cultural diversification; it is inherent in the process of producing meaning; it is a way of life. The symbolism of red lies not simply in the image, but in the radical plurality of meanings. Taking literalness for naturalness seems, indeed, to be as normal as claiming that the sun is white and not red. Thus, should the need for banal concrete examples arise, it could be said that society cannot be experienced as objective and fully constituted in its order, but only as incessantly recomposed of diverging forces wherein the war of interpretations reigns.

Seeing red is a matter of reading. And reading is properly symbolic. In a guide listing the elements of screenwriting, a voice of authority dutifully calls attention to cultural differences and the many ensuing contradictory behaviors of characters in relation to an event; but it further warns: 'If ten viewers can walk away from a film with ten different interpretations, maybe the film was about nothing specific. Perhaps they were looking at the proverbial emperor's new clothes. The marks of the artsy-craftsy film are withholding basic exposition and leaving the viewer confused. The illusion of profundity is not the same as being profound' (Blacker 1986:48). True, in a world where the will to say prevails (a 'good' work is invariably believed to be a work 'that *has* something to say'), the skill at excluding the gaps and cracks that reveal language in its nakedness—its very void—can always be measured, and the criteria for good and bad will always exert their power. The emperor's new clothes are only invoked because the emperor is an emperor. But what if profundity neither makes sense nor constitutes a non-sense? Where, for example, does profundity stand in: 'A, black; E, white; I, red'?[2]

More likely to persist in bordering on both profundity and absurdity, the work of saying in unsaying, or of unsaying in saying again what it has already said and unsaid, seems always uneasily and provocatively fragile. Playing between 'absurdities', anecdotes and decisive analysis, or between non-sense and critical languages, it often runs the risk of being mistaken immediately for a the-sky-is-blue-the-grass-is-green type of work, and can be both condemned and praised within that very reading. It is easy to commit an outrage on those (men) who fulminate against what they call 'those school*boyish* evidences' (referring here to statements in a film whose words are uttered by women's voices), when the work succeeds in luring them into a spectacle that shows neither spectacular beings nor sensational actions; offers neither a personal nor a professional point of view; provides no encased knowledge to the acquisitive mind; and has no single story to tell nor any central message to spread, except the unconcealed one(s) about the spectators themselves as related to each specific context.

The inability to think symbolically or to apprehend language in its symbolic nature is commonly validated as an attribute of 'realistic', clear and accomplished thinking. The cards are readily shifted so as to turn a limit, if not an impoverishment of dominant thinking into a virtue, a legitimate stance in mass communication, therefore a tool for political demagogy to appeal to widely naturalized prejudices. Since clarity is always ideological, and reality always adaptive, such a demand for clear communication often proves to be nothing else but an intolerance for any language other than the one approved by the dominant ideology. At times obscured and at other times blatant, this inability and unwillingness to deal with the unfamiliar, or with a language different from one's own, is in fact a trait that belongs intimately to the man of coercive power. It is a reputable form of colonial discrimination, one in which difference can be admitted only once it is appropriated, that is, when it operates within the Master's sphere of having. Activities that aim at producing a different hearing and a renewed viewing are undifferentiatingly confused with obscurantism and hastily dismissed as sheer incompetency or deficiency. They are often accused of being incoherent, inarticulate, amateurish ('it looks like my *mother*'s first film', says a young to-be-professional male) or, when the initiating source of these activities happens to be both female and 'articulate', of 'intellectualism'—the unvarying target of those for whom thinking (which involves reflection and reexamination) and, moreover, thinking differently within differences, remains a male ability and, justifiably, an unwarranted threat. As the saying goes, He only hears (sees) what He wants to hear (see), and certainly there are none so deaf (blind) as those who don't want to hear (see).

'All the prejudice against intellectuals originates from the narrow-mindedness of small producers,' wrote the *Beijing Review* (1983:115) not long ago to rectify the 'left' mistakes perpetuated from the time of the Cultural Revolution. The moment the female filmmaker opens her mouth, she is immediately asked to show her identification number and to answer the (reluctant) listener in whose name she is speaking. ('Is this a semiological approach?' 'Who taught you?' 'Whose work do you like?' 'What I find badly missing in your talk are the models! Where do we go without models?' 'If it is a deliberate attempt at breaking *the rules*, then I certainly applaud you, but I doubt it is consciously done, and if it is *just a subjective approach* then I don't see where it leads us . . . ') If she relies on names, she finds herself walking in line both with 'the penis-envy' women, and 'the coloured-skin-white-mask' oppressed who blindly praise their oppressor's deeds. If she distrusts names and names no master, she will, whether she likes it or not, be given one or several, depending on the donor's whims ('The film reminds me of Kubelka's *Unsere Afrikareise* and of Chris Marker's *Sans Soleil*'; 'How different are these films from Godard's?'); otherwise, she is bound to face fiery charges of circulating 'schoolboyish evidences'. This type of charge repeats itself endlessly in varying faces. Knowledge is not knowledge until it bears the seal of the Master's approval ('She doesn't really know what she does'). Without the Name, the product is valueless in a society of acquisition. (Thus, after having, for example, taken over the floor during the entire length of a film debate session, where angry reactions were continuously thrown at a woman filmmaker, a number of men approached her individually afterwards to intimate: 'All that is very *cute* . . . and I *commend* you for your effort, but . . . ', 'You can't *have* an answer for every question!')

She is both inarticulate and too articulate. *Although one can*

*speak of intellectuals, one cannot speak of non-intellectuals,
because [they] do not exist . . . There is no human activity from
which every form of intellectual participation can be excluded*
(Gramsci 1988:321). Standardization and sameness in variations
are the unacknowledged agenda of media suppliers and consumers
who, under the banner of 'accessibility', work at levelling out
differences to defend their property, whether this property takes
the form of mercantile monopoly or of political tenure. While the
craving for *accession* to power seems to underlie every intolerance
for alternatives that may expose the totalizing character of their
discourses (whether rightist or leftist), the goal is to render power
sufficiently invisible as to control more efficaciously the widest
number down to the smallest details of existence. ('Self-help' and
'Do-it-yourself' systems are an example.) The literal mind has to
dominate if accessibility is to be equated with efficacy. Literal and
linear readings are thus not simply favoured; they are championed
and validated as the only ones 'accessible' to the wide number, in
all media work, whether documentary or narrative. (Even Francis
Coppola, 'the best of what *we have* in America', is blamed for
emphasizing the visuals at the cost of a good story line.) Mass
production, as Gandhi defined it, is production by the fewest
possible number. The needs (for orderly literal thinking) created
by the few and voiced back in chorus by the many are normalized
to the extent that not only do consumers come to internalize the
suppliers' exploitative rationale, but suppliers more often than not
become the victims of their own practices. 'The greatest error I've
committed in my career is to have once made a film for people
who think,' says a respected Hollywood director (not to name any
names); 'it featured in all the festivals, but never made it at the
box office . . . Don't forget that people in the media are all very
smart and creative, but the audience is invariably simple-minded.'

With such a rationale, the hackneyed question of elitism arises
again, albeit reversed and slightly displaced: who appears more
elitist here? The institutional producer who caters to the needs of
the 'masses' while down- and de-grading their mentality in the
interest of mercantilism (the Master's sphere of having)? Or the
'independent' producer who disturbs while soliciting the audience's
participation in rethinking the conditions of this 'society of the
spectacle', and therefore neither pleases large numbers nor expects
to make it at the box office? My admittedly biased question should
probably remain without answer after all, for in a situation in
which the suppliers are victims of their own supplies, no clear-cut
division operates between makers and consumers. Only the
humanism of the commodity reigns, and the vicious circle, continuously reactivated, provides no response to inquiries such as:

'Is it the media which induce fascination in the masses, or is it
the masses which divert the media into spectacle?' (Baudrillard
1981:105). The media's message may condemn war, violence and
bloodshed, for example, but its language fundamentally operates
as a form of fascination with war; and war scenes persist in
dominating the spectacle. (The only way to represent war or to
speak about it in the language of commodified humanism is to
show war scenes; any form of indirection and of non-literalness
in approaching the subject of war is immediately viewed as a form
of absence of war.) Thus, under the regime of commodities, even
the distinction between institutionalized and independent (or mainstream and alternative) producers becomes problematic; and
within the realm of independent filmmaking, there are nuances to
bring out, there are varied ramifications, and there are crucial
differences.

  If Hollywood films are consistently condemned for their capitalist enterprise and 'apolitical' commitment to film as an
industry, 'political' films (or 'issue films' as Hollywood calls them)
are looked down upon by mainstream feature producers as representative of the unimaginative mediocre's domain: 'Don't apply
the criteria of today's politics in feature films, otherwise they will
all look like PBS products, which are boring as hell!' Whether
political, educational or cultural (if one can momentarily accept
these conventional categories), rational linear–literal communication has been the vehicle of quantified exchange. The imperative
to produce meaning according to established rationales presents
itself repeatedly in the form of moralizing information: every film
made should inform the masses, raise their cultural level, and give
objective, scientific foundation to all explanations of society. *The
revolutionary viewpoint of a movement which thinks it can dominate current history by means of scientific knowledge remains
bourgeois* (Debord 1983:82). Here, there is almost never any
question of challenging rational communication with its normalized filmic codes and prevailing objectivist, deterministic–scientific
discourse; only a relentless unfolding of pros and cons, and of
'facts' delivered with a *sense of urgency*, which present themselves
as liberal but imperative; neutral and value-free; objective or
universal.

> Yesterday's anti-colonialists are trying to humanize today's
> generalized colonialism. They become its watchdogs in the cleverest
> way: by barking at all the after-effects of past inhumanity.
> (Vaneigem 1983:23)

  Red is the colour of life. Nearly all cultures attribute a greater
potency to red than other colours, but red can never be assigned

a unitary character. Giving the impression of 'advancing' toward the viewer rather than receding, it is analyzed as having: 'a great wealth of modulations because it can be widely varied between cold and warm, dull and clear, light and dark, without destroying its character of redness. From demonic, sinister red-orange on black to sweet angelic pink, red can express all intermediate degrees between the infernal and the sublime.' (Itten 1970:86) Thus, whether red radiates luminous warmth or not depends on its contextual placement in relation to other colours. On white it looks dark, while on black it glows; with yellow, it can be intensified to fiery strength. In the costuming and make-up of Vietnamese opera, red symbolizes anger; black, boldness; and white, treachery. In classical Chinese symbolics, red characterizes summer and the south; black, winter and the north; green, the colour of virtue and goodness, represents spring and the east; and white, the colour of war and penalty, stands for fall and the west. The color of life and of revolution may thus remain a transnational sign of warmth and anger, but whether or not it is associated with war, violence and bloodshed—as it unfailingly is in the modern concept of revolution—depends largely on one's praxis of revolution. To think that red is red, no matter whether the red is that of blood or that of a rose, is to forget that there is no red without non-red elements, and no single essential red among reds.

If, in the opening Chinese anecdote, red humoristically incurs the risk of being fixed as a sign 'always indicative of happy events' by 'a local pedant', in Dogon (Mali) cosmology, red is one of the three fundamental colours (with black and white) whose complex symbolism exceeds all linear interpretations and remains inexhaustible. A sign opening constantly onto other signs, it is read in practice with all its signifying subtlety and density. The Dogon myth of the red sorghum tells us, for example, that its grains grew at the time when the pond had become impure, its water having served to wash the corpse of the ancestor Dyongou Serou—the first human dead, also called the 'great mask'. The impurity of death had tainted the pond, and the red colour of the sorghum is a manifestation of this contamination. Red is also the glare of the sun. The latter is associated with putrefaction and death (it rots Dyongou Serou's corpse), although it remains absolutely necessary to agriculture and plants; in other words, to the growth of life.[3] The sun is essentially feminine in Dogon mythology, and its ambivalent character of femininity is asserted here as in many other instances of the culture's symbolics.

Red as the sun is both beneficial and malefic. Women, who are the bearers and givers of life, are also the cyclical producers of 'impurity'. Dogon societies abound with rituals in which 'bad blood'—menstruation, the blood shed at childbirth, the dark blood that clots—is distinguished from the bright healthy blood that flows in the body. The latter, which is evoked when a wife is pregnant ('your body's blood is good'), is also identified with men's semen: it is said to represent the successful, fecund sexual act, while 'bad blood' results from a failure of the couple to reproduce. Yet the bright red flowers of the kapok tree are associated with menstruation and death, and it is from its wood that masks are carved. Women are raised to fear 'the mask with a red eye', for masks are men's domain. He who is angry is said to have 'the red eye', while he whose anger becomes violent has 'the red heart'. However, men are also referred to as 'having their periods' when their blood runs during circumcision or when they carve masks and tint the fibres red. Their words are then 'impure', and women are strictly forbidden to come near them while they carry out these tasks. Paradoxically, to decorate the masks and to tint the fibres amount to nursing the sick; for the white wood and fibres do not look healthy—just like sick people—and to paint and tint them with vivid colours is to 'heal' them.[4]

The reading of red as impurity and death proves appropriate to the eating of red sorghum during mourning in the Chinese anecdote. Should the friend of the dead mother remember this, he or she would have more than one witty answer to give in reply to the pedant. And depending on the context, this friend could also decide whether or not it was at all necessary to resort to another colour for comparison . . . ('Remember' is here adequate, for even without knowledge of Dogon cosmology, the relationship commonly drawn between red and blood evokes meanings that cut across cultural borderlines.) Rich in signification and symbolism, red defies any literal elucidation. Not only do its values vary between one culture and another, but they also proliferate within cultures. The complexities are further multiplied when a reading takes into consideration the question of gender. 'Impurity' is the interval during which the impure subject is feared and alienated for her or his potential to pollute other clean(sed) and clear(ed) subjects. It is also the state in which gender division exerts its power. (Just as women are excluded from the process of tinting the masks, no Dogon man can witness a woman giving birth, nor can he come near her when she has her period. For, like many women from other parts of the world, Dogon women temporarily separate themselves from the community during menstruation, living in confinement—or rather, in differentness—in a dwelling built for that very purpose.)

Many of us working at bringing about change in our lives and in others' in contexts of oppression have looked upon red as a passionate sign of life and have relied on its decisive healing attributes. But as history goes, every time the sign of life is brandished, the sign of death also appears, the latter at times more compelling than the former. This does not mean that red can no longer stand for life, but that everywhere red is affirmed, it im-purifies itself, it necessarily renounces its idealized unitary character, and the war of meanings never ceases between reds and non-reds and among reds themselves. The reading of 'bad blood' and 'good blood' continues to engender savage controversies, for what is at stake in every battle of ideologies are territories and possessions. While in conservative milieux, the heat and anger surrounding the debates are generated from the emblem of red itself ('What can you expect but hostility? You are waving a red rag at a bull!'), in (pseudo-)progressionist milieux they more likely have to do with sanctified territories and reified power. The dogmatic mind proceeds with ready-made formulas which it pounds hard into whoever's ear it can catch. It validates itself through its own network of lawmakers and recruited followers, and constantly seeks to institute itself as an ideological authority. Always ready to oppose obvious forms of power but fundamentally uncritical of its own, it also works at eliminating all differences other than those pre-formulated; and when it speaks, it prescribes. It preaches revolution in the form of commands, in the steeped-in-convention language of linear rationality and clarity. At length, it never fails to speak *for* the masses, *on behalf of* the working class, or *in the name of* 'the American people'.

Nazism and facism were only possible insofar as there could exist within the masses a relatively large section which took on the responsibility for a number of state functions of repression, control, policing, etc. This, I believe, is a crucial characteristic of Nazism; that is, its deep penetration inside the masses and the fact that a part of the power was actually delegated to a specific fringe of the masses . . . You have to bear in mind the way power was delegated, distributed within the very heart of the population . . . It wasn't simply the intensified central power of the military. (Foucault 1989:99–100). Power is at once repulsive *and* intoxicating. Oppositional practices which thrive on binary thinking have always worked at preserving the old dichotomy of oppressor and oppressed, even though it has become more and more difficult today to establish a safe line between the government and the people, or the institution and the individual. When it is a question of desire and power, there are no possible short cuts in dealing with the system of rationality that imprisons the body politic and the people, and regulates their relationship. There are, in other

words, no 'innocent people', no subjects untouched by the play
of power. Although repression cannot simply be denied, its always
duplicative, never original sources cannot be merely pointed at
from a safe articulatory position either. As has been noted, in the
society of the spectacle (where the idea of opposition and the
representation of oppression are themselves commodified), 'the
commodity contemplates itself in a world it has created' (Debord
1967/1983:53).

> A woman viewer: By having the women re-enact the interviews,
> you have defeated your own purpose in the film!
> The woman filmmaker: What is my purpose? What do you think it
> is?
> The viewer, irritated: To show women's power, of course!

Every spectator mediates a text to his or her own reality. To
repeat such a banality in this context is to remember that although
everyone *knows* this, every time an interpretation of a work
implicitly presents itself as a mere (obvious or objective) decoding
of the producer's message, there is an explicit reiteration of the
fetishistic language of the spectacle; in other words, a blind denial
of the mediating subjectivity of the spectator as subject-reader and
meaning-maker–contributor. The same applies to producers who
consider their works to be transparent descriptions or immediate
experiences of reality 'as it is' ('this is *the* reality of the poor
people'; 'the reality of the nine-to-five working class is that they
have no time to think about 'issues' in their lives'). Literal
translations are particularly fond of 'evident truths', and the more
they take themselves for granted, the more readily they mouth
truisms and view themselves as *the* ones and the only *right* ones.
The self-permitting voice of authority is common in interpretation,
yet every decoding implies choice and is interpellated by ideology,
whether spoken or not. Reading as a creative responsibility is
crucial to every attempt at thwarting 'the humanism of
commodity'. Although important in any enterprise, it is pivotal in
works that break off the habit of the spectacle by asking questions
aloud; by addressing the reality of representations and entering
explicitly into dialogue with the viewer/reader. Each work has its
own sets of constraints, its own limits and its own rules, and
although 'anything could be said' in relation to it, this 'anything'
should be rooted in the specific reality of the work itself. The
interpreters' conventional role is disrupted since their function is
not to tell 'what the work is all about', but to complete and
'co-produce' it by addressing their own language and representational subject-ivity. *The Text is a little like a score of this new
kind: it solicits from the reader a practical collaboration . . . The*

reduction of reading to consumption is obviously responsible for the 'boredom' many feel in the presence of the modern ('unreadable') text, the avant-garde film or painting: to be bored means one cannot produce the text, play it, release it, make it go'. (Barthes 1986:63) Ironically enough, both the all-too-familiar (PBS conventions according to Hollywood standards) and the un-familiar have been qualified as boring. In one case, the question is that of instituting representational habits and of providing alibis of ownership, while in the other, it is that of disturbing and dispossessing them of their evident attributes. Yet what links these two 'boring' modes of production is precisely this lack: that of the spectacular, the very power to appeal. In the first instance such a lack usually derives from a normalized deficiency: the (involuntary, hence lesser) spectacle never admits to itself that it is a spectacle; in the second instance, it results from an ambiguous rupture: the spectacle(-on-trial) fractures its own unicity by hold-ing a mirror to itself as spectacle. Being the site where all the fragments are diversely collected, the viewer/reader remains, in this situation of rupture, intimately involved in a dialogue with the work. The latter's legibility and unity lie therefore as much in its origin as in its destination, which in this case cannot be righteously predetermined, otherwise commodity and its vicious circle would triumphantly reappear on the scene. With such emphasis laid on the spectator's creative role and critical resistance to consumption, it is amazing (though not in the least surprising) to hear the unfamiliar or different/autonomous work morally condemned in the name of a humanism which hypocritically demands respect for the viewers/readers, claiming, sure enough, to speak on their behalf and advocate their rights.

Among the many realms of occupied territories, one of partic-ular relevance to the problems of reading here is the concept of the 'political'. Although much has already been said and done concerning the 'apolitical' character of the narrow 'political', it is still interesting to observe the endlessly varying ways in which the boundaries of 'the political' are obsessively guarded and reassigned to the exclusive realm of politics-by-politicians. Thus, despite the effectiveness and persistence of the women's movement in deconstructing the opposition between nature (female) and culture (male) or between the private (personal) and the public (political); despite the growing visibility of numerous Third-Worldist activities in decommodifying ethnicity, displacing thereby all divisions of Self and Other or of margin and centre based on geographical arbitrations and racial essences; despite all these attacks on pre-defined territories, a 'political' work continues unvaryingly for

many to be one which opposes (hence remains particularly dependent upon) institutions and personalities from the body politic,
and which mechanically 'barks at all the after-effects of past
inhumanity'—in other words, one which safely counteracts within
the limits of pre-formulated, codified forms of resistance.

Particularly intriguing here are the kinds of questions and
expectations repeatedly voiced wherever films made on and by
members of the Third World are concerned. Generally speaking,
there is an excessive tendency among members of overdeveloping
nations to focus on economic matters in 'underdeveloped' or
'developing' contexts. It is as if, by some tacit consent, 'Third
World' can/must only be defined in terms of hierarchical economic
development in relation to 'First World' achievements in this
domain. And it is as if the presence and the sight of imported
Western products being 'misused' in non-Western contexts remain
highly compelling and recomforting to the Western viewer on
imaginary foreign land. The incorporation of (if not emphasis on)
recognizable signs of Westernization even in the most remote parts
of the Third World is binding; for exoticism can only be consumed
when it is salvaged, that is, reappropriated and translated into the
Master's language of authenticity and otherness. A difference that
defies while not defying is not exotic, it is not even recognized as
difference, it is simply no language to the dominant ear (only sheer
charlatanism—a 'mother's first [attempt]'; something that infuri-
ates the men who ask: 'What is it!?' 'What can you *do* with such
a film?'). Any film that fails to display these signs of 'planned
poverty' in its images and to adopt the *diagnostic* language of
economic-deterministic rationale is often immediately classified as
'apolitical'. The devices set up by the Master's liberals to correct
his own mistakes thus become naturalized rules, which exercise
their power irrespective of context.

The political is hereby *not* this 'permanent task inherent in all
social existence' which, as Michel Foucault suggests, 'cannot be
reduced to the study of a series of institutions, not even to the
study of all those institutions which would merit the name
'political', but pertains to 'the analysis, elaboration, and bringing
into question of power relations and the "agonism" between
power relations and the intransitivity of freedom' (Foucault
1984:429–430). *The political becomes compulsively instead 'the
legislative, institutional, executive mirror of the social'*
(Baudrillard 1981:18). In this exclusive realm of politics by politicians, the political is systematically depoliticized. The more
'self-evident' the location of politics, the easier it is to claim
knowledge, to gain control and to acquire territory. The progressive 'First World' thus takes as much pride in its 'Third World'

underdeveloped as the church used to take pride in its poor. (As has been astutely pointed out, the humanitarianism advocated through all the 'feed the poor' images of Africa and the 'do good' messages of the television missionaries may ease the consciences of the rich, but what they hide are precisely the ties between world hunger and imperialism (Lesage 1987:18).) Not only must all films related to the Third World show the people's poverty, but whatever they put forth in their critical stance vis-à-vis oppression should not depart from the Master's image of progress, for it is only in terms of progress—more particularly acquisitive, quantified progress—that he conceives of 'revolution' and transformation.

> A woman viewer: In dealing with socialist Vietnam, why don't you show what has been acquired through the Revolution?
> The woman filmmaker: The women in the film wouldn't have spoken as they did without the Revolution.
> The viewer: . . . True, but I mean real acquisitions, real attainments . . . something tangible! Do you understand me?

Poverty and class. Even the notion of class is commodified. Again, it is almost exclusively in the context of films on and by people of colour that middle-class viewers become suddenly over(t)ly concerned with the question of class—more as a classifying term, however, than as a way of rethinking production relations. Class, which is reduced to a fixed and categorized meaning in its common use among the viewers mentioned, has apparently never been their preoccupation in contexts other than those that concern 'their' poor. (For they do not seem to have any qualms about going to see movies whose dominating attractions are the love stories of the Western petty bourgeoisie; nor are they disturbed every time they switch on their televisions, whose visual symbols and chatter are governed by the myths of the upwardly mobile and the tastes of the very affluent.) *[The] attachment to the new insures that television will be a vaguely leftist medium, no matter who its personnel might be. Insofar as it debunks traditions and institutions . . . television serves the purposes of that larger movement within which left and right (in America, at least) are rather like the two legs of locomotion: the movement of modernisation . . . Television is a parade of experts instructing the unenlightened about the weather, aspirins, toothpastes, the latest books or proposals for social reform, and the correct attitudes to have with respect to race, poverty, social conflict, and new moralities.* (Novak 1982:33,36)

The mandatory concern for class in the exclusive context of films on and by Third World members *is in itself a class issue.* The complexity of the problem often goes unnoticed, as the class

bias many of us project onto others is often masked by the
apparent righteousness of these 'correct attitudes' popularized in
relation to race and poverty. The tendency to identify the Third
World with mere economic poverty is always lurking below questions such as: 'The film is beautiful. But some people look as if
they have starched their clothes [sic] for the camera. Why do they
dress so well?' (concerning a documentary shot in villages in
Senegal); or else: 'I am surprised to see how beautiful the women
are. Here [in the US], they would have been fashion models. You
have obviously selected them!' Such a tendency is further recognizable in the way differences in dress codes are often ignored.
While among many progressivist middle-class women today it is
important to signal publicly, by dressing in a very casual way, that
one is sufficiently secure to enact the downwardly mobile, the
situation among the working class is rather the reverse. 'Most
black women don't dress like this [in slacks and shirt],' observes
Julia Lesage, 'nor do most trade union women, if they are gath-
ering in public for a meeting. Many, if not most, women in the
US cherish a notion of dressing up in public or dressing up out
of respect for other people . . . [Blacks] do not have a legacy of
pride in dressing down' (Lesage 1987:15). Nor do most Asians in
the US or elsewhere (including post-Mao China); especially when
it is a question of appearing on camera for thousands of
(respected) others, and of 'saving face' for one's own family and
community. Thus, for example, in a film in which both Asian
middle-class and working-class women are featured, a woman
viewer remarks: 'All the women in the film are middle-class. Can
you talk about this?' The woman filmmaker: 'Oh! . . . How is it
you see them all as middle-class?' The viewer: 'Aren't they?! . . .
the way they dress! . . . ' Whose middle class is it, finally? In
refusing to situate its own legacy in dress codes, hence to acknowledge the problem of class in dealing with class, middle-class
spectatorship believes it can simply evacuate class content from
its safe observer's post by reiterating the objectifying look—the
spectacle's totalitarian monologue.

So gay a colour . . . in mourning. Not too long ago (1986),
in an issue of the weekly *Figaro-Magazine*, one read, in large bold
letters, this title of a feature article by a famed French reporter
who is said to have spent twenty years covering the war in
Vietnam: *'Mon' Viêt-nam d'aujourd'hui, c'est la désolation* ('My'
Vietnam Today Is a Desolation). Vietnam: a sacred territory and
an ideal subject for generalized colonialism. A widely unknown
people, but an exceptionally famed name; all the more unforget-
table as every attempt at appropriating it through the
rejustification of the motives and goals of the war only succeeds

in setting into relief the political vacuum of a system whose desperate desire to redeploy its power and to correct its world image in a situation of bitter 'defeat' unfolds itself through the supremacy of war as mass spectacle. Every spectator has a Vietnam of his or her own. If France only remembers its ex-colony to expatiate forever on its being the model of a successful revolutionary struggle against the largest world power, America is particularly eager to recall its predecessor's defeat at Dien Bien Phu and Vietnam's ensuing independence from French colonialism, whose desperate effort to cling to its Asian possession had led to the American involvement in the war. It is by denouncing past colonialism that today's generalized colonialism presents itself as more humane. North and South Vietnam are alternately assigned the role of the Good and the Bad according to the time, to suit the ideological whims of the two foreign powers. And the latter carefully take turns in siding with the 'winner', for it is always historically more uplifting to endorse the 'enemy' who wins than the 'friend' who loses.

> Yes, we defeated the United States. But now we are plagued by problems. We do not have enough to eat. We are a poor, underdeveloped nation . . . Waging a war is simple, but running a country is very difficult. (Pham Van Dong)[5]

For general Western spectatorship, Vietnam does not exist outside of the war. And since the war has ended, she no longer exists except as a name, an exemplary model of revolution, or a nostalgic cult object for those who, while unconditionally admiring the revolution, do not seem to take any genuine, sustained interest in the troubled reality of Vietnam in her social and cultural autonomy. The more Vietnam is mystified, the more invisible she becomes. The longer Vietnam is extolled as the model of the unequal struggle against imperialism, the more convenient it is for the rest of the world to close its eyes to the harrowing difficulties the nation, governed by a large postrevolutionary bureaucracy, continues to face in trying to cope with the challenge of recovery. (Even when the possessive pronoun 'my' is liberalistically bracketed,) whose Vietnam is the Vietnam depicted in Hollywood films as well as in the daily news and television series that offer to reproduce the 'fresh action from Vietnam [brought] into our living rooms each evening' (Time-Life Books brochure on *Vietnam: A Television History*) and claim to deliver 'the entire story of what really happened in Vietnam' in a few hours for VCR owners? Whose Vietnam is the one presented in the book series *The Vietnam Experience*, 'the definitive work on the Vietnam conflict . . . the whole explosive story . . . the whole astonishing truth

. . . More colorful than any novel, more comprehensive than any
encyclopedia'? Whose conflict triumphantly features in 'The TV
war'? Whose experience finally do Time-Life Books posters herald
in large, bold type that denotes the Vietnam war as exclusively
that of: 'The Men, the Weapons, the Battles'?

Contrary to what has been affirmed by certain Vietnam
experts, America's concept of its own 'exceptionalism', which is
said to have nurtured the roots of American intervention in the
war, did not die on the shores of Vietnam. It is still alive and well
even in its most negative aspects. Vietnam as spectacle remains
passionately an owned territory. Presented through the mediation
of the dominant world forces, she exists only within their binarism; hence the inability to conceive of her outside (or rather, in
the gaps and fissures, in the to-and-fro movement across the
boundaries of) the pro-communist/anti-communist opposition.
Every effort at challenging such reductive paternal bilaterism and
at producing a different viewing of Vietnam is immediately recuperated within the limits of the totalized discourse of red is red
and white is white. Not every Vietnam anti-war demonstration
effort was based on an advocacy of socialism, or on an elaborate
questioning (instead of a mere moral condemnation) of imperialism. Nor was every demonstration based on an extensive
interrogation of the territorial and numerical principle of the war
machine whereby the earth becomes an object. It is interesting to
note the extent to which common reactions presented as oppositions to the government's stance often involuntarily met the latter's
ultimate objective in its foreign interventions, which was to defend
and promote a specific lifestyle—the world of reification. Thus,
despite the anti-war denotation of such a comment as: 'It seems
like we're always getting pulled in by other people's problems.
We've got enough problems of our own to deal with,' what is also
connoted is a certain myopic view of America's 'goodwill', which
reduces the rest of the world to 'beggars' whose misery does not
concern us because *we have our own* beggars here at home.

While, in Vietnam, Party officials readily acknowledge the
severity of their economic crisis and even felt the urge recently to
publicly declare that 'only when we no longer refuse, out of fear,
to admit our own failures and oversights, only when we can
squarely face the truth, even if it is sad, only then can we learn
how to win' (Secretary General Nguyen Van Linh, October 1988);
while, in Vietnam, women reject the heroic-fighter image the world
retains of them and vocally condemn the notion of heroism as
being monstrously inhuman,[6] numerous foreign sympathizers continue to hold fast to the image of an exemplary model of
revolutionary society and to deny the multifaceted problems the

regime has been facing. Thus, all reflections on socialist Vietnam which do not abide by a certain socialist orthodoxy, positively embrace the system, and postulate the validity of its social organization, are crudely distorted as they are forced into the mould of the hegemonic world view and its lifelong infatuation with binary classifications: pro-communist/anti-communist, left/right, good/bad, victory/failure. *'I am not a Marxist!' exclaimed Marx, in despair of his disciples.*[7] In fact, it is imperative that socialist Vietnam remain 'pure' and that it continue to be unconditionally praised, for, through past denunciations of 'America's most controversial war', America can still prove that it is not entirely wrong, that 'the Vietnam failure' should be attributed to a guilty government but not to 'the American people'. The West's friendliness and benevolence toward its others often consist of granting itself the omnipotent right to counteract its own government and to choose, as circumstances dictate, when to endorse or when to detach itself from its institutions, while members of the Third World are required to stand by their kinsmen—government and people alike—and urged to show the official seal of approval 'back home' wherever they go, in whatever enterprise they undertake . . . The commodity contemplates itself in a world it has created. And this world it has created is *boldly* that of 'The Men, the Weapons, the Battles'. To say that the spectacle is always master-owned and that it aspires to genderlessness is to indulge again and again in redundancy. But repetition is at times necessary, for it has a function to fulfil, especially when it does not present itself as the mechanical recurrence of sameness, but rather as the persistence of sameness in difference. If in Dogon rituals men also 'have their periods' and their days of 'impurity,' no such reversal seems to be tolerated in a male-centred context in which the concept of gender is irremediably reduced to a question of sexual difference or of universal sex opposition. And since in such opposition, priority is always given to literal reading and to the validation of 'evidences' (essences), rather than to the interrogation of representation, the tools of (gender) production are bound to remain the Master's (invisible) tools. (Thus, reacting to a film in which women's sufferings have been commented upon by numerous women viewers as being 'very intense and depressive', a male viewer blurts out, after having uneasily embarked upon a lengthy, weasel-worded question: ' . . . The subject of the film is so partial . . . Don't you think it overshadows the rest of the issues? . . . I mean, how can one make a film on Vietnam, where there is so much sufferings [sic] and focus on women?' A number of women in the audience express their approval, others hiss.) While the male-is-norm world continues to be taken for granted as the objective, comprehensive societal world, the world of woman subjects(ivities) can only be viewed in terms of partiality, individuality and incompleteness. The tendency is to *obscure* the issue of women's oppression or of women's autonomy in a relationship of mutual exclusiveness rather than of interdependency. The impetus of the positivist project is first and foremost to supply answers, hence the need to level out all forms of oppression into one. *Not only has the question of women's liberation traditionally been bypassed by revolutionary organisations in the Third World (as it has in the West), but (again this applies to groups in the West) it has also become a target for hostility from the Left . . .* (Davies 1983:iv)

In the society of the male-centred spectacle, gender will always be denied, even and especially when the spectacle exalts feminism (heroic workers who are also good mothers and good wives). For what the humanism of commodity markets is not two, three, but one, only one feminism: one package at a time in a policy of mutual exclusion. *To deny gender, first of all, is to deny the social relations of gender that constitute and validate the sexual oppression of women; and second, to deny gender is to remain 'in ideology', an ideology which . . . is manifestly self-serving to the male-gendered subject.* (de Lauretis 1987:15) The dogmatic, hence genderless mind has never been eager to ask why, for example, the bright red flowers of the kapok tree are associated with menstruation and death in a context where 'bad blood' is identified with dark, çoagulated blood. As mentioned earlier, 'impurity' is the interval during which the impure subject is feared and alienated. It is the state in which the issue of gender prevails, for if red defies all literal, male-centred elucidation, it is because it belongs intimately to women's domain, in other words to women's struggles. To say this is simply to recognize that the impure subject cannot but challenge hegemonic divisions and boundaries. Bound to other marginalized groups, women are often 'impure' because their red necessarily exceeds totalized discourses. In a society where they remain constantly at odds on occupied territory, women can only situate their social spaces precariously in the interstices of diverse systems of ownership. Their elsewhere is never a pure elsewhere, but only a no-escape-elsewhere, an elsewhere-within-here that enters in at the same time as it breaks with the circle of omnispectatorship, in which women always incur the risk of remaining endlessly spectators, whether of an object, an event, an attribute, a duty, an adherence, a classification or a social process. The challenge of modifying frontiers is also that of producing a situated, shifting and contingent difference in which the only constant is the emphasis on the irresistible to-and-fro movement across (sexual and political) boundaries: margins and centres, red and white. It has often been noted that in Chinese ink painting, there is a 'lack of interest in natural colour'. One day, someone asked a painter why he painted his bamboos in red. When the painter replied, 'What colour should they be?', the answer came: 'Black, of course.'

Notes

This essay has also been published in Trinh 1991.

1 Borrowed from Paul Eluard's poem 'La Terre est bleue' in *Capitale de la douleur* (1926, rpt 1966), Gallimard, Paris, p. 153.
2 From Arthur Rimbaud's poem 'Voyelles', in *Rimbaud, Complete Works* (1966), trans. W. Fowlie, Chicago University Press, Chicago, p. 21.
3 For more information, see Calame-Griaule (1987:136, 246).
4 Discussion of the symbolics of red among the Dogon is based on Calame-Griaule 1987.
5 Quoted in Karnow 1983: 27–28.
6 See interviews with Thu Van and Anh in Mai Thu Van, *Vietnam, un peuple, des voix* (1982).
7 Quoted in Solomon 1979:12.

References

Barthes, Roland (1986) *The Rustle of Language*, trans. R. Howard, Hill & Wang, New York.
Baudrillard, Jean (1981) *In the Shadow of the Silent Majority*, Semiotext(e), New York.
Beijing Review (1983) *China After Mao. A Collection of Eighty Topical Essays by the editors of Beijing Review*, Beijing Review, Beijing.
Blacker, Irwin R. (1986) *The Elements of Screen-writing. A Guide for Film and Television Writing,* Collier Books, New York.
Calame-Griaule, Genvieve (1987) *Ethnologie et language. La Parole chez les Dogon*, Institut d'ethnologie, Paris.
Davies, Miranda, ed. (1983) *Third World Second Sex. Women's Struggles and National Liberation*, Zed, London.
Debord, Guy (1967/83) *Society of the Spectacle*, reprinted by Black & Red, Detroit.
de Lauretis, Teresa (1987) *Technologies of Gender*, Indiana University Press, Bloomington.
Eluard, Paul (1926/66) *Capitale de la douleur*, rpt, Gallimard, Paris.
Foucault, Michel (1984) 'The Subject and Power', in *Art After Modernism. Rethinking Representation*, ed. B. Wallis, The New Museum of Contemporary Art and MIT Press, New York, pp. 29–30.
——(1989) *Foucault Live. Interviews 1966–68*, trans. J. Johnston, ed. S. Lotringer, Semiotext(e), New York.

Gramsci, Antonio (1988) *Antonio Gramsci. Selected Writings 1916–1935*, ed. D. Forgacs, Schocken Books, New York.

Itten, Johannes (1970) *The Elements of Color*, trans. E. Van Hagen, Van Nostrand Reinhold, New York.

Karnow, Stanley (1983) *Vietnam. A History*, Penguin, New York.

Lesage, Julia (1987) 'Why Christian Television Is Good TV', *The Independent*, vol. 10, May.

Mai Thu Van (1982) *Vietnam, une peuple, des voix*, Editions Pierre Horay, Paris.

Novak, Michael (1982) 'Television Shapes the Soul', in *Television: The Critical View*, ed. H. Newcomb, Oxford University Press, New York.

Rimbaud, Arthur (1966) *Rimbaud, Complete Works*, trans. W. Fowlie, Chicago University Press, Chicago.

Solomon, Maynard, ed. (1979) *Marxism and Art*, Wayne State University Press, Detroit.

Trinh, T. Minh-ha (1991) *When the Moon Waxes Red: Representation, Gender and Cultural Politics*, Routledge, New York.

Vaneigem, Raoul (1983) *The Revolution of Everyday Life*, trans. D. Nicholson-Smith, Left Bank Books & Rebel Press, London.

Wit and Humor from Old Cathay (1986) trans. J. Kowalis, Panda Books, Beijing.

11 Little girls were little boys: Displaced femininity in the representation of homosexuality in Japanese girls' comics

Midori Matsui

While women's marginality in literary culture has commonly resulted in their silencing by the dominant male order, Japanese women's writing has derived its strength from its 'minority' position, developing its discourses of subversion within the structures of power. This was in contrast to the official 'women's writing' (*joryubungaku*) which fulfilled the definitions of 'feminine sensitivity' prescribed by male critics, a mode dealing with representations of women's feelings developed within the format of popular culture. The transformation of the girls' magazine, *shojozasshi*, in prewar Japanese society exemplifies the paradoxical empowerment of Japanese women through the subversive use of pleasure under the cover of an obedient silence. Originally devised as an educational apparatus to prepare adolescent girls for marriage and motherhood, the magazines became, in the liberal milieu of the 1920s, a medium channelling girls' appetite for pleasure. The constitution by romantic male discourse of the imaginary category of 'girlhood' (*shojo*) as a transient yet unique phase characterized by daydreaming, left female adolescents in a cultural closure in which they discovered 'pleasure' as a private category as opposed to the duties of womanhood imposed by patriarchal discourses. The girls' magazine helped them stage their fantasies by giving them the emergent genre of the girls' novel (*shojoshosetsu*), which celebrated an implicitly lesbian sisterhood complete with aesthetic illustrations; this, together with the all-women theatre Takarazuka, enabled girls to see themselves differently from the way they were represented in images sanctioned by the patriarchal culture (Yonezawa 1980: 14–15).

The girls' comic in the postwar period replaced the girls' magazine as an apparatus for inciting pleasure, combining the hitherto separate genres of the girls' novel and fashion magazines in its dramatic representations. Since its birth in 1947, however, the function of the girls' comic has generally not been at odds with the aims of the commercial mass media, an example of an ideological state apparatus functioning to fortify the hegemony of the capitalist economy by arousing the masses to the imaginary pleasure of consumption (Althusser 1971:162–168). Thus, the majority of girls' comics reiterated stories of adolescent Cinderellas, reinforcing images of passive femininity. The major change occurred with the advent in the late 1970s of a new subgenre, the boy-boy comic, which dramatized implicit or overt homosexual relations. It must be emphasized that these comics were targeted at girl readers. The representative 'works of the ambitious young women writers Moto Hagio, Keiko Takemiya, Ryoko Yamagishi, and Yumiko Oshima, generally referred to as the group of the 1949ers, consciously assimilated the codes and structures of the major Western literary genre the *Bildungsroman* to stage a psychodrama of the adolescent ego achieving its imaginary plenitude through the successful transference of the primary object of its desire from mother to father. While raising the social status of the girls' comic from despised marginality—'soft-brained'; 'too kitschy for the adult male taste'—to subliterary genre by winning major prizes, their works also captivated adolescent female readers, who found in the comics a range of signifiers for their imaginary subjectivities.[1] It was apparent that the boys were the girls' displaced selves; despite the effeminate looks that belied their identity, however, the fictitious boys were endowed with reason, eloquence and aggressive desire for the other, compensating for the absence of logos and sexuality in the conventional portraits of girls. In short, they signified the possession of the phallus as opposed to the feminine 'lack'.

This essay discusses the function of the Japanese boy-boy comic in constituting the imaginary relations of girls to phallocentric culture (Althusser 1971) and to their femininity. Apart from the immense popularity and critical attention enjoyed by Japanese comics, there are reasons for analyzing the significance of this specific genre. First, emerging in the transitional period of contemporary Japanese history in which the postwar struggles for economic restoration had to some degree created the sense of a void in a society without a legitimate father figure (the humanization of the Emperor deepening the spiritual *aporia*), the boy-boy comics rendered heroic the female subject's search for an ideal self, reclaiming an imaginary centrality for both female reader and writer. More significantly, since the search immediately threw the female subject into a confrontation with the patriarchal monopoly of language/culture, its goal was split between, on the one hand, the drive toward achieving a place in the logocentric universe by constituting an illusory mirror image, and on the other, the drive toward dissolving all historical, moral or discursive boundaries by extending the rhetoric of the *feminine* imagination (*shojoshumi*). The apparent contradiction of the female ego masquerading as a boy in such comics embodies this split; its representations of homosexual relations and androgyny, in particular, reflect Japanese girls' rejection of their sexuality as a commodity in the patriarchal structure and, more positively, their attachment to the fictitious category which, embodying the principle of pure play (fantasy), contests the socially determined definitions and parameters of sexuality. The extension of the Lacanian Imaginary through the cultivation of androgynous fantasy is especially crucial to the power of this particular medium. It is the intimation of the erotic, as opposed to the politico-economic category of the sexual, that underlies the subversive effect of the boy-boy comic.

The ambivalent functions of the male masks in the early comics will be analyzed in terms of the contradictory meaning of the phallus for female readers. While the male disguise functions positively in constituting a mirror self-image to assist girls' entry into the dominant speech culture, it also confirms their rejection of their own femininity as it is inscribed within the patriarchal order, where the womb functions merely as an empty vessel for the logos. This reinforcement of female 'lack' is positioned from a male perspective and supports the theory of 'penis envy' and the ranking of women as the second sex. The representation of androgyny is equally ambiguous. While epitomizing the 'golden myth' of sexually undifferentiated childhood, it also draws female readers' attention to the sexual attractiveness of boys, although this is partially undermined by depicting them as children. Nonetheless, the drawings emphasize the erotic effeminacy of the boys. Through their observation of the fantasized male body and their partial identification with it, girls attain the gaze as a means of scopic domination and simultaneously eroticize their own bodies through the mechanism of the mirror image. This surreptitious entertainment reverses the conventional role of the female as an object of male desire and helps girls attain their own aggressivity.

In the following sections, I will examine particular examples of boy-boy comics from the three periods of their advent, variation and maturation (diffusion). These respectively took place in the

late 1970s, the mid-'80s, and the late '80s to early '90s. These
three periods I provisionally name the phallic phase, the parodic
phase, and the nihilistic phase.

From the phallic phase, I will discuss the epochal works *The
Heart of Thomas* (1974) by Moto Hagio and *The Poem of the
Wind and the Tree* (1976) by Keiko Takemiya. While Hagio's
adoption of the *Bildungsroman* with feminine-looking boys
enables the female reader to assert *her* subjectivity in her struggle
with patriarchy, Takemiya's more schizophrenic presentation of
sexuality in the problematic role of the 'male prostitute' Gilbert
reintroduces expelled femininity by the back door, ominously
foregrounding the powers of repressed semiotic seduction, appropriately named *abjection* by Julia Kristeva (Kristeva 1982).

In my discussion of the parodic phase, I will analyze the
representations of homosexuality and androgyny in Tomoko
Naka's comic *The Green Boy* (1989) as an apparatus for eliciting
women's pleasure as well as a satire on patriarchal views of
virginity and marriage.

From the nihilistic phase, I will briefly examine two science
fiction comics staging a sexual dystopia, Hagio's *Marginal* (1987)
and Wakuni Akisato's *Renaissance* (1991), in which the homosexual relationship supplements the nearly defunct heterosexual
relationship as a means of totalitarian control. Their description
of cloning and simulation as sustaining factors in the new sexual
economy demystifies the ideals of the early boy-boy comic: the
erasure of sexual difference in androgyny and the narcissistic
coupling with the other. This phase also exposes the nihilism
which is inherent in the male impersonation that conceals the
regressive attitudes of girls toward their sexuality and which is
characteristic of the whole genre.

My conclusion assesses the subversive significance of the boy-
boy comic within women's writing and refers to Kristeva's concept
of adolescent writing as an open form deliberately exploiting its
'incomplete' status. With this, I hope to reinstate the subversive
potential inherent in the marginal expression that has traditionally
empowered Japanese women's writing.

Early boy-boy comics are highly determined by the oedipal relationship of the authors to patriarchal culture, especially within the
domain of language defined in favour of the male subject. The
psychoanalytic theory of the phallus as the seat of subjectivity and
the mark of sexual difference assists the understanding of these
comics' creative impetus. In Moto Hagio's work, in particular, the
important Freudian concatenation of castration, narcissism and
overcoming of the oedipal complex through possession of the

Erich, who represents the uncanny return of Thomas (Moto Hagio: The Heart of Thomas).

phallus is recapitulated in her treatment of characters and plot. In addition, Hagio's own relationship to patriarchal culture, her ambivalent wish to be included as subject in the realm of language and at the same time to defy the definition of the female subject as castrated and secondary, makes her work an exemplary attempt at the phallic construction of a logical and humanistically ordered textual microcosm.

Thus, *The Heart of Thomas* enacts the psychodrama of the adolescent subjects overcoming their 'narcissistic crisis'—the fear of castration at the loss of the primary nurture of their parents—by transferring the primary object of desire to the asexual other, thus proclaiming their centrality in the oedipal universe. The comic stages the conflicts of three boys—Erich, Yuri and Oscar—over the death of the school idol, Thomas, who is said to have killed himself to prove his unegotistical love for Yuri, the intellectual Narcissus who rejected him. Erich, who resembles Thomas, discovers Yuri's trauma over having been sadistically whipped by a satanic upperclassman to whom Yuri had been attracted. Threatened in his own narcissistic security as a child by the sudden death

Yuri, the object of desire (Moto Hagio: *The Heart of Thomas*).

of his mother, Erich comes to share Thomas's love of Yuri and finally succeeds in curing the latter.

   Their homosexual feelings, expressed purely at the spiritual level, are indicated as a supplement to the 'lack' realized at the loss of their parents, especially their insecurity over the absence of their fathers. Thus, the three main characters are described as partial orphans, and their strong resemblance to their parents and metonymic relationship with one another's parents are repeatedly emphasized. For example, Oscar, who resembles his mother, loves Yuri, whose dark hair and association with Latin countries remind him of his stepfather (who had murdered his mother), to whom he was attached as a child. Erich's conflict and friendship with Yuri reflects the former's ambivalent relationship with his stepfather, also named Yuri. These metonymic clues, which include Erich's uncanny resemblance to Thomas, indicate that the boys inhabit a closed oedipal universe as fragmented personae of the narcissistic ego.

   Hagio reiterates the importance of castration as a primal guilt and cause of the boys' conflict. Erich's description of Yuri's whipping wound on the back as 'scars of broken angel wings' and Yuri's own constant references to his inability to love anyone because of 'the lack of wings' are apparent metaphors of castration. In Freudian theory, castration fear is designated as the cause of the disruption of primary narcissism, which is overcome through the restoration of the shattered mirror image as legitimate heir to culture, at which point the subject enters the phallic phase as opposed to the early oedipal one. Juliet Mitchell's summary illuminates Yuri's problem:

> The concept of castration is the link between narcissism and the Oedipus complex. In the move from auto-eroticism to object-love, the phallus, which symbolizes the ability to connect with the loved object (the mother) is the bridge. The threat to the phallus is, therefore, the greatest threat to the ego's narcissism and it is the greatest threat to the child's object relations . . . in the case of the boy, the heir of the patriarchal law, it is the acceptance of symbolic castration which ends the Oedipus complex that is crucial. (Mitchell 1975:83)

This provides a ground for Lacan's linking of the phallus with logos, the possession of which alone guarantees the child's inclusion in culture: '[the] phallus . . . is the privileged signifier of that mark in which the role of logos is joined with the advent of desire' (Lacan 1977:287). Thus, the departure of Yuri for the seminary to fortify his reawakened faith in an all-forgiving God signifies the reestablishment of his ideal I and his successful reinsertion as a model subject into the patriarchal culture. Meanwhile, reconciliation with their new fathers offers Oscar and Erich the compensation of the 'law'.

Although it is to be read as an allegory of the *girl's* search for the Imaginary, the story faithfully accommodates the Freudian explanation of castration from the dominant male perspective. The formulaic conclusion particularly reinforces the prestige of the phallus as the 'privileged signifier'. Since Lacan's thesis clearly privileges the male ego, the unfaltering affirmation of its legitimacy in *The Heart* appears to indicate the internalization of male values by the author and the subsequent constitution of her subjectivity in phallocentric terms.

Lacan's remark on women's 'rejection of femininity' reinforces Freud's theory of the girl's 'penis envy' (Freud 1914). It reflects the difficulty of the female subject in displacing her memory that she was once a 'little boy' with an aggressive love for her mother in the pre-oedipal world; forced to realize her 'lack' of the phallus, she reluctantly transfers her love of mother to the father; yet the boy in her remains, in the form of the desire for the phallus, if not a desire for mother (Mitchell 1985:6–7). Lacan's equation of the logos with the phallus articulates the predicament of the female subject in the male-defined universe of language: lacking the language to define her independence, the girl is either left on the margin of the speech culture or kept as a subaltern subject in the symbolic order of patriarchy:

> Paradoxical as this formation may seem, I am saying that it is in order to be the phallus, that is to say, the signifier of the desire of the Other, that a woman will reject an essential part of femininity, namely, all her attributes in the masquerade. It is for that which she is not that she wishes to be desired as well as loved. But she finds the signifier of her own desire in the body of him to whom she addresses her demand for love. (Lacan 1977:289–90)

Hagio's text is split between the desire to embrace the imaginary male world of logos through the vicarious possession of the phallus exemplified in the male impersonations and her desire to escape the constraints of the actual patriarchal order by rejecting femininity or sexual difference altogether. Her other works constantly address the predicament of the oedipal girl subject recognizing her 'lack' of the phallus, which is synonymous with her absence *as subject* in the patriarchal culture. Hagio has often dramatized the girl's efforts to regain the illusory 'unity' she had known in her sexually undifferentiated childhood. Her early short comic, *The Snow Child* (1967), stages the tragedy of a girl who, raised as the male heir to her millionaire grandfather, kills herself at the age of thirteen, just before the sexual difference brought about by her growth will shatter her imaginary identity and the complacent unity of her childhood. In this and later comics, Hagio depicts androgynous children who choose to secure an eternal childhood either by dying or by becoming vampires. The latter function as aliens arousing terror and desire in normal children caught in the process of ageing and social integration.

Such children's metamorphosis has been motivated by rejection of the sexual differentiation that leads to women's victim status in the patriarchal order. For example, in *The Tribe of Poe*, the heroine, Mary-Belle, joins the vampires at the age of thirteen to escape the foster-parentage of her oldest brother (who is sexually attracted to her), and dies in order to be integrated into the psyche of her fourteen-year-old brother, Edgar, who lives as an eternal boy—a seductively alien and terrifying vampire who kills his classmates with a kiss. The girl's humiliating sexual role as a potential rape victim is negated by her subtle metamorphosis into an androgynous seducer. While *The Heart* sets up androgyny within a logocentric structure, *The Tribe of Poe* presents it as a threatening otherness to the dominant culture.

Repressing negative femininity in an all-male drama, *The Heart*

Gilbert and Serge (Keiko
Takemiya: *The Poem of the
Wind and the Tree*).

nevertheless gives female readers their mirror image by encouraging their identification with its characters. Thus, Yuri's
'castration', which is a metaphor for rape, makes his re-establish-
ment in the father's name all the more necessary, because his
castration meant essentially the female reader's castration, and
because, as Lacan emphasizes, castration initiates the subject's
entry into the symbolic culture.

Keiko Takemiya's *The Poem of the Wind and the Tree* parodies
Hagio's earlier work by chronicling the homosexual conflicts of
two boys, Serge and Gilbert, at a French boarding school in the
late nineteenth century. While ostensibly a *Bildungsroman*,
Takemiya's work functions as surreptitious pornography for girls.
Unlike Hagio, Takemiya boldly represents boys driven by sexual
desire and engaged in intercourse. Gilbert, in particular, is
described as an effeminate and beautiful boy whose presence alone
provokes the sado-masochistic desire of older males to rape,
humiliate and treat him as a sexual commodity. In addition, he is
characterized as a body of sexual reflexes conditioned by his own
father to feel his tie with the world only through orgasm, unable
to register the value of anything else and incapable of maturing.

The description of Gilbert as a pure object of the male gaze parodies the traditional portrait of the *femme fatale*, that notorious construct of male fantasy. At the same time, his sexuality evokes the subversive element of *abjection*, defined by Kristeva as the 'abyss' within the subject which threatens to disperse ('pulverize') the symbolic control over the semiotic (libidinal) drives, and which for that reason is expelled and repressed by the subject (Kristeva 1982:5). Elizabeth Grosz's description is an apposite summary of Gilbert's place in *The Poem*—his classmates' abhorrence for and exclusion of him as an irresistibly seductive but destructive other—as well as the effect of his horrible sexual defilement, which gratuitously fills the pages of the nine volumes:

> Abjection is the underside of the symbolic. It is what the symbolic must reject, cover over and contain. The symbolic requires that a border separate or protect the subject from this abyss which beckons and haunts it: the abject entices and attracts the subject ever closer to its edge. It is an insistence on the subject's necessary relation to death, to animality, and to materiality, being the subject's recognition and refusal of its corporeality. (Grosz 1990a:89)

Gilbert's repeated rape, often caused by his own manic provocation, functions to arouse readers' fears concerning their own sexuality. At the same time, the humiliation of the adolescent male body distances girls from their own violation within patriarchy and allows them to possess a reversed specular position: girls gain the 'gaze' with which they can reduce the male body to the object of their desire. Gilbert's ignoble death at the end—raped, drugged and made a male prostitute and opium addict, he is run over by a carriage in which he sees the phantom of his father—completes the subject's repression of the abject. Girl readers, partially identifying with Gilbert to satisfy their own libidinal drives through him, ultimately kill off the abject part of their own femininity in order to be accepted by the patriarchal culture that acknowledges the emergence of the phallic subject as the only legitimate constituent of its symbolic order. In other words, while Gilbert's abjection is linked with femininity as a power of seduction through which girls can recognize the 'accursed share' as a refusal of the symbolic order in themselves, its repeated repression through male sexual discourses has conditioned girls to internalize the patriarchal abhorrence of abjection as the 'right' response.

The deployment of sexual pleasure certainly produces contradictions in *The Poem*, foregrounding the power of seduction, which Baudrillard places under the 'feminine' category as on the one hand threatening to usurp the rational authority of the 'masculine' subject, and on the other, reinforcing conventional

Gilbert and Serge
(Keiko Takemiya: *The*
Poem of the Wind and
the Tree).

metaphors of feminine sexuality as dark seducer (Baudrillard
1979; 1990:12). The split between the facade of a *Bildungsroman*
and the undercurrent of pornography indicates the 'abyss' through
which the abject emerges to deconstruct the comic's logocentric
pretext. Such a use of desire within the legitimate structure of an
'educational' fiction liberates girls while letting them stay within
the dominant hierarchy. Nevertheless, the representation of the
erotic body from the predominantly 'male' perspective of pornography does not enable girls to outgrow the hackneyed code of sex
as commodity. Moreover, by giving them the specular position that
remains ineffective outside the comic's domain, it encloses girls'
desire within the circumscribed 'freedom' pertaining to all marginal culture. Finally, implicating pleasure in the context of
voyeurism and the subjugation of the other, the representations of
homosexuality in *The Poem* merely perpetuate the phallocentric
conflation of sex with aggression.

   The illustrations of *The Poem* epitomize its contradictions. Not
only is Gilbert indistinguishable from a girl, but his erotic postures
are those of women in conventional films. At the same time, the
childish sleekness of the boys' bodies emphasizes their make-

Hanako as Ranmaru having an affair with a boy (Tomoko Naka: *The Green Boy*).

believe character, reducing the impact of the sex act to the safety level of a puppet show. In addition, the frequent use of window frames to display the boys' eroticized bodies invites the reader's voyeuristic participation.

Although rejected by many male readers as a second-rate imitation of Hagio's work, Takemiya's comic had a deeper impact in the long run. From the late 1970s to the early '80s, comics featuring a boy-boy relationship enjoyed a boom, and in turn induced readers to write similar 'homosexual' comics in fanzines which ignored plot coherence or the emergence of the Imaginary as an ultimate goal, but endlessly reproduced romantic conversations and erotic intercourse between boys.

The second phase of the boy-boy comics produced writers who consciously exploited the function of homosexuality as a pleasure machine for girls. From the displacement of girls' reaction to the 'castration' fear, androgyny became a style in the works of Tomoko Naka, Yasuko Aoike and Hiroko Kishi, who playfully incorporated real personages from glam rock and *kabuki*, sanctioning androgyny as art, into their overtly fantastic stories. Tomoko Naka's *Green Boy*, however, is unique for its sharp satire on conventional sexual stereotypes; against the double standards that demand virginity from girls but allow promiscuity for boys, Naka uses androgyny as an anarchic alternative that breaks down the priggish definitions of male and female sexuality.

The story is a farcical fantasy in which the hedonistic heroine aims to marry into a rich family by using her graceful appearance and the prestige of her school. Her contradictory desires for free sex and respectable marriage are fulfilled when her favourite plants suddenly produce two beautiful boys, Rintaro (a 'grove boy') and Ranmaru (an 'orchid boy'), who can magically transform themselves into different figures and change Hanako's shape and sex. Disguised as a pretty boy, Hanako has an affair with the former boyfriend of her fiancé, Mikihiko (a 'trunk boy'): Ranmaru, disguised as Hanako, makes love with Mikihiko to conceive his child. Hanako discovers her fiancé's bisexuality and his double standard about male promiscuity and female chastity while hiding her own perversion from him; Mikihiko's blindness to the identity of his lover (male or female, virgin or nymphomaniac), coupled with his complacently sexist assumptions, provokes a good laugh from the reader, especially in the final scene. In front of the plant bearing its fruits, Hanako remarks to Mikihiko, 'Your child may perhaps be born of them.' Mikihiko interprets this as a sign of Hanako's sexual ignorance and loves her all the more for her 'innocence'. The irony represents a counterattack against the patriarchal culture that has placed women under surveillance to ensure they retain their virginity before marriage and has confined their sexuality to the biological function of childbearing, keeping the pleasures of sexual freedom as a male privilege.

The comic ridicules male fantasies concerning virginity by grotesquely parodying the romantic portrayal of a girl with a flower. Not only does it equate the ornamentality and passivity of the flower with those of the girl, but the portrait functions in Japanese culture as an instant signifier of the shojoshumi—a childish, ornamental, narcissistic, whimsical and insignificant taste supposedly characteristic of adolescent girls—for which girls' comics have been despised by male readers. At the same time, the kitschy sweetness of a girl talking to her flower heightens her desirability for men by eliciting their complacent protectiveness. Yet Hanako's plants are cacti with erotic dints in their trunks; a different sort of 'faery' is born of them, one which enjoys sex with men and women. In addition, the fragrance of flowers that supposedly induces the romantic dreams of virgins functions in The Green Boy as the hallucinogen that breaks down gender distinctions and the boundaries between proper and improper. The picture of coy chastity is cynically discredited by the drug use and free sex it conceals.

Hanako and her plants (Tomoko Naka: *The Green Boy*).

The Green Boy doubly deconstructs the conventional view of
feminine sexuality as passive or empty (waiting to be filled in by
the signifiers of male desire), first by Hanako's activity and second
by the parody of *shojoshumi* ('girls' taste'). At the same time,
Naka exploits the graphic conventions of *shojoshumi* to the
extreme by punning on the names and filling the background
behind the highly stylized characters with superfluous illustrations
of flowers. This constant foregrounding of the ornamental aspects
of the girls' comic no longer intoxicates readers into a sweet
fantasy, but makes them conscious of the artificiality of the
discourse they read. Naka's comic may not give readers the
narcissistic signifier that might shape a new representation of
femininity, but it does deploy both patriarchal discourses and the
codes of the marginalized 'feminine' culture in order to convey a
critique of 'virginity', while still preserving the comic or erotic
entertainment.

Although *The Green Boy* relies on the legitimacy of the
institution of heterosexual marriage in its exploration of bisexual
adventure, the comic also manages to play a complex game with
power. As Foucault argues, power secures its hegemony by letting
the discourses about what it controls—sexuality, madness, etc.—
proliferate under its surveillance. The regulation of sex, for
example, through public discourses facilitates its control; at the

same time, the diversification of discourses allows the dissenting
elements to grow within its structure:

> . . . one is dealing with mobile and transitory points of resistance,
> producing cleavages in a society that shift about, fracturing unities
> and effecting regroupings . . . Just as the network of power
> relations ends by forming a dense web that passes through
> apparatuses and institutions, without being exactly localized in
> them, so too the swarm of points of resistance traverses social
> stratifications and individual unities. (Foucault 1980:96)

The Green Boy's use of parody precisely fractures the network
of power without ever going outside the symbolic order. If there
is a possibility for nurturing the dissenting voices in the girls'
comic, it may be found in the deployment of the conventional
discourses on and stereotypes of femininity for the deconstructive
purpose of exposing their arbitrary genealogy. With the discovery
of this use of the feminine, the girls' comic no longer has to
centralize the symbolic persona of the boy as phallic subject, or
homosexual relationships as a narcissistic fulfilment of the desire
for the other. The transformation of the boy-boy comic from the
phallic to the parodic (playful) phase may indicate the changing
attitudes of writer and reader toward the values of the dominant
culture and their acceptance of the feminine (seduction) as a
discursive weapon.

As Foucault remarks, points of resistance within hegemonic power
are transitory and scattered. Although boy-boy comics have
become a cultural phenomenon recognized by many as an important subculture, their partial integration into Japanese cultural
discourses has also resulted in the dispersion of their impact and
message. The third stage is characterized by the polarization of
the boy-boy comic between the pornographic expressions in
fanzines and in science fiction or more intellectual forms adopted
by major writers (publishing solely in comic magazines) which
target an older, educated audience. I interpret the phenomenon as
signifying the hypostasization of homosexuality as an erotic or
intellectual commodity. With the gradual acceptance of homosexuality as a cultural phenomenon, the discrepancy between the
realities of gay life and their representation in girls' comics have
been pointed out and criticized. Consequently, the boy-boy comic
has closed itself within the private pleasure of the naive reader or
within the autonomous artistic performance.

The choice of science fiction as a representational format, on
the other hand, indicates the increasing distance between the
comics' textual fantasy and the reality of the readers. Incorporated
into an already major mode of popular representation, the boy-boy

comic no longer particularly addresses the unique problems of the adolescent female subject.

As if to reinforce the nihilism, two excellent sci-fi comics, *Marginal* and *Renaissance*, resolve the problems of gender and sexual difference through the ironic apparatus of cloning and simulation by depicting the earthly community as a sexual dystopia. In *Marginal*, the all-male society is given children from a single Mother, who is a male with brain control and organ transplantation, used to camouflage the artificial production of children by the Centre. Sexual relations are restricted to those between older males and adolescent boys; yet, due to defective genetic traits which also cause sterility, no one lives much past the age of 30.

Marginal is a negative version of *The Heart of Thomas*, lacking the former's faith in phallic authority. In fact, the portrayal of Marginal, inhabited by an artificially produced, all-male race destined to die when they are scarcely past their youth, is a grotesque parody of the gymnasium as a crystallization of adolescent experience. The society is watched over as a spectacle and a simulation by the scientist who has provided his genes for the experiment on this planet and whose decaying mechanism and swollen right breast make a mockery of both the logocentric Creator and the phallic mother. The entire situation demystifies Hagio's own early logocentrism and the idealistic assumptions of the early boy-boy comics by parodying and exposing the function of the boy-boy comic as a simulacrum of female subjectivity.

Homosexuality is treated as an apparatus of totalitarian control in *Renaissance*, a parodic adaptation of the pornographic sci-fi novel *The Cattle-Men Japoo*, by Shozo Numa. Its creator, Wakuni Akisato, describes a society controlled by the coloured races after the virtual extinction of the white race by skin cancer. The name 'Renaissance' refers to the perverse project of the Japanese corporation Hara, which raises Caucasian clones in underground pastures on the moon, without giving them language, and checks them out as prostitutes to a select few of the dominant races. Despite an apparent permissiveness which allows bisexuality and homosexual marriage, the society regulates sexuality as an important means of mind control. Akisato explicitly links sexual desire with aggression, showing the sadistic love of the young president of Hara for a white girl; his youngest brother, an androgyne, also fulfils his unrequited love by killing his sister's lover and having him cloned for his own sexual use. The world is presented as a circular and thus atemporal one in which people return through cloning. As some Japanese critics have suggested, 'sexual difference' is transcended in this perverse recurrence of the same

(Fujimoto 1990), but ironically and horribly. For, as Baudrillard says, cloning signifies the death of the original while securing the eternity of the individual organism; dispensing with parents and thus with the problems of gender, clones erase the subject as difference, reducing everything to a simulacrum (Baudrillard 1990:167–171).

In *Marginal* and *Renaissance*, the homosexual 'utopia' is constantly watched over by the rulers on the moon as an object of specular domination. The theatrical metaphor indicates the condition of the boy-boy comic as empty signifier; equally, Akisato's refusal to make any one of her characters register emotions in order to encourage the reader's identification also suggests the exhaustion of the boy-boy comic as a signifier for the girl's imaginary subjectivity.

It may be too early to declare the demise of the boy-boy comic as a vehicle for creative feminine fantasy. But the literalization characterizing the works of major writers brings to the surface the contradiction inherent in the genre's initial aspirations. Incorporating the major literary mode of the *Bildungsroman*, the pioneers of the boy-boy comic attempted to transcend its limits as a minor form. Yet the contradiction lay in the fact that their experiments were permitted only because of the marginality of the genre, whose 'imperfection' was an accepted attribute. The 'childish' characters with enormous eyes, and the backgrounds superfluously sprinkled with flowers, camouflaged their subversive content. The diffusion of the impact of the boy-boy comic began when the writers started to give their characters more-adult features. Similarly, the pursuit of 'artistic' prestige made those writers construct their narratives more closely in line with the conventions of science fiction, history and myths, at the price of the unique features differentiating comics from other representational modes: feminine day-dreaming as a matrix of world-transforming fantasy (Watanabe 1987:63).

The merging of the girls' comic with other literary modes and discourses increased its assimilation into the hegemonic culture. As Raymond Williams says, emergent cultures are rarely allowed to stay on the margins long enough to form a truly alternative position (Williams 1980:41). Foucault also says that no resistance is exterior to power, that one is 'always inside power' (Foucault 1980:95). Girls' comics are also firmly inserted into the capitalist economy, which legitimizes their existence within the free market but limits their expression. A big business, with sales of 1 million books a month, girls' comics are largely under the surveillance of the publishing editors, whose judgment is influenced by the laws of the market. Conforming to the tastes of a conservative public, profit-conscious judgments are frequently made to appease patriarchal authority.

The question remains whether the boy-boy comic has exhausted its possibility as an alternative signifier for the ambiguous subjectivity of girls. Even if it has, Kristeva's definition of 'adolescent writing' provides clues to understanding the significance of the boy-boy comic as a semiotic practice toward the attainment of creative subjectivity in the most fruitful sense:

> During adolescence, this reactivation of the symbol . . . is accompanied by a more or less free phantasmatic elaboration, which permits an *adjustment of drives* subjacent to the phantasms *and of the signs* of spoken or written language. In this sense, imaginary activity, and imaginary writing even more so . . . gives the subject an opportunity to construct a discourse that is not 'empty' but that he lives as authentic. (Kristeva 1990:1)

To this one could counter that the vicarious attainment of subjectivity in the boy-boy comic was not altogether escapist but positive, enhancing girls' ability to turn their lack—the absence of a penis—into a sense of the 'real', that is, a regaining of the wholeness lost through the fear of castration by 'performing' that situation. In fact, Kristeva's definition of the adolescent novel as an 'open' and 'incomplete' form that represents fantasies driven by the semiotic flow recapitulates the specific position of boy-boy comics in Japanese culture. Just as the 'adolescent novel' represents 'subjectivity in crisis', split between its drive toward symbolic authority and its attraction to fantasies, the boy-boy comic represents the girl subject split between her loyalty to phallic authority and her attraction to the subject-less freedom of abjection-seduction.

In Kristeva's theoretical universe, the semiotic is firmly rooted in the feminine as well as in the adolescent. The Japanese boy-boy comic, in its most imaginatively ambitious mode, is a remarkable amalgam of the feminine and the adolescent imagination; its best effects naturally realize the semiotic, including the ambiguous charm of androgyny. In fact, the sexual indeterminacy at the heart of serious or parodic performances of the boy-boy comic almost achieves 'seduction' as an 'ironic alternative form' that 'breaks the referentiality of sex and provides a space . . . for play and defiance' (Baudrillard 1990:21).

Yet this transgressive play can easily slide into self-indulgence, an intellectual equivalent of drug-taking (Kristeva 1990:22). Regrettably, the current situation of the boy-boy comic indicates that its initially 'defiant' seduction has turned 'soft', recapitulated by the 'technology of desire', creating situations that mechanically feed sexual curiosity, a ritual transgression only to provide a transitional stage for individual integrations into smooth social relations (Baudrillard 1990:174–175).

Being transitional may be the inevitable destiny of a representational mode whose strength derives from 'adolescent' indeterminacy; the moment it achieves a 'major' expression, it destroys its own foundations. Yet the 'feminine' power of perceiving and reconstructing reality semiotically, once released through the adolescent male mask, should not diminish with the degeneration of the boy-boy comic. The boy-boy comic has revolutionized the genre of comic writing as well as providing readers with subtle means for distancing themselves from ideologically regulated sexual discourses through the radical and ironical use of play. Its influence has branched out to create the new genre of sexual comics written by women, represented by the 'new pornographic comics' of Kyoko Okazaki and Erika Sakurazawa. Meanwhile, the 'classic' works discussed here continue to form important points of reference in the broader application of adolescent culture to the problems of women's writing in Japan.

Notes

1 The reference is to Lacan's concept of the Imaginary, in which the ego imagines an illusory unity with its counterpart or specular ego (usually the mother's gaze), as revised by Julia Kristeva. She analyses this concept in a historical and social context as well as giving it a wider sensory dimension than Lacan, who relegated it to the visual. See Grosz 1990:157.
2 The reference is to Kristeva's concept of the semiotic as described in Kristeva 1980. See also Grosz 1989; 1990a.

References

Althusser, Louis (1971) *Lenin and Philosophy and Other Essays*, trans. Ben Brewster, Monthly Review Press, New York.

Baudrillard, Jean (1990) *Seduction*, first pub. as *De la Séduction*, Editions Galilée, Paris; trans. Brian Singer, St. Martin's Press, New York.

Fletcher, John & Benjamin, Andrew, eds. (1990) *Abjection, Melancholia and Love*, Routledge, London.

Freud, Sigmund (1914) 'On Narcissism: an Introduction' (1984), in *On Metaphyschology: The Theory of Psychoanalysis*, Pelican, London.

Foucault, Michel (1980) *The History of Sexuality*, vol.1, trans. Robert Hurley, Vintage, New York.

Fujimoto, Yukari (1990) 'The Spiritual Crossing of Gender' (*Tamashii no Seibetsu Ekkyo*), unpublished paper read at Pacific Rim Conference of Women's Studies, Tokyo.

Grosz, Elizabeth (1989) *Sexual Subversions: Three French Feminists*, Allen & Unwin, Sydney.
——(1990) *Jacques Lacan: A Feminist Introduction*, Routledge, London.
——(1990a) 'The Body of Signification', in Fletcher & Benjamin, *Abjection*, pp. 80–103.
Kristeva, Julia (1980) *Desire in Language: A Semiotic Approach to Literature and Art*, Blackwell, Oxford.
—— (1982) *Powers of Horror: An Essay on Abjection*, trans. Leon S. Roudiez, Columbia University Press, New York.
——(1990) 'The Adolescent Novel', in Fletcher and Benjamin, *Abjection*, pp. 8–23.
Lacan, Jacques (1977) *Écrits: A Selection*, trans. Alan Sheridan, Norton, New York.
Mitchell, Juliet (1975) *Psychoanalysis and Feminism: Freud, Reich, Laing and Women*, Vintage, New York.
——(1985) 'Introduction—1' in Mitchell & Rose, *Feminine Sexuality*.
Mitchell, Juliet & Rose, Jacqueline, eds. (1985) *Feminine Sexuality: Jacques Lacan and the Ecole Freudienne*, trans. Jacqueline Rose, Norton, New York.
Watanabe, Tsuneo (1987) 'Trans-Gender Adventure', *Eureka*, Seidosha, Tokyo.
Williams, Raymond (1980) *Problems in Materialism and Culture*, Verso, London.
Yonezawa, Yoshihiro (1980) *The History of the Post-War Girls' Comic*, Shinpyousha, Tokyo.

12 Sexism, racism and Canadian nationalism

Roxana Ng

My concern about the dynamics of sexism and racism and the interrelationship of gender, race/ethnicity and class arose out of my experience as a 'visible minority' immigrant woman and a member of the intelligentsia living in a white-dominated Canada. Working politically in the immigrant community, I and other women of colour frequently feel that the weight of our status as women is not equal to that of our status as members of minority groups. Our interests and experiences are subsumed under the interests of immigrant men, especially 'community leaders'. This situation is analogous to the classic position of the left: women's issues are secondary to the class struggle. Women are often told that their interests can be taken up only after the revolution.

Working in the women's movement, on the other hand, women of colour also feel silenced from time to time. Our unique experiences as women of colour are frequently overlooked in discussions about women's oppression. At best, we are tokenized; at worst, we are told that our concerns, seen to be less advanced, have to do with a patriarchy characteristic of our indigenous cultures.[1] There is something missing from the women's movement which gives us an increasing sense of discomfort as we continue to participate in struggles in which only a part of our experiences as women of colour is/can be taken up.

Analytically, in standard social science debates (which filter to the left and to the women's movement through people's multiple roles and locations in society), there is a tendency to treat gender, race and class as different analytic categories designating different domains of social life. While I continue to experience gender and race oppression as a totality, when I participate in academic and intellectual work I have to make a theoretical and analytical separation of my experience and translate it into variables of 'sex', 'ethnicity' and 'class' in order for my work to be acceptable and understandable to my colleagues. It is not uncommon, when I present papers at conferences, for me to receive comments about the lack of definitional clarity in my use of concepts of gender, race/ethnicity and class. I am asked to spell out clearly which category is more important in determining the position of immigrant women, for example.

It was out of these experiences and concerns that I began, more than ten years ago, to search for a way of thinking about the interrelationship of categories of gender, race/ethnicity and class that would account for the lived experiences of people of colour; a way of understanding their experiences that does not fragment them into separate and at times opposing domains of social life.

Furthermore, as I continue to teach and do research in ethnic and women's studies, and especially since my two-year sojourn in New Brunswick, it has become clear to me that we cannot understand gender and ethnic relations in Canada without attending to the ways in which these relations have been/are mediated and organized by the Canadian state. (Let me remind the reader that Nova Scotia and New Brunswick are the oldest provinces in Canada, settled and dominated not only by Irish and Scottish immigrants, but by Loyalists.) Indeed, it is not enough for feminists and ethnic historians to rewrite women's history and ethnic history. In order to understand how Canada came to be a nation with its present configuration, we have to rewrite the history of Canada.

This essay does not address problems of racism and sexism in the left and in the feminist movement directly. It is a methodological essay, which calls for a different conceptualization of gender, race/ethnicity and class, one that grounds these relations in the historical development of the Canadian state. In it, I shall challenge current theorizations of ethnicity and class and demonstrate the interlocking relationships of gender, race and class by means of historical examples. My method is informed by Marx's analysis of capitalism in the nineteenth century (see Marx 1954; Sayer 1983) and by feminist interpretations of Marx's method (see Hartsock 1987; Smith 1987a).[2] In developing the analysis I put foward here, I ask myself: How do I account for the silencing I and other women experience in our diverse social locations? How do I have to understand history in order to understand my experience as a totality lodged in a particular social formation? I don't claim to put forward a complete or definitive theory or argument; it is very much a start in developing a method of thinking and practice that will, I hope, ultimately give us women of colour a voice in Canadian society and a way of understanding our oppression so that we can work in concert with other Canadians toward eradicating it.

Before I proceed, let me pause for a couple of qualifications. First, I use the concepts 'ethnicity' and 'race' interchangeably throughout this essay. Although I am aware of the technical differences between the two concepts, I want to draw attention here to their socially and culturally constructed character. While the difference between people of Irish and Scottish descent in New Brunswick is seen as a subcultural one nowadays, at one time the two groups treated each other as people belonging to different races. Today, the term 'ethnic groups' is used primarily to refer to immigrants from non-British and non-French backgrounds, especially those from Third World countries. In the past, immigrants were referred to as 'Europeans', 'Orientals', 'Negroes', etc., signifying their different racial origins. In this connection, we should bear in mind that the change of studies in race relations to studies in 'ethnic relations' in the late 1960s and early 1970s was a political move on the part of the state to diffuse rising racial tensions among different groups in both the United States and Canada. Today, in Ontario, the reverse movement, toward policy development in race relations as opposed to multiculturalism, signals the increasing militancy and political clout of minority groups in the changing political economy of that province.[3] Thus, it is important to bear in mind that definitions and meanings of ethnicity and race are social constructions that shift constantly, reflecting the changing dynamics of gender, race/ethnic and class relations over time.

Second, I use the term 'the Canadian state' as a shorthand for the multiplicity of institutions and departments which administer and coordinate the activities of ruling. It therefore includes the formal government apparatuses and the various policies and programs which come under their jurisdiction, and the functions performed therein. But more importantly, I wish to advance the notion of the state as the central constituent in the developing relations of capitalism in Canada (see McIntosh 1978). This set of relations didn't drop from the sky. As Corrigan (1980: xxii) points out, it was constructed through time, by the complicated and extensive struggles of people grouped together by their differing relationships to the emerging dominant mode of production.

Indeed, as we shall see, the history of ethnic and gender relations is the history of the Canadian state.

Ethnicity, class and gender: Standard conceptual problems

In his book *Ethnic Canada*, Driedger (1987) distinguishes three views of the interrelationship of class and ethnicity. The first view states that ethnicity is a by-product of the class structure and reducible to class. The second view holds that ethnicity may or may not be reducible to class, but that it certainly is a drawback to social mobility. The third view, held by Driedger himself, suggests that ethnicity and class are separate phenomena, and should be examined separately (Driedger 1987: 6). Certainly, both ethnicity and class are observable features of social life. Both have an objective reality. While orthodox Marxists contend that ethnicity is a product of the class structure (e.g. Cox 1948), Depres (1975) maintains that ethnicity and class are different bases of sociality, although at times they overlap.

I suggest that the difficulties encountered by these theorists in understanding the interrelationship between ethnicity and class have to do with the fact that they treat these phenomena as analytic categories whose relationship to each other can be established only abstractly, through the construction of clever analytic schemas developed to discover correlations between variables. In this kind of approach, ethnicity and class are conceptualized as variables which have no actual relationship to one another in the everyday world. The indicators for 'ethnicity' as an analytical category are descent, common religion, and a shared feeling of belonging to the same group. This list can be expanded and changed depending on the group the researcher is investigating; however the criteria used do not change the procedures and conceptual schemas adopted. Class, on the other hand, is an economic category which has to do with occupations, level of education, income, etc. Class is relevant to researchers of ethnic groups only if they wish to study the economic participation of these groups. The issue then becomes: how do particular groups rank in terms of this socioeconomic classification (class)? (See, for example, Pineo 1977; Pineo & Porter 1985.)

Standard approaches to ethnicity, then, treat the ethnic phenomenon as a separate ontological and epistemological domain, in much the same way that scholars of Orientalism treat the study of the Orient, according to Edward Said (1979: 2). In this way, what is considered as 'the ethnic phenomenon' (VanderBerghe 1981) is severed from the relationships that give rise to it. Its ontological domain is one whose relevance resides in race, kinship and, following from these two major attributes, a sense of belonging and a shared identity. Seen in this light, ethnicity can be considered apart from and as unrelated to the political and economic processes of any particular society; it is detached completely from the context within which the phenomenon arises. Similarly, the phenomenon of class, for these researchers, arises in terms of people's relative statuses in a stratified society. Since class and ethnicity are seen to be different variables designating different social phenomena, their relationship has to be derived by examining their correlation (or the lack thereof) in a conceptual schema devised by the researcher. Their interconnection in the shaping of social life is left unexaminable.

Gender usually falls outside the realm of analytical relevance for ethnic theorists. Implicitly, like other areas of sociology, women's experiences are subsumed under those of men. More often, the significance of gender (read woman) is overlooked or treated as a separate field of investigation. Thus we find women being included in the study of the family or the domestic labour debate, for example, but political economy remains completely sex-blind (for a critique see Smith 1987b). While there have been increasing efforts by feminists to incorporate women into the study of ethnicity and class, these efforts are only at a preliminary stage. Frequently, the similarities between racism and sexism are compared (see Ng 1984, endnotes 1&3), and parallels between the experience of women and the experience of ethnic minorities are drawn (Juteau-Lee & Roberts 1981). Recently, feminists such as Roberts and Juteau-Lee (1981) have attempted to conceptualize the relationship between gender, ethnicity/race and class by suggesting that they are three different systems of domination which overlap (Juteau-Lee & Roberts 1981). Their inclusion of gender in ethnic studies is a major breakthrough, but the question of the precise relationship between these three systems of domination remains to be conceptualized and investigated.

Gender, race/ethnicity and class as relations

This essay calls for a different conceptualization of ethnicity/race, gender, and class: they must be treated as social relations which have to do with the ways in which people relate to each other through productive and reproductive activities. This conception is consistent with Marx and Engels' (1967, 1970) treatment of class, which refers to people's relationships to the means of production rather than to an economic category. As Braverman (1974: 24) eloquently explains, class, properly understood, never precisely designates a group of people; rather, it is the expression of a process whose result is the transformation of sectors of society. When we speak of class, then, we are referring to a process whereby people construct and alter their relationships to the productive/reproductive forces of society using whatever means they have at their disposal.

When we review the historical development of Canadian society, we find that family and kinship, perceived or real, are means people deploy to exert their domination or overcome their subordination. Theorists have identified the deployment of kinship ties and of common descent as the salient features of ethnic groups. However, as Weber has pointed out, descent itself is not a sufficient condition for ethnic-group formation. He observes:

> . . . it is primarily the political community, no matter how artificially organized, that inspires the belief in common ethnicity. This belief tends to persist even after the disintegration óf the political community, unless drastic differences in the custom, physical type, or above all, language exist among its members. (Weber 1968: 389)

In terms of gender relations, women's work within and outside the family is completely taken for granted. It is not deemed worthy of consideration in ethnic studies.

Weber's contribution lies in his identification of political and ideological factors in the formation of ethnic groups. In particular, he draws attention to the importance of colonization and emigration as an important basis for group formation (Weber 1968). In this sense, his conception of ethnicity coincides nicely with Marx's conception of class: they both see these two phenomena as arising out of the struggles for domination and control, notably in colonization as capitalism emerged as the dominant mode of production in the Western world.

Similarly, gender relations are crucial and fundamental to the division of labour in any society. In most societies, gender is the basic way of organizing productive and reproductive activities. But gender relations are not the same in all societies. Furthermore, like ethnic and class relations, they change over time in response to changing social, political and economic relations. My investigation of immigrant women's domestic work, for example, reveals the transformation of their domestic labour after immigration to Canada. Whereas in a less industrialized setting, women's work is organized organically in relation to farming and other subsistence activities, in Canada it is organized industrially according to the husband's waged work outside the home, school schedules, the degree of mechanization of the household (e.g. the use of vacuum cleaners and other appliances), public transportation systems, distances to shops, and so on. The change in women's domestic labour in turn creates new areas of contestation and conflict between immigrant women and their husbands, as well as upsetting the previous balance of power among all family members (Ng & Ramirez 1981). Smith observes:

> In pre-capitalist societies, gender is basic to the 'economic' division of labour and how labour resources are controlled. In other than capitalist forms, we take for granted that gender relations are included. In peasant societies for example, the full cycle of production and subsistence is organized by the household and family and presupposes gender relations. Indeed, we must look to capitalism as a mode of production to find how the notion of the separation of gender relations from economic relations could arise. It is only in capitalism that we find an economic process constituted independently from the daily and generational production of the lives of particular individuals and *in which therefore we can think economy apart from gender.* (Smith 1983:2, emphasis in original)

Thus gender relations, as well as those of ethnicity and race, are integral to the organization of productive activities. The theoretical and analytical separation of gender from the economy (productive relations) is itself the product of capitalist development, which creates a progressive separation between civil society, politics and the economy in the first place, and in the second place renders relations of gender, race and ethnicity more abstract and invisible to productive processes (see Smith 1983, 1985; Mole 1979–80, Sayer 1979).

When we treat class, ethnicity and gender as relations arising out of the long-term processes of domination and struggles over the means of production and reproduction, a very different picture of their interrelationship emerges. We find that we don't have to develop a set of criteria, be they 'economic' or pertaining to descent, for defining gender, ethnicity and class. We see that these are relations which have crystallized over time as Canada developed from a colony of England and France to a nation built on male supremacy. Indeed, we can trace ethnic-group formation and gender relations in terms of the development of capitalism in Canada, first through its history of colonization, then through immigration policies which changed over time in response to the demands of nation-building. People were recruited firstly from Ireland, then from the Ukraine and Scandinavia, to build up an agrarian base for England and Canada; they were imported from China through an indentured labour system to build the railways for Canada's westward expansion; more recently people from southern Europe were recruited to fill gaps in the construction industry. In the overall framework of immigration, men and women were/are treated differentially. For example, Chinese men were not allowed to bring their wives and families to Canada so they could not propagate and spread the 'yellow menace' (Chan 1983). Even today, men and women enter Canada under different terms and conditions. The majority of Third World women enter the country either as domestic workers on temporary work permits or as 'family class' immigrants who depend for their livelihood on the head of household or the sponsor (see Estable 1986; Djao and Ng 1987).

Indeed, the emergence of the Native people as a group, not to mention the Metis subgroup, is the result of the colonization process which destroyed, reorganized, fragmented and homogenized the myriad tribal groups across the continent. Until recently, the differential and unequal status of Indian women was set down by law in the Indian Act (see Jamieson, 1978). Ethnicity and gender are essential constituents of the Canadian class structure.

When we treat gender and ethnicity as relations constituted through people's activities, we also begin to see the different kinds of work carried out by men and women in nation-building. Examining the history of nation-building from a feminist perspective, Roberts (1990) divides this work between 1880 and 1920 into two aspects. The first had to do with developing the infrastructure of the economy: a nationwide transportation system, a manufacturing base and a commodity market, and so on. The development of this aspect of the economy was the domain of men. The second aspect had to do with the building of the human nation: the development of a population base in Canada. Women reformers (whom Roberts calls upper-class 'ladies') were the active organizers of this aspect of nation-building. To ensure the white character and guarantee the Christian morality of the nation, upper-class British women worked relentlessly to organize the emigration of working-class girls from Britain to serve as domestics and wives in the New World (see also Lay 1982). They were the first people to establish immigration societies in Canadian cities to oversee the plight of immigrants.

Similarly, Dehli's (1990) research on school reforms in Toronto at the turn of the century shows how middle-class mothers of (mainly) Anglo-Saxon background worked to enforce a particular version of motherhood on working-class immigrant women. In the 1920s, Toronto experienced a serious depression. During this time, many working-class immigrant women were forced to engage in waged work outside the home. Alarmed by the declining state of the family (many working-class children attended school hungry and poorly dressed), middle-class women worked hard to propagate and enforce 'proper' mothering practices on working-class families. This is when the notion of 'proper motherhood' gained prominence in the organization of family life through the school system (Dehli 1990; Davin 1978). These examples point to the class-based work done by men and women to preserve Canada as a white nation and to enforce a particular ideology to guarantee white supremacy.

But as ruling-class men consolidated their power over the state apparatus, they also began to take over and incorporate women's work into the state. Thus, Roberts found, by 1920, control over immigration and the settlement of immigrants had shifted from the hands of the ladies to the hands of state officials. As state power was consolidated, women's work was relegated more and more to the domestic sphere (Roberts 1990; Smith 1985). Similarly, community work has been incorporated into the local state, in boards of education (Dehli 1990). The central role played by middle-class women in school reform was supplanted by the development of an increasingly elaborate bureaucracy at different levels of the state. Interestingly, it was also as the state consolidated its power that sexuality became controlled by law. During this time, homosexuality became a crime, and sexual intercourse was legitimized within legal marital relationships (see Kinsmen 1987).

I am not arguing that gender and ethnicity are reducible to class. I maintain that the examination of gender, ethnicity and class must be situated in the relations of a specific social formation which have to do with struggles by groups of people over time for control of the means of production and reproduction. An examination of the history of Canada indicates that class cannot be understood without reference to ethnic and gender relations, and that gender and ethnicity cannot be understood without reference to class relations.

It should now be clear why I asserted earlier that gender, ethnic and class relations are inextricably linked to the formation of the Canadian state, if we see the state as the culmination and crystallization of struggles over the dominant (in the case of Canada, capitalist) mode of production. The history of the Native people, from the fur trade period to their entrapment in reserves, is the most blatant example of this. The Loyalists' expulsion of the Acadians, a primarily agrarian group with a subsistence economy, from the rich arable lands of the Atlantic region, offers further historical testimony to the consolidation of power and control by the Anglo-Saxons. The struggles among groups of Irish, Scottish and English descent in the Maritimes (Acheson 1985) is yet another example.

Although we don't have an encompassing picture of the detailed interplay of gender, ethnicity, class and the formation of the Canadian state, because few systematic studies based on this conceptualization have been carried out, we can begin to see the centrality of these elements through a review of selected historical studies. Armstrong's (1987) research on the Family Compact during the eighteenth and nineteenth centuries, for example, begins to pinpoint the genesis of the Ontario establishment. He describes the ways in which groups of Scottish and English origin consolidated their power through the acquisition of land and wealth, marriage, and connections with British officialdom, which eventually culminated in the formation of the Canadian elite. He ends by suggesting that once in power, the elite tended to 'de-ethnicize' themselves (Armstrong 1987:290).

The process that Armstrong describes becomes, in the twentieth century, what Porter (1967) has called 'the vertical mosaic'. While Porter's empirical study of the interrelationship between ethnicity and class is essentially correct, his positivism has prevented him from coming to grips with the actual connections between ethnicity, class and the state. While he rightly points out that the upward mobility of certain groups tends to be curtailed by their ethnicity, he fails to understand that ethnic relations are part of the organization of productive relations in Canada, and that the state is the culmination of the struggles between the various groups over time. The framework proposed here also explains the emergence of what some researchers have called 'ethnic nationalism' (e.g. Richmond 1983; Nagel 1987) which is being played out at the present historical juncture, in which capital is undergoing a major global restructuring.

In sum, I have presented some historical sketches illustrating ways in which the dynamic relations of gender, race/ethnicity and class underpin the development of Canada as a nation-state. It is important to note that these sketched events are not presented as instances to support a particular theoretical proposition. Rather, I have made use of a way of understanding the world that does not splinter different historical events and moments into compartmentalized fields or areas of study (see Smith 1974, 1987b). In the latter approach, what upper-class women did would be seen as 'women's history', which has little to do with the organization of the labour market and the continuance of Anglo supremacy in nation-building, which in turn would be seen as 'imperial history'. The framework I put forward enables us to assemble a picture of the formation of Canada as a nation-state with strong racist and sexist assumptions and policies from the seemingly separate pieces of history which are in fact pieces of the same jigsaw puzzle. We may thus come to see racism and sexism as the very foundations of Canadian nationalism.

Political implications

What can be learned from this discussion? I want to end by exploring how we may work to eradicate sexism and racism from our praxis as feminists, as intellectuals, and as people of colour.

The first thing that needs to be said is that gender, race/ethnicity and class are not fixed entities. They are socially constructed in and through productive and reproductive relationships in which we all participate. Thus, what constitutes sexism, racism, as well as class oppression, changes over time as productive relations change. While racism today is generally defined in terms of discriminatory practices directed mainly at dark-skinned people (Blacks, South Asians, Native people, for example), skin colour and overt physical differences were not always the criteria for determining racial differences. Historically, the Acadians were treated, by the Scots and the Irish, as people of a different race, and were discriminated against and suppressed accordingly. Their experience of racial oppression is no less valid than that encountered by the Native people and today's ethnic and racial minorities. Within each racial and ethnic group, men and women, and people from different classes, are subject to differential treatment. For example, while virtually no Chinese labourer or his family was allowed to enter Canada at the turn of the century thanks to the imposition of the head tax, Chinese merchants were permitted to immigrate during this period (Chan 1983).

Thus, our project is not to determine whether gender, race/ethnicity, class or the economic system is the primary source of our oppression. The task is to discover how sexism and other forms of gender oppression (e.g. compulsory heterosexuality,[4] racism, and class oppression) are constituted at different historical junctures so that the dominant groups gain hegemony over the means of production and reproduction—bearing in mind that the state in modern society is a central site of the struggles among groups. Recognizing ways in which the state divides us at each historical moment would enable us to better decide how alliances could be forged across groups of people in order to advance the struggle against racial, sexist and class oppression.

From the above analysis, it becomes clear that racism and sexism are not merely attitudes held by some members of society.

I am beginning to think that they are not even just structural, in the sense that they are institutionalized in the judicial system, the educational system, the workplace, etc. (though of course they are). More fundamentally, they are systemic: they have crystallized over time in the ways in which we think and act regardless of our own gender, race and class location, and the ways in which business is ordinarily conducted in everyday life. This is what Bannerji (1987) has called 'common sense racism'.

Thus, we cannot simply point the finger at the media, the schools, etc. and accuse them of gender and racial discrimination. While we begin from a recognition of the fundamental inequality between women and men, and between people from different racial and ethnic groups, at the everyday level we have to recognize that we are part of the institutions that perpetuate this, and pay attention to the ways in which our own practices create, sustain, and reinforce racism and sexism. These include the mundane and unconscious practices of what and to whom we give credence, of the space we take up in conversations with the result of silencing others, and of the space we don't take up because we have learned to be submissive. We need continuously to re-examine our history, as well as our own beliefs and actions, so that we are better able to understand and confront the ways in which we oppress others and participate in our own oppression. While this in itself will not liberate us completely from our own sexist and racist biases, it is a first step in working towards alternative forms of alliances and practices which will ultimately help us transform the society of which we are a part.

Notes

1 See, for example, the charge of racism by Native and Black women of Toronto's International Women's Day Committee (IWDC) in 1986, and the subsequent debates in socialist feminist publications such as *Cayenne* in 1986 and 1987.
2 Harding (1986) has called this 'the standpoint approach'. But while both Hartsock and Smith insist on the primacy of women's standpoint in social analysis, their theories differ in important ways. The way I make use of their work is to begin with the experiences of women of colour and to situate their experiences in the social organization of Canadian society. I make no claim to follow their theories exegetically. See Ng (1982).
3 See various Ontario Ministry of Education documents since the mid-1980s. A pivotal document is 'The Development of a Policy on Race and Ethnocultural Equity', Report of the Provincial Advisory Committee on Race Relations, September 1987.
4 This term is used by Adrienne Rich (1983) to describe the institution

of heterosexuality which discourages and stifles intimate relationships among women.

References

Acheson, T.W. (1985) *Saint John: The Making of a Colonial Urban Community*, University of Toronto Press, Toronto.

Armstrong, Frederick H. (1987) 'Ethnicity and the Formation of the Ontario Establishment' in Leo Driedger ed. *Ethnic Canada: Identities and Inequalities*, Copp Clark Pittman, Toronto.

Bannerji, Himani (1987) 'Introducing Racism: Notes Towards an Anti-Racist Feminism' *Resources for Feminist Research*, 16(1):10–12.

Braverman, Harry (1974) *Labour and Monopoly Capital: The Degradation of Work in the Twentieth Century*, Monthly Review Press, New York.

Chan, Anthony B. (1983) *The Gold Mountain: The Chinese in the New World*, New Star Books, Vancouver.

Corrigan, Philip ed. (1980) *Capitalism, State Formation and Marxist Theory*, Quarter Books, London.

Cox, Oliver C. (1948) *Caste, Class and Race: A Study in Social Dynamics*, Doubleday, NY.

Davin, Anna (1978) 'Imperialism and Motherhood' *History Workshop* 5:9–65.

Dehli, Kari (1990) 'Women in the Community: Reform of Schooling and Motherhood in Toronto' in Roxana Ng, Gillian Walker & Jacob Muller (eds), *Community Organization and the Canadian State*, Garamond Press, Toronto.

Depres, Leo ed. (1975) *Ethnicity and Resource Competition*, Mouton, The Hague.

Djao, Angela W. & Roxana Ng (1987) 'Structured Isolation: Immigrant Women in Saskatchewan' in Kathleen Storrie (ed), *Women: Isolation and Bonding: The Ecology of Gender*, Methuen, Toronto.

Driedger, Leo ed. (1987) *Ethnic Canada: Identities and Inequalities*, Copp Clark Pittman, Toronto.

Estable, Alma (1986) *Immigrant Women in Canada: Current Issues*, a background paper prepared for the Canadian Advisory Council on the Status of Women, March.

Harding, Sandra (1986) *The Science Question in Feminism*, Cornell University Press, Ithaca.

Hartsock, Nancy C.M. (1983, 1985) *Money, Sex and Power: Toward a Feminist Historical Materialism*, Northeastern University Press, Boston.

Jamieson, Kathleen (1978) *Indian Women and the Law in Canada: Citizens Minus Ottawa*, Canadian Advisory Council on the Status of Women and Indian Rights for Indian Women, April.

Juteau-Lee, Danielle & Barbara Roberts (1981) 'Ethnicity and Femininity: d'après nos experiences', *Canadian Ethnic Studies*, 13(1):1–23.

Kinsmen, Gary (1987) *The Regulation of Desire: Sexuality in Canada*, Black Rose Books, Montreal.

Lay, Jackie (1980) 'To Columbia on the Tynemouth: The Emigration of

Single Women and Girls in 1862' in Barbara Latham & Cathy Kess
(eds) *In Her Own Right: Selected Essays on Women's History in B.C.*,
Camosum College, Victoria.
Marx, Karl 1954 *Capital. Volume 1*, Progress Publishers, Moscow.
Marx, Karl and Frederick Engels (1967) *The Communist Manifesto*, trans.
by Samuel Moore, Penguin Books, New York.
——(1970) *The German Ideology*, International Publishers, New York.
McIntosh, Mary (1978) 'The State and the Oppression of Women' in
Annette Kuhn & Ann Marie Wolpe (eds) *Feminism and Materialism:
Women and Modes of Production*, Routledge, London.
Mole, David (1979–80) Lectures on 'Marx and Political Economy' Depart-
ment of Sociology, Ontario Institute for Studies in Education.
Nagel, Joan (1987) 'The Ethnic Revolution: Emergence of Ethnic
Nationalism' in Leo Driedger (ed) *Ethnic Canada*.
Ng, Roxana (1982) 'Immigrant Housewives in Canada: A Methodological
Note' *Atlantis* 8(1):111–118.
——(1984) 'Sex, Ethnicity or Class: Some Methodological Considerations'
Studies in Sexual Politics 1:1–45.
Ng, Roxana and Judith Ramirez (1981) *Immigrant Housewives in Canada*,
Immigrant Women's Centre, Toronto.
Ontario Ministry of Education (1987) *The Development of a Policy on
Race and Ethnocultural Equity*, Report of the Provincial Advisory
Committee on Race Relations. September.
Pineo, Peter C. (1977) 'The Social Standing of Ethnic and Racial
Groupings' *Canadian Review of Sociology and Anthropology*,
12(2):14–15.
Pineo, Peter C. & John Porter (1985) 'Ethnic Origin and Occupational
Attainment' in M. Boyd, *et al.* (eds) *Ascription and Achievement:
Studies in Mobility and Status Attainment in Canada*, Carleton Uni-
versity Press, Ottawa.
Porter, John (1965) *The Vertical Mosaic*, University of Toronto Press,
Toronto.
Rich, Adrienne (1983) 'Compulsory Heterosexuality and Lesbian
Existence' in Elizabeth Abel & Emily K. Abel (eds) *The Signs Reader—
Women, Gender and Scholarship*, University of Chicago Press, Chi-
cago.
Richmond, Anthony (1983) 'Ethnic Nationalism and Postindustrialism' in
Jean Leonard Elliot (ed), *Two Nations, Many Cultures: Ethnic Groups
in Canada*, 2nd ed. Prentice-Hall, Scarborough.
Roberts, Barbara (1990) 'Ladies, Women and the State: Managing Female
Immigration, 1880–1920' in Roxana Ng, Gillian Walker & Jacob
Muller (eds) *Community Organization and the Canadian State*, Gar-
amond Press, Toronto.
Said, Edward (1979) *Orientalism*, Vintage Books, New York.
Sayer, Derek (1979) *Marx's Method: Ideology, Science and Critique in
'Capital'*, Harvester Press, Sussex.
Smith, Dorothy E. (1974) 'Women's Perspective as a Radical Critique of
Sociology' *Sociological Inquiry*, 44(1):1–13.
——(1983) 'Women's Equality and the Family' in Allan Moscovitch &

Glenn Drover (eds) *Inequality: Essays on the Political Economy of Social Welfare*, University of Toronto Press, Toronto.

——(1985) 'Women Class and Family' in Varda Burstyn & Dorothy E. Smith, *Women, Class, Family and the State*, Garamond Press, Toronto.

——(1987a) *The Everyday World as Problematic: A Feminist Sociology*, University of Toronto Press, Toronto.

——(1987b) 'Feminist Reflections on Political Economy', paper presented at the annual meeting of Political Science and Political Economy, Learned Societies Meetings, Hamilton, June.

VanderBerghe, Pierre L. (1981) *The Ethnic Phenomenon*, Elsevier, New York.

Weber, Max (1968) *Economy and Society: An Outline of Interpretive Sociology*, Bedminister, New York.

13 Slash and suture: Post/colonialism in *Borderlands*/La Frontera: *The New Mestiza*

Annamarie Jagose

Recent feminist theorizations of difference have invoked Gloria Anzaldúa's *Borderlands/ La Frontera: The New Mestiza*,[1] with its foregrounding of the figures of the border and the *mestiza*, as demonstrating the possibility of a radically new, utopic hybridization.[2] Such readings of *Borderlands* are also misreadings. They remain oblivious to the duplicity of those figures (the border, the *mestiza*), to their internal resistance to utopic recuperation. Moreover, the attempt to project a postcolonial politics as the undoing of differences and distinctions is itself, as Homi Bhabha suggests, to represent the very condition of the colonial relationship.

For Anzaldúa, as for Foucault, modern power is at once prohibitive and productive (Foucault 1980:12). In *Borderlands*, the border is emblematic of this duality. It is a legislative line which insists on demarcation and separation. Yet equally it is an interface, a conjoining of the categories it distinguishes. The border, therefore, is the mark of both a regulatory demarcation and a prohibited intermixture. The slash of the border is the very site at which the taxonomic closure it effects is also indefinitely deferred. In this respect, the border is always in excess of itself.

Anzaldúa's discussion of the border is centred primarily, but not solely, on the American/Mexican border:

> The actual physical borderland that I'm dealing with in this book
> is the Texas–US Southwest/Mexican border. The psychological
> borderlands, the sexual borderlands and the spiritual borderlands
> are not particular to the Southwest. In fact, the borderlands are
> physically present whenever two or more cultures edge each other,

212

where people of different races occupy the same territory, where under, lower, middle and upper classes touch, where the space between two individuals shrinks with intimacy. (Preface)

Borderlands provides an elaboration of the border's adjudication of such binarily opposed terms as inside and outside, American and Mexican, heterosexual and homosexual, same and different, familiar and alien. This elaboration continually demonstrates that the border, that site of simultaneous prohibition and production, is never only the site of distinction but also and equally the site of undifferentiation. Nevertheless, and despite her insistence on the double function, the slash and the suture, of the border, Anzaldúa's final utopic projection attempts to install the *mestiza* beyond distinction and demarcation, as the harbinger of a global miscegenation and hybridization which eliminates forever the possibility of difference and separation. In this sense, *Borderlands* replicates the mechanisms of defence that it critiques. In order to reclaim the border as a utopic site, *Borderlands* must disavow the border's difference from itself. This disavowal is an instance of the taxonomic closure which, for *Borderlands*, is properly symptomatic of prohibitive power. Ironically, then, this nostalgia for the border and the *mestiza* as the site of a utopic intermixture, hybridization and confluence merely inverts the privileging, in the discourse of colonialism, of the slash of the border as the site of taxonomic closure.

The classic geometric representation of the border is the line, a representation which is certainly typographically prominent in *Borderlands*. However, the *function* of the border is better represented not as the single stroke of the dividing line, nor even as the twin categories it bisects, but as a tripartite structure constituted by the line of the border and its flanking binarisms. For if the line of the border is deceptively simple, its force field, the intermeshing operations of attraction and repulsion which it simultaneously prohibits and allows, is inevitably more complicated. The border's linear stroke initiates the interaction of three components, the line of the border itself and the two oppositional categories it paradoxically conjoins in an elaboration of their distinctness. This representation of the border as initiating a fundamentally trichotomous structure provides a model capable of inscribing the border's dynamics, the way in which its interposition between categories enables the at times simultaneous opposition, codependence, and even coincidence of those categories.

On the front cover of *Borderlands*, and reproduced (in black and white) on the title page, the title of the book and the author's name appear. A thick, horizontal line subdivides the typographical block. Its central position provides balance, signalling an equivalence between the two groups of words—one upper, one lower—that it separates. Above this line, in large plain type, is the word 'Borderlands'; below this line, in an identical but italicized typeface, are the words '*La Frontera*'. Above 'Borderlands', distinguished from it by a 75 per cent reduction in size and a more elaborate typeface, are the words 'Gloria Anzaldúa', justified to the right-hand margin. Below '*La Frontera*', typographically identical to the author's name but justified to the left-hand margin, are the words 'The New Mestiza'. The equivalence, across the dividing line of the border, of 'Borderlands' and '*La Frontera*', of 'Gloria Anzaldúa' and 'The New Mestiza', is further emphasized on the front cover by the fact that while the former pair is printed in orange, as is the border's broad stroke, the latter pair is printed in yellow.

The secondary importance of the author's name and the book's subtitle, suggested on the front cover by their appearance in a smaller size and different colour, is further emphasized in two places within the book: on the page before the title page and on the page between the title and contents page. Here, the subtitle and the author's name are omitted entirely as the details of the cover and title page are circulated in a condensed version by the abbreviated fraction formed by 'Borderlands', '*La Frontera*' and the horizontal border which marks them off from each other. Further, it is this more compact rendering of the text's title which is imitated typographically by the titles of *Borderlands*' two internal sections. The title of the first section holds its two parts—'*Atravesando Fronteras*' and 'Crossing Borders'—separate, above and below the by now familiar border of the heavy horizontal line. Similarly, the title of the second half of the book, '*Un Agitado Viento*/Ehécatl, The Wind', is presented as typographically equivalent, its two halves horizontally divided.

This proliferation of titles wherein the domain of the primary title is divided between two secondary titles which moreover replicate the original title's form, foregrounds the border's horizontal cleavage. In each of these three titles the border negotiates a translation, a carrying over. Again, in the form of each title—the Chicano/Spanish, the English and the horizontal bar which determines their relationship—a tripartite figure is described. As a figure of translation, each title describes both the equivalence of the original and the translation, the way in which the one may be substituted for the other, across the divide of the border, and their incommensurability, the way in which the interface of the border, functioning not as a slash but as a suture, negotiates their

inevitable difference. For is it not a deferred mitosis that governs
these fractional titles whose hybridized halves, in that they are
translations of each other, are always the same and, insofar as
they are translations, always different?

The dark line of the border, then, which demarcates the site
of translation, the very site of transition, also refuses that translation. In a continual redramatization of the impossibility of the
'dream of translation without remnants', the border neither marks
a translation from Chicano Spanish to English nor one from
English to Chicano Spanish but enables a relationship between
both (Derrida 1979:119). The border's horizontal bar simultaneously denotes, through its function as an axis of symmetry,
sameness and, given that one half of each title is not substituted
for but supplements the other in a recognition of the inherent
asymmetry of translation, *difference*. The border, in short, divides
without division.

The preface (any preface) takes up an ambivalent position in
relation to the text. As that which precedes the text, it is clearly
distanced from that text; yet equally, as an introduction to the
text, it is not properly outside the text. Both within and without,
its very nature raises questions about interiority, exteriority and
the difficulty of categorically distinguishing one from another. The
preface to *Borderlands* specifically addresses issues of interiority
and exteriority with its shifting structures of address inscribed
across the inside/outside opposition and its foregrounding of the
border as the site which both undoes and reformulates the distinction between inside and out. The passage in which the
opposition between inside and outside is most clearly delineated
and equally, most overtly confounded, foregrounds the threshold
through its focus on entrance and invitation:

> Presently this infant language, this bastard language, Chicano
> Spanish, is not approved by any society. But we Chicanos no
> longer feel that we have to beg entrance, that we need always to
> make the first overture—to translate to Anglos, Mexicans and
> Latinos, apology blurting out of our mouths with every step.
> Today we ask to be met halfway. This book is our invitation to
> you—from the new mestizas. (Preface)

Anzaldúa, having emphasized the devalorization and illegitimacy of Chicano Spanish, identifies herself, through her use of the
first-person plural pronoun, with the group 'Chicanos'. The limits
of this group are defined in opposition to a second group, 'Anglos,
Mexicans and Latinos'. Or are they? For the last sentence, whose
second-person pronoun recasts the group 'Anglos, Mexicans and
Latinos' as the implied readers, also demonstrates a certain pro-

nominal slippage about the possessive 'our'. Initially, the 'our' of 'our invitation' appears equivalent and identical in reference to the previous 'our' of 'our mouths': both possessive pronouns seem to refer to 'Chicanos'. However, retrospectively, it becomes clear that this second 'our' refers to another subject, the group introduced in the passage's final phrase, 'the new mestizas'. It is not that the swerve effected by the substitution of 'mestizas' for 'Chicanos' takes place simply at the level of the signifier. Any synonymity between the two nouns is undermined entirely by their differentiated inflections as the feminine 'mestizas' supplants the (generically) masculine 'Chicanos'.

The various slippages and consolidations that are effected around the twin poles, the 'we' and the 'you', of Anzaldúa's address are further complicated by the reversibility of the categories of inside and outside; the way in which interior is reinscribed as exterior and *vice versa*. Initially, the illegitimacy of Chicano Spanish, 'this bastard language', ensures its exterior location. It is not simply outside the dominant language system of English but exterior to all legitimate, recognized language systems since it 'is not approved by any society'. By corollary, the exteriority of Chicano Spanish is extended to those who speak it, Chicanos. The outside position of Chicanos is evident in that they are represented as previously having had 'to beg entrance', 'to make the first overture', 'to translate'. However, these past strategies of gaining admission are now rejected by Anzaldúa on behalf of '[us] Chicanos'. Translation is not only refused but characterized as demeaning apology and, through a series of grammatical equivalences, represented as an act of supplication. Nor does translation ensure the passage of outside inside. Rather, it ensures that at the point at which the outside gains entrance to the inside, it *becomes* the inside. Translation does not transgress but reinforces the border's jurisdiction, its production of the oppositional and hierarchical categories of inside and outside.

This refusal of translation is markedly different from the refusal signalled by the back-cover blurb: 'Interspersing Spanish phrases that English readers will understand in context, she [Anzaldúa] gives us a powerful and cohesive book.' Anzaldúa's refusal of translation is primarily a consequence of her recognition (and rejection) of the linguistic dominance of English and, less so, Castilian Spanish. Her refusal to translate her hybridized language, her desire to 'write bilingually and to switch codes without always having to translate' (59), is a refusal to subordinate her text to the demands of dominant-language speakers and for linguistic purity.

The blurb, through a series of omissions and collapses, centralizes English (and the English speaker) while minimizing or totally excluding other languages. In this way, 'Spanish' is inaccurately used as an umbrella term to designate Chicano Spanish, which is elsewhere referred to by Anzaldúa as a hybrid language composed from Castilian Spanish, North Mexican dialect, Tex-Mex and Nahuatl and, moreover, specifically contrasted with the hegemonic system of 'pure' Spanish. Not only is the text misconstrued as an interaction between English and Spanish language systems but the blurb prioritizes the English part of this conglomeration through the uneasy, if implicit, conflation of 'English readers' with 'us'. Furthermore, the rewriting of the text as 'gift' rather than, as the preface maintains, 'invitation' again reworks the nature of the transaction between the text and the reader. It reinscribes the movement of the reader to the text as the movement of the text to the reader, and consequently affirms the bastard status of Anzaldúa's hybrid language since 'as long as I have to accommodate the English speakers rather than having them accommodate me, my tongue will be illegitimate' (59).

As Anzaldúa's refusal of translation suggests, interiority is no longer what is sought: 'Today we ask to be met halfway.' However, the apparent neutrality of this threshold between outside and inside, this liminal 'halfway' point, is soon reinscribed within the very inside/outside dichotomy it appears to transcend. For the 'halfway' point between the language systems earlier identified as outside and inside, and spoken by 'Chicanos' and 'Anglos, Mexicans and Latinos' respectively, is precisely the continual movement 'from English to Castilian Spanish to the North Mexican dialect to Tex-Mex to a sprinkling of Nahuatl to a mixture of all these.' This 'halfway' point of hybridized languages negotiates a new inside, a prioritized space equivalent to the text of *Borderlands*. The text, therefore, is both an invitation to this liminal space and the site of liminality itself, as what was once outside and begging entrance is now inside and issuing invitations: 'This book is our invitation to you.'

Many of *Borderlands'* figural strategies converge at the term 'invitation'. An invitation is, after all, one possible negotiation of the border; a negotiation which necessarily contravenes the border's demarcation between categories, for example, of inside and outside, even while acknowledging it. Indeed, the various shifts evident around the terms 'inside' and 'outside' are preceded and, in some senses, predicted by similar reversals and collapses which occur earlier in the preface around another pair of dichotomously opposed terms, 'familiar' and 'alien':

Living on borders and in margins, keeping intact one's shifting and

multiple identity and integrity, is like trying to swim in a new
element, an 'alien' element.. .And yes, the 'alien' element has
become familiar—never comfortable, not with society's clamor to
uphold the old, to rejoin the flock, to go with the herd. No, not
comfortable but home. (Preface)

Here, having been worked through a series of other oppositions—
tradition as opposed to innovation, the old versus the new—the
category 'alien' is collapsed into its opposite, the 'familiar'. In
Anzaldúa's account, living on the border, between classificatory
categories, entails a familiarization of the alien. For the inhabitant
of the border, paradoxically what is familiar is precisely that which
is unfamiliar, foreign. Finally, Anzaldúa describes that which is
alien as 'home'. With this word, the divergent etymological origins
of 'alien' and 'familiar' are, at once, insisted upon and denied.
For while the concept of *home* allies itself with 'familiar', that
which is connected with the household, and in doing so emphasizes the difference between this term and 'alien', that which
belongs to another person, place or family, that which is not one's
own, it nevertheless rewrites the latter in terms of the former.
Home becomes an increasingly central term for Anzaldúa, negotiating a new relationship between such oppositions as 'interior'
and 'exterior'; 'familiar' and 'alien'; 'true' and 'false'. Anzaldúa's
construction of *home*, therefore, negotiates a triangulated connection between opposing terms.[3] It is also itself oppositionally
constructed, being both that which is familiar yet alien and that
which is alien, therefore familiar.

Anzaldúa writes that the nearly 2000-mile-long chain-link
fence that divides Mexico from the United States creates 'a third
country—a border culture'(3). 'The prohibited and the forbidden'
are the inhabitants of this border culture. '*Los atravesados* live
here: the squint-eyed, the perverse, the queer, the troublesome, the
mongrel, the mulato, the half-breed, the half dead . . . ' (3). Of
this illegitimate hybridization, this outlawed borderland, Anzaldúa
writes, 'This is my home/this thin edge of/barbwire' (3). Home,
then, is that which is alien; from *alius*, that which is other. Yet
there is another otherness, that of the lesbian (and the homosexual), which is, in turn, alienated from the alien: '[t]he secret I tried
to conceal was that I was not normal, that I was not like the
others. I felt alien, I knew I was alien. I was the mutant stoned
out of the herd, something deformed with evil inside' (2–3). 'The
queer' (18), the lesbian and the homosexual, mark a further site
of alienation. They are cast out from the cast-offs; dispossessed
by the dispossessed. It is this aspect of home which is

foregrounded by Anzaldúa's punning definition, 'Fear of Going Home: Homophobia' (19).[4]

In her opening pages, Anzaldúa conflates the lesbian body and her homeland, metaphorically describing each in terms of the other—the land as injured body, the body as divided land:

> 1,950-mile-long open wound
>   dividing a *pueblo*, a culture,
> running down the length of my body,
> staking fence rods in my flesh,
>   splits me   splits me
>   me raja   me raja. (2)

The last two lines typographically reinforce the ideas of incision and partition, since the body of the text is also divided. Furthermore, since the division holds apart two identical segments, it acts as a textual prefiguration of Anzaldúa's construction of the border as that which separates itself from itself. The border is that cleavage which brings oppositional categories into existence, this cleavage being always already the symptom of a repressed synonymity.[5]

The attempt to segregate a domestic from an alien space, to hold an interior place of safety distinct from an exterior place of danger, founders on the equally fundamental indistinguishability of these oppositions:

> In the Borderlands
>   you are the battleground
>   where enemies are kin to each other;
>   you are at home, a stranger . . . (19)

Consequently, the border presides equally over hospitable and hostile interactions of familiar and alien and *divides while rendering indistinguishable* the categories of inside and outside.[6]

Sexual exchange in *Borderlands* is explicitly characterized and valorized as an operation whose traversals of the border between inside and outside ensure only a utopic undifferentiation, merging and indistinguishability. However, I want to argue that, given Anzaldúa's own insistent articulation of the border as that which simultaneously holds apart and brings together, the sexual exchange transacted across that border is more properly represented as operating in two congruous yet contradictory ways. Furthermore, it is this necessarily and irresolvably contradictory nature of the border, and consequently the contradictory nature of sexual exchange whose operations the border structures, which enables and is ultimately disavowed by Anzaldúa's text. For on the one hand, the formalized transgression of the border between kinship groups through the reciprocal exchange of women, while facilitating a relationship between groups, nevertheless also ensures, through the woman's role in patronymic reproduction, the continuing discreteness of these kinship groups, the maintenance of a distinct inside and outside. On the other hand, sexual exchange is equally that which obscures the distinction between kinship groups through the installation of kinship relations which breach the border's line of demarcation. The utopic (cl)aims of *Borderlands*, of the *mestiza*, of 'hybrid progeny' (77), of '*la primera raza síntesis del globo*' (77), of 'crossbreeding' (81), of 'blood . . . intricately woven together' (85), in emphasizing only the confounding of the categories of inside and outside by sexual exchange, describe that classic defence mechanism of disavowal, of not knowing what is known. Having been structured around a representation of the border as that which both separates and conjoins, the text attempts in its final polemical statements to distance itself from this knowledge.

Borderlands argues for the political radicalness of hybridization and intermixture and, by corollary, for the political conservatism of separatism and classificatory demarcation. This is evident in Anzaldúa's self-descriptions; in, for example, her sexual and ethnic identifications. Anzaldúa defines her identification as a lesbian in terms of gender-integrative transitivity,[7] emphasiszng in this way the equivalence of her location at the border between genders with that of gay men:

> There is something compelling about being both male and female, about having an entry into both worlds . . . I, like other queer people, am two in one body, both male and female. I am the embodiment of *hieros gamos*: the coming together of opposite qualities within. (19)

In a similar manoeuvre, Anzaldúa defines her identification as Chicano through a hybridization of geographically and historically opposed terms:

> We call ourselves Mexican-American to signify we are neither Mexican nor American . . . we don't identify with the Anglo-American cultural values and we don't totally identify with the Mexican cultural values. We are a synergy of two cultures with various degrees of Mexicanness or Angloness. (62–63)

Here, with the valorization of the 'coming together of opposite qualities', of 'synergy', the border's function of commingling opposite qualities is prioritized over its function of distinguishing between them. Finally, *Borderlands* fixes the border as only the site of indistinguishability and not also of distinction, of conflu-

ence and not also of divergence. Furthermore, in insisting on a
difference between these two opposites, the border as slash and
the border as suture, in maintaining that they can be held separate
and distinct from each other, *Borderlands* replicates, at the border
of the border, precisely that defensive mechanism of disavowal
that elsewhere it attributes to the operations of colonialism.

Anzaldúa's historical account of the original peopling, the
invasions, the territorial remapping of the land on either side of
what is the modern American/Mexican border, with its focus on
interracial union and genetic intermingling, is also an account of
an evolutionary development which produces as its most highly
evolved form the figure of the *mestiza*. Beginning with a documentation of the sixteenth-century intermixture of the
'pure-blooded Indians' and the conquering Spaniards which
resulted in *'una nueva raza, el mestizo, el mexicano'* (5) and
proceeding with the ensuing 'continual intermarriage between
Mexican and American Indians and Spaniards [which] formed an
even greater *mestizaje'* (5), *Borderlands* envisages a future when
'la raza cósmica, a fifth race embracing the four major races of
the world' (77) will eradicate racial difference through an internationally realized genetic intermingling. The *mestiza* is the utopic
forerunner of *la raza cósmica*:

> At the confluence of two or more genetic streams, with
> chromosomes continually 'crossing over,' this mixture of races,
> rather than resulting in an inferior being, provides hybrid progeny,
> a mutable, more malleable species with a rich gene pool. From this
> racial, ideological, cultural and biological cross-pollinization, an
> 'alien' consciousness is presently in the making—a new *mestiza*
> consciousness, *una conciencia de mujer.* (77)

In that this passage's vocabulary of eugenics is reiterated in both
descriptions of the bilingualism of Chicano Spanish and the
generic intermixture of *Borderlands*, the *mestiza* functions as a
figure of the text itself.[8] The same notions of evolutionary development through hybridization which characterize *Borderlands'*
construction of the *mestiza* also structure its description of Chicano Spanish:

> Chicano Spanish is a border tongue which developed naturally.
> Change, *evolción, enriquecimiento de palabras nuevas por
> invención o adopción* have created variants of Chicano Spanish, *un
> nuevo lenguaje.* (55)

Chicano Spanish is represented as a linguistic hybridization whose
natural evolution is in response to the deficiencies of either
standard English or standard Spanish. It is 'a language with terms

that are neither *español ni inglés*, but both'; 'a forked tongue, a variation of two languages' (55). Similarly, *Borderlands'* bilingualism, its oscillation between Chicano Spanish and English, and its generic intermixture, its shifts between poetry and prose, history and autobiography, is constituted by the text itself as a merging of different parts, a hybridization; as an entity 'with pieces of feather sticking out here and there, fur, twigs, clay'; as '*Coatlicue*, dove, horse, serpent, cactus' (66–67).

Yet this valorization of the border as the site of linguistic or generic confluence, is itself structured by the repression of the border as site of linguistic or generic demarcation. For, in the terms of *Borderlands'* own argument, intermixture is possible only where there is segregation. The attempt to celebrate the Chicano's location as a linguistic and genetic switchpoint, a point of evolutionary conflux, is undermined by the insistent return of repressed notions of partition and division which equally characterize his position: *Quién está tratando de cerrar la fisura entre la india y el blanco en nuestra sangre? El Chicano, si, el Chicano que anda como un ladrón en su propia casa* (63). Here, having answered the question of who is endeavouring '*cerrar la fisura entre la india y el blanco*', to heal the rift between racial others, with the emphatically repeated '*el Chicano, si, el Chicano*', the text describes this (r)evolutionary figure of utopic union with the simile '*como un ladrón en su propia casa.*' As in Freud's characterization of repression as the struggle between host and guest over the domestic threshhold, this description of the Chicano as a thief in his own house exposes the safe interior of the domestic space as not only unprotected against, but always already infiltrated by, the threatening exterior. Here, the figure of the Chicano, like the border at which he is located, violates that space at the very moment of securing (in the double sense of obtaining and making safe) a triumphally new space of undifferentiation, breaking and entering it by the same means which enabled it in the first place, difference and distinction.

In a passage which strongly recalls the famous Kristevan denunciation that 'the very dichotomy man/woman as an opposition between two rival entities may be understood as belonging to *metaphysics*' (Kristeva 1981:33), Anzaldúa maintains, through a similar metaphor, that the rift marked by the border can be sealed:

> But it is not enough to stand on the opposite river bank, shouting questions, challenging patriarchal, white conventions . . . At some point, on our way to a new consciousness, we will have to leave the opposite bank, the split between the mortal combatants

somehow healed so that we are on both shores at once and, at
once, see through serpent and eagle eyes (78–79).[9]

After all the talk of blood flowing together, of chromosomes
crossing over, of genes intermingling, it comes as no surprise that
the *mestiza* with her mixed racial origins stands as the actual and
potential site of this utopic merger: 'That focal point or fulcrum,
that juncture where the *mestiza* stands . . . is where the possibility
of uniting all that is separate occurs' (79). The *mestiza* is '*un
amasamiento*, . . . an act of kneading, of uniting and joining'; she
is the 'evolutionary step forward', 'the great alchemical work', 'a
product of crossbreeding' (81).

However, despite the text's promotion of the *mestiza* as the
site of confluence and intermixture, as the point at which the
border's suture triumphs over the border's slash, there is an
undeniable sense in which the very concept of the *mestiza*, not to
mention those closely associated concepts of alchemy, hybridization and crossbreeding, intrinsically depend on concepts of
diversity, distinction and difference. Equally, the textual strategies
of bilingualism and generic intermixture, represented by the text
as operations of unification and confluence, are similarly marked
by the repressed operations of division and separation. It is not,
then, that the *mestiza* is an inadequate figure of the text. Rather,
in that what is represented as most foreign to the concept of the
mestiza, segregation and distinction, is also always that which is
most familiar to it, the *mestiza*, in reproducing the border's
inseparable functions, provides the perfect figuration of the text.
The *mestiza* and indeed all the other privileged textual figures of
conflux, including those of bilingualism and generic intermixture,
demonstrate that the continual transitions of the border which
they effect not only obscure the border's demarcation of oppositions but also and equally reinscribe that very demarcation.

In the final chapter of *Borderlands*' first section, the *mestiza*
is privileged for her transcendence of difference. She is the pro-
genitor of a prospective *raza cósmica* whose subsumption of the
existing four races will effectively eliminate the possibility of racial
difference. However, this utopic homogenization denies what *Borderlands* elsewhere demonstrates, the necessary coincidence, at the
border, of difference and undifferentiation, of separation and
conjunction. Arguing, against Anzaldúa's final figuration of the
mestiza but in accordance with her earlier elaboration of the
border's dual function, that the *mestiza* is at once a figure of
intermixture *and* demarcation, is not simply to reinscribe that
figure within the original structure of dominance and inequality
against which it struggles. It is to argue that any prioritization of

the *mestiza* must not be on account of her alleged ability to secure a space beyond the border's adjudication of cultural difference but on account of her foregrounding of the ambivalence which enables even as it destabilizes the colonial relationship.

Thus the border trope of the *mestiza* does not mark the end of the colonial relationship; it represents its very condition. As a cultural and racial hybrid, the *mestiza* does not prefigure some eugenically sanctioned exit from those operations of recognition and disavowal, energized by the border's simultaneous conjunction and cleavage, which *Borderlands* documents. Rather hybridity, insofar as 'it is not a third term that resolves the tension between two cultures . . . in a dialectical play of "recognition" ' (Bhabha 1985:98), continually remarks upon the inevitable ambivalence which marks the colonizer's attempts to fix the relation between same and different, between familiar and alien, between inside and out. The *mestiza*, that hybrid colonial subject, that 'mimic [wo]man' (Bhabha 1989:236) who is at once similar and different, does not move beyond, but replicates the function of, the border in producing an uncanny effect for the colonizer, implicating him or her in relations of identification which must then be disavowed.

Bhabha writes that 'the hybrid is finally uncontainable because it breaks down the symmetry and duality of self/other, inside/outside' (Bhabha 1985:100). This uncontainability of the hybrid, of the *mestiza*, does not signify a triumphant excess of the border's legislation. Rather, it demonstrates the way in which the border's legislative authority is always already in crisis. In this respect, my reading of the *mestiza* reinstalls her within that economy of the border from which Anzaldúa represents her as making a break. It posits her as the paradoxical site of undifferentiation and distinction, a contradiction which *Borderlands'* representation of the border demands but ultimately represses. In agreement with Bhabha's argument that 'the production of hybridization', far from initiating an escape from, *is* 'the effect of colonial power' (Bhabha 1985:97), my reading of the *mestiza* represents her not as transcending but as figuring that fundamental irresolution of the legislative border which, as *Borderlands* demonstrates, structures colonialism.

Notes

With the appearance of this article, I would like to thank Linda Hardy for walking (and talking) me through my doctoral thesis, of which this is a revised chapter. Its present form is due, in large part, to Linda's thoughtful editing, whose strenuousness easily outstrips the—admittedly complex—operations of slashing and suturing.

1 Anzaldúa 1987. Future quotations from the text will include page numbers only.

2 See, for example, Nelson 1989 in *Trivia*'s special issue on language and difference, which significantly also includes an interview with, and an article by, Anzaldúa. See also the mobilization of one of Anzaldúa's key terms— *mestiza*—in both Engelbrecht 1990 and de Lauretis 1990.

3 Since my discussion here attempts to articulate the instability of the signifier 'home' in Anzaldúa's text, in order to avoid confusion (although at the same time demonstrating precisely how, through the oppositional construction of that term, this confusion is articulated), my text will distinguish typographically between the three uses of the term whenever such a distinction is possible. Accordingly, the italicized *home* will be the umbrella term which indicates the general category; the unadorned *home* indicates the childhood home of the narrator; 'home' in inverted commas refers to that home which the narrator constructs for herself. These last two typographical distinctions are used in the same way in *Borderlands*.

4 Given their mutual concern with the intersections of racism, colonialism, sexism and heterosexism, it is interesting to compare Anzaldúa's construction of *home* with that of bell hooks. Whereas for Anzaldúa, *home* is the site of a radical division, for hooks it is the site of resistance to a divided world:

> Historically, African-American people believed that the construction of a homeplace, however fragile and tenuous (the slave hut, the wooden shack), had a radical political dimension. Despite the brutal reality of racial apartheid, of domination, one's homeplace was the one site where one could freely confront the issue of humanization, where one could resist. (hooks 1990:42)

Whereas for Anzaldúa, *home* is a site of further fragmentation, for hooks it is 'that space where we return for renewal and self-recovery, where we can heal our wounds and become whole' (hooks 1990:49). For a related commentary on the ambivalent fascination for *home* in the writings of women of colour, see Martin & Mohanty 1986.

5 See Freud's 'The Uncanny', where he argues that the semantic coincidence of the antonyms *heimlich* and *unheimlich* signals a disavowed connection between them: 'the *unheimlich* is what was once *heimisch*, familiar; the prefix 'un' ['un'] is the token of repression' (Freud 1919:24).

6 Freud's essay 'Repression', characterizes repression as a conflict between a host and a guest over the disputed territory of home (Freud 1915:153). His account both confirms and problematizes *Borderlands*' triangulation of the terms 'familiar', 'alien' and 'home'. In Freud's account, the host/guest relationship, of invitation and acceptance, is reinscribed as one of siege and defence. The threshold's liminal border both marks, and fails to make, a distinction between the defensive host and the aggressive guest. For a more detailed deconstruction of the opposition between the terms guest and host, see Miller 1979.

7 See Sedgwick 1990:86–90, for the definition of this and other terms

used to negotiate constructions of heterosexuality and homosexuality with regard to systems of sexuality and gender.

8 Interestingly, given the *mestiza*'s construction as hybrid and its figuring of the text's bilingualism, the word 'mestiza' appearing both italicized and unitalicized in the text, functions as a typographical border between English and Chicano Spanish, uniting and separating the two language systems.

9 The reference to the serpent and eagle is contextualized earlier by Anzaldúa: '*Huitzilopochtli*, the God of War, guided them to the place (that later became Mexico City) where an eagle with a writhing serpent in its beak perched on a cactus. The eagle symbolizes the spirit (as the sun, the father); the serpent symbolizes the soul (as the earth, the mother). Together they symbolize the struggle between the spiritual/ celestial/male and the underworld/earth/feminism' (5).

References

Anzaldúa, Gloria (1987) *Borderlands*/La Frontera: *The New Mestiza*, Spinsters/aunt lute, San Francisco.

Beaver, Harold (1981) 'Homosexual Signs', *Critical Inquiry* 8(1):99–119.

Bhabha, Homi K. (1985) 'Signs Taken for Wonders: Questions of Ambivalence and Authority Under a Tree Outside Delhi, May 1817', *Europe and Its Others*, ed. Francis Barker *et al.* vol. I. University of Essex, Colchester, pp. 89–106.

——(1989) 'Of Mimicry and Man: The Ambivalence of Colonial Discourse', *Modern Literary Theory: A Reader*, ed. Philip Rice and Patricia Waugh, Hodder & Stoughton, London. pp. 234–241.

de Lauretis, Teresa (1990) 'Eccentric Subjects: Feminist Theory and Historical Consciousness,' *Feminist Studies*, 16, pp. 115–150.

Derrida, Jacques (1979) 'Living On: Border Lines', *Deconstruction and Criticism*, Harold Bloom *et al*, Seabury Press, New York.

Engelbrecht, Penelope J. (1990) ' "Lifting Belly Is a Language": The Postmodern Lesbian Subject', *Feminist Studies*, 16:85–114.

Foucault, Michel (1980) *The History of Sexuality*, vol. 1, trans. Robert Hurley, Vintage Books, New York.

Freud, Sigmund (1915) 'Repression', *The Complete Psychological Works of Sigmund Freud*, vol. 1, trans. and ed. James Strachey, Hogarth, London, 1957, pp. 146–158.

——(1919) 'The Uncanny', ibid., vol. 17, pp. 219–252.

Hooks, bell (1990) 'Homeplace: a site of resistance', *Yearning: Race, Gender and Cultural Politics*, South End Press, Boston.

Kristeva, Julia (1981) 'Women's Time', trans. Alice Jardine and Harry Blake, *Signs: A Journal of Women in Culture and Society*, 7:13–35.

Martin, Biddy & Mohanty, Chandra Talpade (1986) 'Feminist Politics: What's Home Got to Do with It?' *Feminist Studies/Critical Studies*, ed. Teresa de Lauretis, Indiana University Press, Bloomington, pp. 191–212.

Miller, Hillis, J. (1979) 'The Critic as Host', *Deconstruction and Criticism*, Harold Bloom et al. Seabury Press, New York, pp. 217–253.

Nelson, Linda (1989) 'After Reading: *Borderlands*/La Frontera by Gloria Anzaldúa', *Trivia: A Journal of Ideas*, 1:90–101.

Sedgwick, Eve Kosofsky (1990) *Epistemology of the Closet*, University of California Press, Berkeley.

14 Voice and representation in the politics of difference

Anna Yeatman

In the contemporary era of multiply contested oppressions, feminism has been forced to lose its innocence. It has had to discover that it is predicated on the assumption that gender is the most salient base of oppression, and that this assumption is always going to be most compelling for those women who do not experience ethnicity, race and class as additional bases of oppression. Feminism has had to discover its partiality in a context where its insistence on the primacy of gender oppression is incommensurable with the emphases of emancipatory movements oriented to different axes of oppression. Even the oppression of non-heterosexist sexualities enjoins a politics only partly commensurable with that of feminism.

To put this differently, the distinct bases of oppression do not add up in the same direction. Women may be oppressed by men, where these positionings are assumed to be cross-class and cross-race; but when blacks are oppressed by whites, these are cross-gender and cross-class positionings. All of which puts paid to the old Hegelian/Marxist emancipatory universal subject. It is impossible to find a practical bearer of this subjectivity, i.e. a social movement which can stand in for and represent all the various and distinct interests in emancipation.

Multiple interests in emancipation have tabled difference as a central axiom in the contemporary politics of justice. Not only do the various emancipatory movements have to accept each other's presence, but they have to work with this presence as part of their *internal* politics.

Feminism indeed has developed an internal politics of difference, a politics of contestation in respect of dominant and marginalized voices within feminism. A politics of difference *within* an emancipatory movement makes explicit the contradictory nature of emancipation itself, its orientation by both interest and ethics. When an emancipatory movement develops an internal politics of difference, a chronic tension and degree of contestation attends all its work of self-representation, when this self is made to appear a categorical identity: 'women' as distinct from 'men'. Identity works to foreclose politics, to substitute interest for ethics, in this case by suppressing the contested differences among women. When these differences are uppermost, their acknowledgment as legitimate requires the identity of the movement to subside so that its internal politics may be practised.

Political contestation is always in the name of an ethical universal, equality in this case. Equality is claimed but its achievement is perpetually deferred. This is because each reforming achievement, which transforms policy in the name of equality, establishes a new regime of governance. All governance works in terms of a bounded community, a community of identity, and thus establishes insiders and outsiders. Reformed policy may radically alter the established political community's identity and thus the nature of its distinction between insiders and outsiders, but this distinction is always generated by policy. Emancipatory politics concerns the assertion of the claim for equality in relation to the wrongs of exclusion generated by policy. This has an ethical-universal dimension which is irreducible.

Emancipatory movements have never been very good at the appreciation and elaboration of this ethical dimension of politics. For reasons of their critical rejection of established policy, they focus their attention on how the custodians of the established order discursively cast the universals of politics in ways which preserve their own privileged relationship to voice and representation. When it is understood that the universal has to be particularized in order to exist, it is all too easy to assume that there is no universal dimension of politics, but only 'interest'. This is a conclusion easy and even comforting to adopt when the subject is positioned within politics as the righteous emancipatory contestant vis-à-vis the custodians of the established order. It is a conclusion very much more difficult for those who are positioned as custodians of the established order within an emancipatory politics to accept. Yet this is precisely the positioning of white, western and middle-class women within contemporary feminism.

If theirs is a position which invites a closer look at the nature of emancipatory politics, indeed a look that does not elide the ethical dimension of this politics into the economic category of 'interest', this may conduce to a more adequate understanding of politics. Politics is the space between established policy and an emancipatory movement's claims on equality. These claims are made through showing how policy wrongs the emancipatory subject by excluding or marginalizing the category of persons to whom this subject belongs. Politics requires and depends on the interlocutory and performative dynamics of what is a contestatory *relationship*, demanding an ethical response from both those who are positioned as privileged by policy and those who are positioned as wronged by policy. If the custodians of established policy move to foreclose politics in favour of a quick and dirty adoption of new protocols of inclusion, we can be sure that the inclusion is token only and that the core policy order remains unreformed. For policy to be genuinely reformed, it has to be understood in an ongoing process of re-formation precisely because it is continuously accountable to politics. Among other things, this means that policy requires to be informed by an ongoing and openly contested politics of voice and representation.

Politics can be foreclosed from the other direction, by the emancipatory subject when it attributes to the custodians of the established order nothing more than an interest in perpetuating it. The result of this type of foreclosure is that this subject is forced to define itself in terms of the status of exclusion, namely as lying outside positive, political capacity. A politics of *ressentiment* follows whereby the emancipatory subject turned victim alternately practises moral appeal to and blackmail of what is now hypostatised as the dominant subject custodian of the established order. This is a pseudo-politics oriented to the exercise of force, moral terror in this case.

Ressentiment is a recurrent theme within the history of feminism (on this see also Tapper 1992). However, it is all the more problematic when feminism has to encounter its own internal politics of emancipation. When it is an internal politics, there are many inhibitions working against the acting-out of a simple manichean struggle between a victim and an oppressor class. This chapter is designed to explore some of the possibilities of insight which arise from an internal politics of emancipation within feminism. It concludes with a brief examination of 'the Bell debate' as an instance of an emerging politics of difference within Australian feminism.

Justice and the contemporary politics of difference

The politics of difference requires as perhaps no other politics has done a readiness on the part of any one emancipatory movement to show how its particular interest in contesting oppression links into and supports the interests of other movements in contesting different kinds of oppression. However, if this is a requirement it must be because it has more than practical force. In other words, if the internal politics of difference within the contemporary feminist movement practically requires of this movement an acceptance of an inclusive politics of voice and representation, practicality does not automatically translate into a just acceptance of an inclusive politics of voice and representation. By 'just acceptance', I mean an ethical orientation to such a politics.

As James Flynn (1992) shows, in a well-made critique of feminist theorists of the politics of difference such as Iris Young, Moira Gatens, and myself, an empirical approach to social differences guarantees nothing in relation to how they should be politically arbitrated and negotiated. There has to be an intervening ethic or value which indicates how these differences should be arbitrated and evaluated in a way which ensures just process and outcomes. Here I define the ethic or value which I wish to interpose in this way in terms of a participatory democratic construction of a politics of voice and representation. Once this kind of intervention is made within a politics of difference it offers an ethical criterion of which 'differences' are acceptable or unacceptable. As Flynn (1992) again points out, those of us who have adopted a postmodern approach to a feminist politics of difference have committed ourselves to the post-Enlightenment proposition that there is no ethical truth, i.e. there is no transcendental God, reason or nature which can guarantee the truth value of our ethics. This notwithstanding, once we become aware of the intervening ethical term in a democratically oriented politics of difference, we are responsible for arguing its value in a logically coherent manner and for operationalizing this value in a way which makes it adequate to the historically specific pragmatics of the present.

This task faces two distinct inhibitions. First, emancipatory movements are situated as marginal to the terms of participation within established political discourse. When they claim to be wronged by their exclusion from established political discourse, they demonstrate this wrong by showing how the political discourse fails to live up to its own professions of universalism. Yet, inevitably, the emancipatory movement converts its marginality into an oppositional relationship to established political discourse wherein the dependency of this movement's terms of critique on established discourse is completely occluded. This occludes also the possibility of discerning common ground with the emancipatory movement's antagonist.

The second inhibition arises from the equally inevitable tendency of the emancipatory movement to highlight the partiality, the bias, of the universalistic-ethical professions of established political discourse. They thereby appear as the rhetorical mask of something which lies outside ethics: interest. This inhibition conduces to a cynical and instrumental approach to politics. It is regarded as a contest ultimately settled by force, where force is directed by interest.

Both of these inhibitions contribute to a lack of understanding of the importance of democratic procedure and process as conditions of politics. Emancipatory movements tend to deploy the historically achieved democratic features of an established political discourse in an irresponsible way. They make two gestures in relation to democratic values, both of which elide the task of democratic acceptance of them.

The first gesture is a utilitarian acceptance of what already exists by way of democratic institutional process and guarantees of rights. This acceptance is implicit in the street demonstration, which actualizes the formal democratic freedom of assembly and, in so doing, may remind the less than democratically oriented local police force and provincial government that this is a widely accepted component of formal democracy. Such implicit reliance on formal democracy (for this concept, see Heller 1988) does not necessarily translate into an ethical reiteration of the importance of this value. Rather the value can be taken for granted as one's due, as something for which one is not responsible but which is owed one by those who are powerful.

The second gesture is to criticize the inadequacies of the extant institutions and culture of democracy by showing how they are specified in ways which mirror the kind of human nature that characterizes those who belong to the dominant oppressor/exploiter group. Such critiques are critically important to the advancement of claims on justice on the part of minority social movements. But they are rarely sufficiently developed to become a positive contribution to contemporary policy debate about how the extant institutions and culture of democracy need to be changed so as to become more inclusive. If this contribution were to be made, it would have to be linked into an *explicit* appreciation of what has already been achieved by way of these institutions, and thus into a metaphor of building on and extending these achievements.

This would accord what is typecast as the oppressor/exploiter dominant group something other than that status, namely one of possessing a more or less shared ethic with the minority movements. It would also involve these minority movements in the assumption of a leadership role in the explicit constructions of this ethic, a business which is usually left to the philosophical and jurisprudential minds of the dominant group. For minority movements to explicitly construct this ethic is to participate in its reconstruction. That is, their historical positioning of relative exclusion from the modern democratic ethic means that when they reiterate this ethic they are actually recasting it. Reconstructive work of this kind draws emancipatory movements into the political domain of policy-making, a step which threatens their outsider and contestant status and one which minority movements, for reasons of both guarding their contestatory *hubris* and political independence, are usually reluctant to take.

The two gestures of contestation combine to allow minority group movements to 'stand outside looking in', and to maintain a contradictory position of both dependency on and critical rejection of the *status quo*. 'Difference' in this context is underspecified in its potential politico-ethical significance for recasting the universalistic presuppositions of modern democratic values.

Minority group movements are assumed to have in common their respective differences from the dominant subject norm, and in this sense to have something in common in respect of their claims on justice, but what this may be is left unexplicated.

It is not surprising that these emancipatory movements tend to evade the responsibility their own successes in contemporary political life have earned them in contributing positively and creatively to the reconstruction of a democratic polity. After all, these are movements of subjects who have been interpellated within the terms of modern democracy as immature, emotional, irrational and uncivilized. When these movements 'stand outside looking in' they act to confirm these interpellated identities, not to challenge them. An orientation to ethics is viewed as a privilege of the ruling elite—of those who can impose their own ethos as an ethics which others those whom it exclude—and is thereby reduced to interest.

This reduction of ethics to interest is endemic in contemporary politics. It arises from a misunderstanding of what happens to the intrinsically universalistic cast of ethics when this universalism is shown to be perpetually inflected by the partiality and particularity of the voice by which it is expressed. The standard response to the discovery of the 'interested' character of all universalistic, ethically oriented politics is to propose that the universalism is the rhetorical mask for interest, and that, therefore, a universally oriented politics is a contradiction in terms. The reduction of ethics to interest inevitably substitutes an economics for a politics.

If universalism is not simply or only the rhetorical mask for interest, it follows that all professions of universalism have an ethical component. Thus, when the established participants in politics profess attachment to universal values like democratic participation, freedom and equality, this attachment is *both* interested and ethical. On the one hand, it is an attachment to the current restrictions on political participation, to the ways in which the current discourse of political participation elicits and positively mirrors their voice while excluding the voice of those whom this discourse others. On the other hand, it is an attachment to the universalizable features of these values.

This latter attachment interpellates or calls into being those who contest the established political discourse because of the ways in which it constitutes them as excluded from it (for an account of how modern republican discourse interpellated feminism in this way, see Landes 1988). Universalism not only interpellates the contestatory other but, when this contestatory other argues that established policy wrongs equality, this process and relationship of contestation is *politics*. Let us examine what happens at this point more closely.

Universalism and the politics of difference

In this discussion I have been using Jacques Rancière's conception of the political. Rancière (1992:58) argues that 'the political is the encounter between two heterogeneous processes'. The first is the process of governance, namely a process which manages the political process by stabilizing it procedurally, bounding who can participate and who cannot, and which orients it to consensus formation and decision-making. Rancière appropriately terms the process of governance *policy*. The second concerns the process of emancipation, 'a set of practices guided by the supposition that everyone is equal and by the attempt to verify this supposition' (Rancière, 1992:58). This process is enacted and developed by emancipatory movements which contest established policy and show how it wrongs particular categories of people by excluding or marginalizing them. Contestation of this kind is made in the name of equality. Equality is a value that does not refer to what is already achieved—to, for instance, the equality of all Australians—but is always enunciated in terms of what is not achieved, in terms, that is, of the exclusions of the established system of governance. Conceived in this way, equality is a value which arises only within the politics which opens up between emancipatory claims and established policy. Rancière (1992:59–60) puts this point thus:

> . . . the process of emancipation is the verification of the equality of any speaking being with any other speaking being. It is always enacted in the name of a category denied either the principle or the consequences of that equality: workers, women, people of color, or others. But the enactment of equality is not, for all that, the enactment of the self, of the attributes or properties of the community in question. The name of an injured community that invokes its rights is always the name of the anonym, the name of anyone.

This is a promising approach for a democratic politics of difference precisely because it insists on the relational nature of this universal value, equality. Equality does not reside in a community that exists prior to politics, and therefore it has no ontological referent. Any such referent—'we Australians' or 'we human beings'—is, as we know, always specified to a particular and exclusive political community whose identity establishes unambiguous boundaries between who belongs and who does not. Equality exists only within the relationship of political contestation, where those who are excluded by established policy both show its bias *and* make a claim on a prospectively more inclusive policy. It is this relationship of political contestation which equalizes the voices of those who represent respectively both established policy and the emancipatory movement. This equalizing process is in the nature of politics. If those who are given voice in and through established policy should act to foreclose this politics in any way, the equalizing process is halted. Such foreclosure can happen in a number of ways: via for example, the simple re-assertion of established policy and a correlative refusal to listen to the contestatory voices of emancipation; or a more subtle version, the appropriation of the contestatory and emancipatory voice by the custodian subject voice. The first temptation of the custodians of established policy is to monopolize the arbitration of how this policy is to be interpreted in the face of such contestation. For such monopoly rights to operate, the custodians have to 'speak for' those who represent the emancipatory movement. We shall see how this operates in a moment when I turn to an Australian case study of the contemporary politics of voice and representation within feminism.

If the custodians, as I term them, are continually stepping back from the *politics* of voice and representation into established policy, when they *participate* in this politics they are contributing to the development of the value of equality. This they do when they listen to the contestatory voices, the act of listening already transforming the established procedures of who gets to participate within the process of governance. This they do also when they invite the contestatory voices to work with them to determine how established policy needs to change to become more inclusive. Theirs, then, is by no means a consistently conservative role even if, at the point at which they enter the universalism of an equality-oriented politics, their mode of entry must always be inflected by their privileged discursive positioning.

What of the contestatory voices? As long as they articulate the gap between established policy and their claims on inclusion/participation, theirs is a selfhood which does not translate a prior identity into politics. Instead it comes into being through this politics of emancipation. Rancière attempts to specify the peculiar properties of this politically interpellated selfhood, here in reference to the distinctively nineteenth-century emancipatory subject, the proletarian:

> . . . proletarian was not the name of any social group that could be sociologically identified . . . In Latin, *proletarii* meant 'prolific people'—people who make children, who merely live and reproduce without a name, without being counted part of the symbolic order of the city . . . *Proletarians* was the name given to people who are together inasmuch as they are between: between several names, statuses and identities; between humanity and inhumanity, citizenship and its denial . . . Political subjectivization is the enactment of equality—or the handling of a wrong—by people who are together to the extent that they are between. It is a crossing of identities, relying on a crossing of names: names that link the name of a group of class to the name of no group or class, a being to a nonbeing or a not-yet-being. (Rancière 1992:61)

Strictly speaking, the emancipatory voice exists only within this in-between: the in-between of existence as those who are excluded from the established symbolic order of governance and as those who aspire to enter what would have to become a new symbolic order of governance. Theirs is an existence in between 'difference' and 'equality'. Inevitably, those who are interpellated as the voices of the emancipatory movement move outside the politics of this relationship of contestation. No one can live in politics all the time. When they move outside politics, they are tempted to ontologize their condition, to articulate their emancipatory contestant status within politics so that it becomes their 'identity' for all purposes associated with social life. Thus, the feminist lives her life as a feminist and subjects all aspects of her everyday life to the political discourse of emancipation. Sometimes this is appropriate, as when 'politics' opens up in the space between the established policy of a household and a claim on equality. However, much of the time it involves the inappropriate subjection of social and personal life to what becomes a pseudo-politics, namely a politics without contestation or dialogue wherein the ethical features of political discourse become empty and righteous slogans.

When the custodians of the established discursive order of governance observe this of those who have been interpellated as emancipatory subjects, the conditions are ripe for a reciprocal cynicism. Each group reduces the complexities of its quite differently positioned participation in an emancipatory politics to an interested, to indeed an identity, politics. The custodians are made to appear to only use universalistic rhetoric to conserve their established privileges. The emancipatory subjects are made to appear to use universalistic rhetoric to advance a new claim on privilege. In each case, the identity which is the referent for the interest concerned is made to appear as though it precedes and is given to politics.

When this happens for an emancipatory movement, the identity of the emancipatory subject concerned is not only ontologized but retroactively established. Thus, 'women' is made to appear a stable identity, with its own culture, which has existed for all time. This is quite different from the contingencies and fragility of the category 'women' as it comes into being in the space in between a phallocentric symbolic order of governance and the no-name for those who are excluded from this order.

In the case of the custodians, they are made also to appear as though they inhabit a given identity, one which confers on them the same culture of selfhood and interest. This being the case, they must subordinate claims on equality to their interest in conserving their privileges, that is, they must subordinate ethics to interest. Again, the ontologizing of their identity requires it to be projected back into the past, to be assumed as though it has always been what it is.

When (in this way) the politics of emancipation is converted into a politics of identity, the potential for change contained in the former is made over into a no-change politics. For if those who are positioned differently, in terms of privilege and its lack within a politics of emancipation, are simply articulating given and opposed interests, there can be no change. One interest must dominate the other, and politics be subordinated to economics.

An economic approach to politics occludes the universalism of politics as it has been defined by Rancière. This universalism resides in the space which politics constitutes, 'the political being the field for the encounter between emancipation and policy in the handling of a wrong' (Rancière 1992:59). The ethical or universal quality of politics develops precisely in the specification in the name of emancipation of how established policy excludes, marginalises, others certain categories of persons.

Of course, such specification indicates directions for how policy needs to change, to become more inclusive in relation to the particulars of these claims on emancipation. Policy can and does change in these ways, and sometimes the nature of the change can be considerable depending on the contingent aspects of how a politics of emancipation is followed into the policy arena. This notwithstanding, one thing is clear: changed policy always brings about a new discursive order of inclusions and exclusions. There can be no positive categorical specification of what it means to be human in a particular societal type without this specification working to generate those who belong and those who do not. In this sense, policy always works on behalf of a politics of identity, reformed or otherwise. Policy must always presuppose a political community that is already defined. This is why Rancière (1992:59) argues that policy must always wrong equality. The truth of this point does not obviate the critical and practical importance of struggles to successfully reform policy.

Voice and representation in contemporary feminist politics

It is a salutary and uncomfortable experience for subjects who have been interpellated as emancipatory voices to find themselves the custodians of policy. This, of course, is what has happened to those of us who are positioned as the custodians of feminism, namely white, Western and middle-class women. We have been challenged as voices privileged by the discursive economies of feminism by those whom these same economies disprivilege: women who are not white, Western, middle-class.

Historically, the custodians of feminism drew discursive legitimacy from the universal civilizing mission of the middle class in extending to their less fortunate sisters a matronizingly appropriative embrace. They could speak on behalf of *all* women, including those less privileged than themselves. It is this which the new emancipatory movements within feminism specifically contest. Within the nature of this contest, the custodians of feminism are inevitably caught within the question of how far they can be affiliated with these new movements without simultaneously appropriating their voice. Yet, as I have argued above, those who are interpellated as the custodians of an existing symbolic order cannot simply walk away from the fray. They have to enter it, and they can do so more or less 'politically', i.e. in a way more or less oriented to the universalistic and ethical aspects of this contestation. One particular issue which the custodians of an established order confront is how far can they advocate for the voice of new emancipatory contestants without beginning to appropriate this voice.

A case study of some of these issues is afforded by the Bell debate. This debate signals an emergent politics of voice and representation within Australian feminism, where, in this instance, Aboriginal women are contesting the historically established dominance of white settler women in Australian feminism. In other instances, women marked as 'ethnic' or 'migrant' women in the Australian context of governance are contesting how established Australian feminism reproduces the unmarked status of the model Australian white settler as British (Anglo-Celtic) in origin (see Gunew, Chapter 1, this volume).

The institutions of Australian feminism, and their established custodians, belong clearly to what Rancière terms the domain of governance or policy. In what follows, it becomes clear that 'the Bell debate' is more of a debate between the custodians as to which of them is the better 'advocate' of Aboriginal women than it is yet an elaborated politics of difference within Australian feminism. This would be a politics whereby not only Aboriginal but non-English-speaking-background feminist voices have become prominent emancipatory voices to the extent both that the custodians no longer monopolize agenda-setting within the movement, and that the differences within the movement can not be arraigned within any one binary (white settler/Aboriginal, migrant-non-English-speaking-background/English-speaking-Anglo-Celtic, lesbian/heterosexual, and so on).

In September 1990 I intervened, through a paper presented to the plenary session of the second Australian Women's Studies Association national conference in Melbourne, in the debate concerning Diane Bell's (1989) article 'Speaking about Rape is Everyone's Business' in *Women's Studies International Forum*. The debate was occasioned by a protest letter to this journal from a group of twelve Aboriginal women who took issue with Bell, with this white Australian feminist's assumption that she could speak on behalf of Aboriginal women, and, in particular, with Bell's use of Topsy Napurrula Nelson's name as co-author of the article.[1] Topsy Napurrula Nelson was an informant/friend to Diane Bell during the years in which she was undertaking anthropological field work in Central Australia, working particularly with Aboriginal women, and offering consultancy advice on their pursuit of

particular land claims. This debate has already assumed clear
historically sequential contours. The primary documents, as it
were, are now tabled in the public domain of feminist academic
publishing. The letter of protest from the twelve Aboriginal
women—Jackie Huggins, Jo Willmot, Isabel Tarrago, Kathy Wil-
lets, Liz Bond, Lillian Holt, Eleanor Bourke, Maryann Bin-Salik,
Pat Fowell, Joann Schmider, Valerie Craigie, Linda McBride-Levi—
which was not published by *Women's Studies International Forum*
for more than a year, has now been published with a comment
from the editors and a long reply by Diane Bell. In the same issue
Bell (1991) restated and elaborated her original argument that
rape of Aboriginal women by Aboriginal men in the Northern
Territory is every feminist's business.[2]

My manifest intentions in intervening in this debate were, first,
to accord more public representation of the objections to the Bell
piece from Huggins *et al.* on the assumption that they were
opening up an important politics of voice and representation in
respect of Aboriginal women and white Australian feminists. I saw
it as a straightforward act of advocacy, extending my access to
the public space of a plenary session at the Australian Women's
Studies Association to Huggins *et al.*'s voices. In so doing, I
understood myself to be asking my sister white feminist audience
to determine where they stood on the issues opened up by Huggins
et al.'s contestation of Bell's assumption that there is a universal
feminist voice which can speak on behalf of all women. I argued
that 'we' were positioned by our shared historical location as racist
and that it was important that we listen to Jackie Huggins *et al.*'s
challenge to our racism:

> . . . just because you are women doesn't mean you are necessarily
> innocent. You were, and still are, part of that colonizing force.
> Our country was colonized on both a racially and sexually
> imperialistic basis. In many cases our women considered white
> women worse than men in their treatment of Aboriginal women,
> particularly in the domestic service field.

I proposed that the issue was whether we were prepared to
acknowledge both the fact and the implications of our shared
positioning as racist in relation to Aboriginal women. I suggested
not that Bell was any more racist than the rest of us, but that her
presentation of herself as an authoritative speaker in the matter
of intra-Aboriginal rape involved the familiar claim of modern
Western professional–scientific authority to speak about and on
behalf of others without their voices being present to arbitrate,
complicate and even contest this claim. Bell, it has to be said,
would fiercely contest this proposition: as she understands it she

also is using her access to cultural resources to open up an important politics, she is keeping faith with Topsy Napurrula Nelson by quoting her verbatim within the written text and by respecting the spirit of their conversations about how rape and violence are damaging Aboriginal women.

The issue as I have posed it cannot be settled by Bell's type of response. It is an issue of whether those who would contest our representations—whoever 'they' or 'we' turn out to be, these pronominal identities shifting with each context of positioning in relation to a politics of representation—are present to undertake this contestation. It is certainly the case that such presence cannot be left to the professional advocate quoting the contestant voice as I did with the letter from Huggins *et al.* in my conference paper.

If the politics of representation at hand is located within an academically institutionalised forum—an academic conference, seminar series, publication, classroom, etc.—then it is clear that the conditions for this kind of contestability depend on the presence of those who are positioned as minority group feminist intellectuals. This is who Huggins and her eleven co-signatories are. Contestability is possible only to the extent that those who would contest are able to directly enter the forum concerned. When, in the matter at hand, those positioned as subaltern intellectuals contest the way in which those positioned as hegemonic intellectuals engage in representation, a favourite response of the latter is to call into question the 'representative' status of the former. The former are both asked to stand in for their subaltern constituency—all Aboriginal women, in the instance discussed—and refused representative status because they are intellectuals, thus in this case identified with urbanized privileges which separate them from the vast majority of Aboriginal women in remote, rural areas. The hegemonic feminist intellectual thus plays out the same/difference game, in which these become mutually exclusive options: you are like us so we do not have to create space for your voice; you are the other, so when we invite you to speak, please speak on behalf of all others, all minorities, all difference. What is avoided is the complexity of dialogue that arises between subjects who understand themselves to be complexly like and different from each other, in this instance, between differently positioned intellectuals who have different constituencies in relation to their shared academic conventions of dialogue and debate.

This is not to suggest that intellectuals should not engage in wider forums of dialogue and debate concerning who we are and what we should do in relation to the shared conditions of our lives. This is the role of the public intellectual, who has to learn to communicate with non-academic audiences and interlocutors.

It is clear, I think, that the contemporary politics of difference inside the academy is likely to become corrupted by the introversion of academic competitive narcissism unless it is answerable to and located within this wider politics of representation.

Academic feminists are rarely let off this particular hook: they are asked to articulate a relationship between their movement and their academic identities. Often this becomes a relationship between institutional/policy and intellectual roles within the academy. In extra-academic contexts of representational politics, professional advocates (whether they be academics or other kinds of professionals) should be required to account for their professional advocacy in relation to the self-advocacy of those who use their services either as professional practitioners or as intellectuals. The opening up of public space here involves the process of developing this accountability within a dialogic partnership between professional and self-advocates (see Yeatman, 1992b). Bell may have contributed her share to the development of this accountability between herself as a professional advocate and the Aboriginal women like Topsy Napurrula Nelson who were positioned as self-advocates, but who lacked direct access to the written, policy-oriented text. This I cannot determine or evaluate. I am criticizing her in respect of her relationship to the politics of voice and representation among feminist intellectuals, a politics whereby professional and self-advocacy can be combined in the same participants.

What advocacy for and self-advocacy mean change fundamentally depending on the dialogical context. Within the academy and all forms of intellectual debate, as Spivak (1988:275) makes clear, intellectual re-presentation of other subjects inevitably drifts into political representation ('speaking for' these subjects in a political sense). In this respect, all intellectuals are positioned to speak *for*, to act as professional advocates. When, however, a politics of identity enters into intellectual representation, and an Aboriginal intellectual feminist contests white settler feminist representations of Aboriginal women's needs, self-advocacy has entered into the business of intellectual representation. This is no different from what feminist intellectuals do when they undertake self-advocacy in contesting the ways in which academic men engage in the various permutations of patriarchal universalism. In these contexts of contestation, the custodians of established policy are positioned as ones who would speak for, because they are appropriating the voice of, others. Their self-advocacy is revealed as the imperial project of self-aggrandizement through appropriation of the identity of others. It would seem that when I am positioned as a custodian of established policy in such a context of contestation,

I am not permitted a self-advocacy relationship to the politics of representation without this 'self' acquiring imperialistic appropriative qualities. Even if I am positioned contradictorily across multiple selves, some of them permitting access to the experience of social marginality, these cannot be harnessed to self-advocacy within this context without their being instrumentalized on behalf of my custodian positioning as one who would imperially appropriate the subaltern voice.

Let me give an example from a service delivery context. A professional member of the management commitee of an advocacy service for the carers of disabled people may herself be disabled. When she speaks on this committee, however, her voice is that of the professional advocate (one who 'speaks for'). It may acquire additional legitimacy as such because she has insight into what it means to be disabled, but it does not position her as a consumer voice on the management committee. If she achieves this position it is because the other professionals on the committee successfully collude with her to permit her to appropriate the direct voice of the consumer of the service, to ensure in effect that it not be heard. In another context altogether this disabled professional may be present as the voice of the consumer, her professional subject positioning assisting her in the articulation of the voice but not displacing it. This time she is positioned as an emancipatory subject engaged in contesting the custodians of established policy. On the former occasion it was the other way around.

In the case with which we are dealing, self-advocacy is a claim on recognition for selves which have been accorded no prior legitimacy within the politics of representation of Australian feminism. All forms of self-advocacy, in contesting the established relational dynamics of reciprocal recognition of selves, change the ways in which the previous participants understand themselves. In this instance, the previous participants are reconstituted as selves who are historically and contemporaneously positioned as colonizing selves in relation to the new claimants on participation. The contestatory subject is also reconstituted as selves who are now participant in the politics of Australian feminism. Change in self-understanding means a change in who we are.

In this case the change in who 'we' (white settler Australian feminists) are is to be situated within the coevality of our standing as participants with that of Aboriginal women within the polity of Australian feminism. This means that our vision for change for this polity and the larger national polity within which it is situated has to take up this relationship and work with it. Such work cannot occur without the participation of the actors concerned.

Notes

I would like to thank Margaret Wilson especially for the many conversations we have had that have enabled the analysis offered here; and Valerie Hazel for her critical and helpful reading of a draft of this chapter.

1 It is clear that if the text as such is considered Topsy Napurrula Nelson is not a co-author: the semiotic conventions of this text are not hers but it is important to point out that this would be no different if her voice were cited within a government policy report on violence and rape within Aboriginal communities.

2 The key documents and events in this debate were in the following order: Diane Bell's (1989) original article; the letter from Jackie Huggins *et al.* originally dated 1 February 1990, followed by correspondence to and fro with the editors of *WSIF*; the circulation within Australia of this letter and much of the ensuing correspondence at a Women and Anthropology Conference convened by Julie Marcus in Adelaide, April 1990; followed by discussion within the Women's Broadcasting Collective's 'The Coming Out Show' on ABC Radio, May 1990; my intervention in a presentation titled 'Feminism and the Politics of Difference' to the plenary session of the second Australian Women's Studies Association National Conference, University of Melbourne, 25–27 September 1990; the AWSA AGM's resolution at this conference urging the editors of *WSIF* to publish the letter from Huggins *et al.*; Jan Larbalestier's (1990) article; the follow up in *WSIF* by a further article by Bell (1991), and an Editorial/Letters to the Editor (1991) section, where the original letter by Huggins *et al.* and replies from the editors and Bell were published.

References

Bell, D. (1989) 'Speaking About Rape is Everyone's Business', *Women's Studies International Forum*, 12:403–416.

——(1991) 'Intraracial Rape Revisited: On Forging a Feminist Future Beyond Factions and Frightening Politics', *Women's Studies International Forum*, 1(5):385–412.

Connolly, W. (1984) 'The Politics of Discourse', in M. Shapiro ed. *Language and Politics*, New York University Press, NY.

Editorial/Letters to the Editors (1991) *Women's Studies International Forum*, 1(5):505–513.

Flynn, J. (1992) 'Postmodernism and Empiricism: No Substitute for Moral Principles', *Political Theory Newsletter*, 4(2):138–156.

Heller, A. (1988) 'On Formal Democracy,' in J. Keane ed. *Civil Society and the State*, Verso, London.

Landes, J. (1988) *Women and the Public Sphere in the Age of the French Revolution*, Cornell University Press, Ithaca.

Larbalestier, J. (1990) 'The Politics of Representation: Australian Aboriginal Women and Feminism', *Anthropological Forum*, 6(2):143–166.

Rancière, J. (1992) 'Politics, Identification and Subjectivization', *October*, 61, Summer: 58–65.

Spivak, G. Chakravorty (1988) 'Can the Subaltern Speak?' in *Marxism and the Interpretation of Culture*, eds. C. Nelson & L. Grossberg, Macmillan, London: 271–313.

Tapper, Marion (1992) 'Feminism and Ressentiment', *Arena Magazine*, no. 1, 41–44 (also in Paul Patton ed. *Nietzsche, Feminism and Political Theory*, Sydney: Allen & Unwin, forthcoming).

Yeatman, A. (1992a) 'Minorities and the Politics of Difference', *Political Theory Newsletter*, 4(1):1–11.

——(1992b) 'A Vision for Women's Studies at the University of Waikato', *New Zealand Journal of Women's Studies*, 8(1):30–47.

Index

abject, foreign languages as, 17
abjection, concepts of, 13–14, 16–17;
  sexual, in Japanese girls' comics, 186
Aboriginal culture, 61, 62; multiculturalism
  and, 5
Aboriginal feminists, Australian feminism
  and, 239–42, 243; Bell debate and,
  239–40
Aboriginal history, 61–4
Aboriginal painters, Aranda watercolour
  school, 75
Aboriginal people, dispersion, 62–4; forced
  adoption, 74; genealogies, 63; housing
  discrimination, 68; racist definitions, 64,
  70–2 n 2; tribal languages, 62, 63
Aboriginal rights, 66
Aboriginal studies, 62–3
Aboriginal women, Aboriginal feminist
  representation, 241, 243; Australian
  feminist representation, 239–41, 243;
  domestic servants, 65; representation, 35
Aboriginal writing, 45–6; *Auntie Rita*
  (Jackie Huggins), 70; authenticity, 12;
  history and, 61–2; image of 'indigene'
  in, 44–5
Aboriginals' Preservation and Protection
  Acts 1939–1946 (Qld), 65
academic discourses, othering and, 25
Acadians, Canadian nation-building history,
  205, 207
adoption, forced, Aboriginal assimilation
  policy, 74
affirmative action, economic rationalism
  and, 130–1
Akerman, Chantal, 74

Akisato, Wakuni, 180, 192
American civil rights movement, 66
American/Mexican border history,
  Borderlands/La Frontera: *The New
  Mestiza* (Gloria Anzaldúa), in, 221
androgyny, in Japanese girls' comics, 179,
  188, 189
Anglo-Celtic Australian male, oppression
  of, 131
anthropology, feminism and, 20, 23, 25,
  26–31; insider, 27; patriarchy and, 28;
  postmodernism and, 20, 23, 30; shared,
  27
anti-racist politics in feminist publishing,
  35–55 *passim*
anti-racist writing, guidelines, 39–42
Aoike, Yasuko, 188
appropriation, cultural, 36, 37, 38–42
  passim; English-Canadian fiction, in,
  42–8; minority representation and,
  xvii–xviii
Araeen, Rashid, 23
Aranda watercolour school, 75
Armstrong, Jeanette, 47
Aryan Nation, 37
assimilation, policies of, 13, 74
assimilationism, liberalism and, 128–9
Atwood, Margaret, 44, 147
Australia, cultural independence, 4;
  multiculturalism in *see* multiculturalism
Australian culture, Irish factor, 4;
  recognition, 5
Australian literature, 4; plurality of, 7–8;
  recognition, 4